# SERIAL KILLERS
# on the
# INTERSTATE

*200 Highway Killers by State*

by
Lori Carangelo

Access Press

## DEDICATION

*In memory of the thousands of*
*known and unidentified victims*
*of the highway killers.*

ISBN: 978-0-942605-33-4

# CONTENTS

(Multi-State Highway Serial Killers are cross-referenced with
the state where committed or where convicted)

INTRODUCTION - 7
Hitchhiking with Serial Killers

ALABAMA - 13

ALASKA - 19

ARIZONA - 23

ARKANSAS - 26

CALIFORNIA - 29

COLORADO - 51

CONNECTICUT - 55

DELAWARE - 63

FLORIDA - 65

GEORGIA - 74

HAWAII - 76

IDAHO – 77

ILLINOIS - 79

INDIANA - 83

IOWA - 85

KANSAS – 86

KENTUCKY – 87

LOUISIANA - 89

MAINE - 92

MARYLAND - 93

MASSACHUSETTS - 95

MICHIGAN - 97

MINNESOTA - 99

MISSISSIPPI - 101

MISSOURI - 105

MONTANA - 107

NEBRASKA – 111

NEVADA - 113

NEW HAMPSHIRE - 115

NEW JERSEY - 117

NEW MEXICO - 119

NEW YORK - 121

NORTH CAROLINA - 125

NORTH DAKOTA - 126

OHIO – 127

OKLAHOMA - 130

OREGON – 132

PENNSYLVANIA – 133

RHODE ISLAND - 135

SOUTH CAROLINA - 136

SOUTH DAKOTA - 137

TENNESSEE – 139

TEXAS - 143

UTAH - 153

VERMONT - 155

VIRGINIA - 157

WASHINGTON - 159

WASHINGTON D.C. - 167

WEST VIRGINIA - 169

WISCONSIN - 170

WYOMING – 171

ADDENDUM:
55 Facts About Serial Killers - 175
Serial Killer Memorabilia - 181

BIBLIOGRAPHY – 185
HIGHWAY KILLERS INDEX –  187
GENERAL INDEX – 193
RESOURCES – 199
ABOUT THE AUTHOR – 201
MORE BOOKS - 202

**38 OF THE 200 SMILING HIGHWAY KILLERS IN THIS BOOK
WHO WOULD HAVE OFFERED YOU A RIDE:**

Row 1:  Aileen Wuornos, Kenneth Bianchi, Angelo Buono, Allen Anderson,
        Tommy Sells, Lawrence Bittaker, Ted Bundy;
Row 2:  Henry Lucas, Peewee Gaskins, Randy Kraft, William Bonin, Jon Jobert;
Row 3:  Dale Hausner, Michael Ross, Gerard Schaefer, Israel Keyes, Herbert Mullin,
        Ray Norris, Keith Jesperson;
Row 4:  Dean Corll, Bruce Mendenhall, Gary Ridgway, Randy Woodfield,
        William Suff, William Boyette and Mary Rice, Michael McLendon;
Row 5:  Joseph Duncan, Herb Baumeister, Wayne Ford, Jesse Matthew, Melvin
        Rees, Patrick Kearney, Joel  Rifkin, Hayward Bissell, David Berkowitz

*"I think there is a mentality that hitchhikers 'deserve what they get' for being out on the road."*
-Judy Jackson, "Highway Injustice"
Texas Observer, 11-7-12

# INTRODUCTION
## Hitchhiking with Serial Killers

Throughout the 1960s and 1970s, California led the nation in promoting free love, enlightenment, protests against the Vietnam War, and a romance with the open road. Hitchhiking was a common mode of travel, especially in California among young surfers, students and free spirits along popular coastal communities connected by the state's freeways. But also the 200 highway serial killers and "spree" killers featured in this compilation evidence that America's interstate highways and truck stops are used by these killers to randomly choose their victims, or to dump their bodies. With rare exception, the killer is male; but the victims may be all males, or all females or both, adults or children. The victim may have been picked up where the killer assumes that a specific group he's targeting, such as prostitutes or homosexuals, may congregate. Often, the only thing that many of the victims have in common is that they were *hitchhiking* when abducted. In fact, the terms, "hitchhiking" and "rape" occur so frequently with regard to these killers that it would be useless to include these terms in the Index. But two extensive Indexes are provided for researchers – a "Highway Killers Index" by killers' names and nicknames, and a "General Index" by subject.

Famous hitchhikers reminisced about their hitchhiking days:
Ronald Reagan: *"I stood on the corner of Routes 26/ 29 in Ohio, thumbing a ride to Dixon."*

Willie Nelson: *"I was about 20, hitchhiking through California, Oregon and Washington, riding freight trains, sleeping under bridges and viaducts -- I didn't like that at all... It's like picking cotton. It's something you did, but never want to do again."*

<u>Paul McCartney</u>: *"John and I slept together as teenagers, top-and-tailed, in millions of hitchhiking places."*

<u>Dan Rather</u>: *"I hitchhiked up to Sam Houston State Teacher's College, which was on the Dallas Highway, 70-some odd miles north of Houston... And I hitchhiked back home... It was a different era."*

<u>Jewell</u>: *"...had a boyfriend for awhile who worried about me hitchhiking, because I'm from Alaska and you hitchhike everywhere, but he was from California."*

<u>Janis Joplin</u>: *"Dear Mom, I've hitchhiked to San Francisco. Don't be mad."* Joplin is remembered for her wailing *"Bobby thumbed a diesel down... it rode us all the way to New Orleans...We sang every song that driver knew... feeling good was good enough for me, good enough for me and Bobby McGee."*

<u>Keith Richards</u> of The Rolling Stones recalls an era when one felt safe with a trucker: *"I met this chick from Montreal on the road in the States. She was going to every Stones gig, hitchhiking blind as a bat to get to the next concert. I said 'This is not safe' and I would fix her up with truckers because I thought she's going to do it anyway, and I didn't want her to get run over."*

At the same time, infamous highway serial killers also reminisced:

<u>Ted Bundy</u>: *"I just liked to kill; I wanted to kill... all the hatred vanished, but only for a short time"*

<u>David Berkowitz</u>: *"I didn't want to hurt them, I just wanted to kill them."*

<u>Edmund Kemper</u>: *"Even when she was dead, she was still bitching at me."*

<u>Henry Lee Lucas</u>: *"I hated all my life... I was treated like what I call the dog of the family."*

<u>Aileen Wuornos</u>" *"To me, the world is nothing but evil, and my own evil just happened to come out..."*

Have you ever accepted a ride from a stranger? I did once, in Santa Barbara, California... It was a perfect sunshiny day in the 1970s at the only place on the state-long 101-Freeway where, there was a Stop sign. That's where a stranger pulled over his Volkswagon "Bug" to ask me directions. I was 25, petite, curly haired, and long-legged in my mini-skirt and open-toed platform sandals. He was a tattooed "hippie" with long gray hair tied back in a ponytail, a huge, disarming smile, quick wit, and a "laid back" demeanor of someone who had as many miles on him as on his worn out VW. He quickly engaged me in interesting conversation. His name, if he had shared his true name at the time, is now forgotten, so I'll call him "Max." Max seemed harmless enough and I was easily tempted by his suggestion of a drive along the coast to enjoy ocean breezes. During the drive down the 101 Freeway, Max stopped at a small strip mall of Christmas novelty stores near Carpinteria, named "Santa Claus, California," a tourist attraction that has since disappeared from the landscape. He offered to lock up my large wicker basket style purse in the trunk while he went to get refreshments and while I browsed the shops. Upon returning to the VW, I was relieved to find both the car and the stranger still there. But when he opened the trunk, the basket he handed me, although identical down to its red and white polka dot lining, was one-third the size of what we had put in the trunk. We had a good laugh at his seizing the opportunity to pull off such a joke which eased any worry I may have had about his intentions.

However, that trust was tested on the way back to Santa Barbara where he decided to stop *on the railroad tracks*, to share his bottle of peppermint schnapps and his philosophy of life, while I kept an eye out for any approaching train and mentally composed my epitaph. Fortunately, no train showed up and he dropped me off near my home. I never saw him again, but the memory of that carefree day still evokes a smile... and a shudder.

Another Santa Barbaran, Gillian Christie, president of Christie Communications, discovered that hitchhiking during the '70s was the perfect way to escape a sheltered youth and meet the "real" people of America. During a college break, she hitchhiked from Colorado to Alaska. But while thumbing in Los Angeles, she was picked up by a man in an old restored truck that was painted bright yellow. *"He pulled off on some old back road in the middle of nowhere and tried to attack me. I hauled off and hit him in the face and told him never to do that again to me, nor to any woman, and to take me back to the main road."*

Christie and I were lucky. Our encounters with strangers on the highway was at a time when California's multiple "Freeway Killers" were operating independently of each other, having discovered the multitude of hitchhikers along the freeways were easy prey.

*"There is no safe place in the world,"* says Tom Mercer of *"Let's Go"* publications, *"but travelers still find success hitching in certain countries and regions around the globe. In Europe, it's still easy to catch rides in Britain, Ireland and Scandinavia. Hitching is also common in New Zealand, Chile, Argentina, and rural areas of Central America and China."*

Then why is hitchhiking in America so much more dangerous?

Highway violence followed on the heels of construction of the U.S. interstate system that was begun in the 1950s. On June 26, 1956, when Congress approved the Federal Highway Act signed by President Eisenhower, over $30-billion was allocated for the construction of 41,000 miles of interstate highways that fueled a surge in the interstate trucking industry, the auto industry, the domestic shipping market and fostered the growth of roadside businesses such as restaurants, food chains, hotels and amusement parks. Hitchhiking hippies were replaced by hitchhiking ex-cons, and, before the concrete was dry on new roads, a specter began haunting them: highway serial killers.

The new highway projects employed tens of thousands of construction workers. Homicide investigators have always had a difficult time establishing the movements of construction workers, due to the seasonal and transient nature of their work, and these workers had immediate access to the highways they were building, and along which they may have picked up and deposited victims unnoticed. Most notably, one serial killer, Mack Ray Edwards, who is featured in this compilation, worked on early freeway construction in Los Angeles County as a heavy equipment operator for CALTRANS, and other agencies, starting in 1941 and during the freeway building boom of the 1950s and '60s. He was convicted of murdering at least 6 children, and claimed to have actually murdered 18 children. The body of one of his victims was found *buried underneath the Santa Ana Freeway*; he claimed to have disposed of another beneath the Ventura Freeway.

In the 1980s, the FBI launched an initiative called "The Violent Crimes Apprehension Program," better known by its acronym, "VICAP," which relied on voluntary submission of murder reports by local law enforcement agencies. And in 2004, the FBI launched its "Highway Serial Killings Initiative," creating a repository specifically for information about serial murders gleaned from law enforcement nationwide. By 2009, the Initiative identified 600 victims and over 275 suspects, forming the basis for the FBI's "**Highway Murders Map**" (see next page). By 2010, Texas led the nation for unsolved serial highway homicides, with California a close second. One reason it was so hard to catch highway serial killers is that law enforcement agencies hardly communicated with each other. And submission of highway homicide cases to central state agencies like VICAP was voluntary. The most recent (2016) FBI statistics find roughly 3.5-million truckers on the road today; 25 long-haul truckers are serving time for serial murder and several cold cases were tied to truckers who were already serving time. Today, highway killers find or dump their victims in towns along the interstates that cross state lines, eluding local law enforcement. According to the FBI's behavioral unit: " *To date, this coordinated database has identified more than 750 people whose bodies were found near U.S. highways and has identified 500 potential suspects. Over 6,000 people per year die at the hands of serial killers and there are currently close to 300 highway serial killers on the loose in the United States prowling the nation in big rigs. Top serial murder suspects are long-haul truckers who may pick up prey in one state and dump the body several states away due to the job's mobility, lack of supervision, and access to victims in remote locations.* "

The FBI is quick to point out that "not all truckers are dangerous."

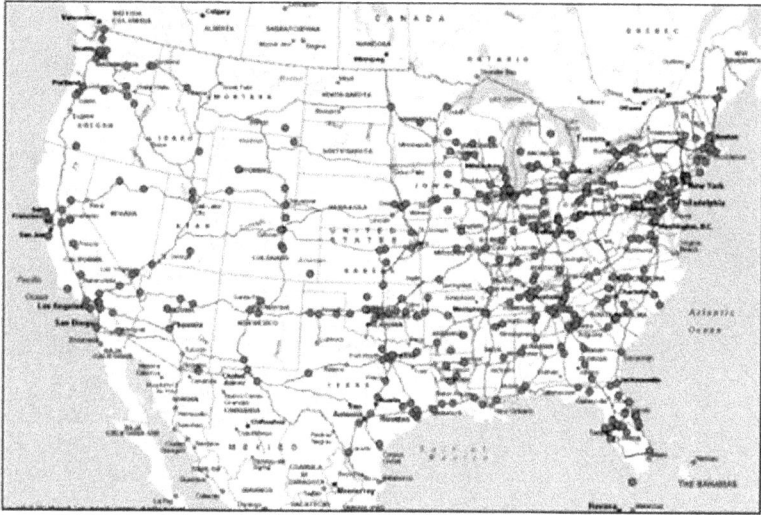

The "**FBI Highway Murders Map**" represents 500 Highway Serial Killings currently in their nationwide database - The dots only mark where those bodies or remains have been found along highways over the past 30 years  - *not intended to be all inclusive* (many more victims are named in this book). Routes whose numbers end in zero, such as U.S. 40, once traversed the entire United States -- an ideal route for multi-state serial killers such as Larry Eyler whose victims were found in Illinois and Indiana; others were found in Kentucky and Wisconsin.  And even before the new interstates, back in 1934, Clyde Barrow and Bonnie Parker ("Bonnie and Clyde") drove existing highways, criss-crossing the central states from Texas to Minnesota on their 2-year multi-state killing spree, finally meeting their demise in a hail of bullets on a dusty stretch of Highway 154 in Louisiana. Billy Cook traveled from Missouri to California killing 6 strangers in 22 days -- *not by picking up hitchhikers but by posing as a hitchhiker.*

Bonnie and Clyde on Route 66

11

# ALABAMA

## BISSELL, Hayward
### ("The I-117 Murders")

On January 23, 2000, Hayward Bissell, a 6-foot 400-pound madman, was hurtling down Alabama State Highway 117 near Mentone in a Lincoln Town Car on a murder rampage. He had driven his girlfriend, Patricia Ann Booher, from Ohio to Georgia, where he stabbed her to death, cut off her leg and hand, cut out her heart, windpipe and eyeballs, then buckled her back into his passenger seat and drove her into DeKalb County, Alabama. Also on the I-117, less than an hour after his first murder, he rear-ended a car, causing the occupants to get out, then purposely accelerated and ran over the driver of the wrecked car, Donald Pirsch, dragging him 150 feet as Bissell sped the scene down the I-117 to Mentone. There, he pulled into the driveway of James Pumphrey, who, like the Pirsch couple, was a stranger, and began stabbing Pumphrey in the stomach, whereupon the family's two Labrador retrievers attacked Bissell who stabbed the dogs and cut their throats. While Bissell was warding off the dogs, Carolyn Pumphrey grabbed a .22 rifle, scaring off Bissell who didn't know the rifle had jammed. Pumphrey survived the attack. When Dekalb County, Alabama sheriff's deputies caught up with Bissell on the I-117 and pulled him over, they discovered the partially dismembered body of his pregnant girlfriend, Patricia Ann Booher, in the passenger seat beside him, her esophagus in Bissell's shirt pocket. In 2002, Bissell pled "Guilty but Insane" and was sentenced to Life in prison.

--Source: "Blood Highway," by Sheila Johnson, Pinacle Books (2008); Robert Waters, "An Extraordinarily Gruesome Case," www.KeepAndBear Arms.com

## BOYETTE Jr., William & Mary Craig RICE"
### ("I-10 Spree Killers")

In 2016, William Eugene "Billy" Boyette, 44, and Mary Rice, 37, went on a week long carjacking and killing spree along the I-10, with a manhunt that spanned Baldwin County in Alabama across Escambia and Santa Rosa counties in Northwest Florida. Boyette, who was known to be a drug user, had a lengthy criminal history going back to 2002, but never served more than a year in jail, for Domestic Violence, Kidnapping, Aggravated Assault. Charges were dropped in 2016 when the victim could not be found, so he served only 3 months in jail on a probation violation. Mary Craig Rice, of Milton, Florida, also had a criminal record - arrests and convictions for Driving with a Suspended License, Failure to Appear in court, Obstruction of Justice, Drug Possession, Possession of Drug Paraphernalia and Check Fraud. Boyette was a "person of interest" in the shooting deaths of his ex-girlfriend, Alicia Ann Greer, 30, and her friend, Jacqueline Jeanette Moore, 39, at Emerald Sands Inn on U.S. Highway 90 in

Milton, (Escambia County), Florida. Boyette then drove Greer's car about an hour on the I-10 and randomly shot and killed Peggy Phillips Broz, 52, in her front yard in Lillian, Alabama during a carjacking. Authorities confirmed that Boyette abandoned the car stolen after the shooting at the Alabama/Florida Welcome Center Rest Stop on I-10 and Nine Mile Road outside Pensacola. Boyette next shot and killed Kayla Crocker, 28, the mother of two young children. Boyette and Rice managed to elude capture by staying very mobile. The pair were seen at a Shell station and when they stopped at a Hardee's for breakfast. Boyette stayed in the car while Rice made the purchases; her hair had been dyed orange. Authorities emphasized that they had no information to determine whether Rice was being held by Boyette against her will or if she was an accomplice. The manhunt for the pair spanned more than a week before ending in a Georgia motel room February 7, 2017, when Rice surrendered into custody moments before Boyette shot himself after a tense standoff. Rice alone then faced not 2 charges of First-Degree Murder, Accessory After the Fact charge, and the wrath of a community looking for answers that only she could provide
--Source: Arden Dier, "*Pair Accused of Murder in Florida, Alabama,*" Newsr.com. 2-7-17; Emma Kennedy, "*Mary Rice: Victim or Murder Accomplice?*" Pensacola News Journal, 4-26-17; "*Fugitive Boyette Shoots Woman in Pensacola Home Invasion,*" nwfDailyNews.com, 2-6-17; Tom Cleary, "*William 'Billy' Boyette and Mary Craig Rice: 5 Fast Facts You Need to Know,* " heavy.com, 2-7-17

# DAUGHTREY JR., Earl Llewellyn
(see GEORGIA)

### FREE, Lewis Lamar
### (*"The Highway 21 Sniper"*)

On November 20, 1981, Lewis Lamar Free, 27, fired dozens of shots at passing motorists while standing behind his pickup truck on Alabama Highway 21, killing Bernice Harville, 56, who was holding her 2-year old granddaughter on her lap in the passing car when hit by the bullet. Injured was Nellie Shook who was with her husband in their passing car; bullets also struck other cars. Free had been shooting for about 15 minutes until he was captured after being wounded in his hip from a barrage of gunfire by officials from nearby Fountain Correctional Center. He pled "Innocent by Reason of Mental Defect or Insanity," and testified that he and his pregnant girlfriend had a fight before he went to Pensagoula, Mississippi in search of his son. He had attempted suicide by slashing his wrists and had consumed a case of beer and 15 amphetamine pills before the shootings. Free was convicted of Murder and 12 counts of Assault with Intent to Murder.
--Source: New York Times, 11-21-81; Eugene Register, 11-21-81; Golden Times, 6-18-83

## JONES Jr., Timothy Ray
### ("The Highway 10 Killer")

The bodies of 5 children were found in garbage bags off Highway 10 near Camden, Alabama. Timothy Ray Jones Jr., 32, was charged only with Unlawful Neglect of a Minor by a Legal Custodian, despite that he confessed to killing his children, and had even told authorities that he dumped their bodies off on Alabama Highway 10 between Camden and Greenville were the children's bodies were located with assistance from federal, state and local law enforcement. The children's mother, who was divorced from Jones, reported the children missing on September 3, 2014, after she couldn't get in contact with Jones. Authorities believe he killed the 5 children before leaving South Carolina, so he was extradited back to South Carolina.

--Source: *"Bodies of 5 Children Found in Garbage Bags Near Greenville, Alabama, Will Be Transported to South Carolina,"* Montgomery News, 9-9-14.

## KNOWLES, Paul John *("The Casanova Killer")*
(see FLORIDA)

## LEE, Deandra Marquis
### ("The Highway 21 Murders")

The bodies of Deandra Lee Marquis, 32, were found along Alabama Highway 21, 3 miles south of U.S. Highway 80. A year after Deandra Lee was acquitted of Murder charges in the December 29, 2008 shooting deaths of Ramon Hale, 18, and Dalvyn Tyre, 17, he was also a "person of interest" in the murders of two 9-year old twins, Jordan and Taylor Dejerinett, and their 73-year old babysitter, Jack. Lee was charged with Resisting Arrest, Possession of a Firearm with Altered Serial Number, and other charges. There had also been a warrant out for Lee's arrest for Bank Robbery. The babysitter's car was later found in another county with all 4 doors missing.

--Source: Greenville Advocate, 6-8-12

## LEWIS, Gerald Patrick
### ("The Highway 80 Killer"; "The Twilite Killer")

Gerald Lewis was convicted in both Alabama and Georgia for killing several women. He claimed to have murdered 72 people in a 10-year murder spree across 21 states. In Daphne, Alabama, where Lewis hid out at his mother's home, he abducted a teenage girl from a parking lot at a WalMart Super Center just off Highway 98. His self described killing spree ended when the body of Kathleen Bracken, 32, was found at the Twilite Motel on Highway 80. After his arrest, Lewis led authorities to the shallow grave off Baldwin County Road 66 in Daphne, where

he had buried Misty McGugin, 22, whose car was found abandoned on the Causeway. Born August 10, 1965 in Jacksonville, Florida, his parents, Edward and Linda Lewis, a computer designer and draftswoman, frequently moved between Atlanta, Georgia and Boston, Massachusetts. In childhood, Lewis exhibited what police call the *"triad of behavior"* almost always found in serial killers -- fire-setting, chronic bed-wetting and animal torture. In one example, he put a milk jug over his dog's head so it could not see and placed the dog in the middle of the road until it was run down and killed. At age 4, while his parents were asleep, he was playing with matches and dropped a lit match onto his pajamas he was burned across his chest and shoulders, leaving permanent scars. He said there were *multiple* fires as he grew up... *"...one in a wooded area and at a couple of apartment complexes -- I wasn't scared -- I was never afraid of fire."* When he was 11, his parents divorced and he discovered his birth certificate named another man as his father. In teenage years he committed burglaries to buy drugs. In between jail times, he could not hold a job long. Hoping to change his life, Lewis got a job at a Kentucky Fried Chicken, where he met Lena Santarpio, 16, and fell in love with her. But he couldn't stand his job frying chicken so switched to pumping gas a few blocks away while he. and Lena, who didn't know about his past, stayed in touch. He saved his money and bought a Firebird hot rod to take her out on dates. They had been dating about 6 months when Lena was hospitalized for a blood clot. Lewis couldn't stand the separation and had sex with her in her hospital bed, which is where they both say their twins were conceived, although one, a girl, died in the womb. While awaiting the birth of the surviving twin, they both had to move in with her parents who weren't thrilled. Lena's mother constantly picked on Lewis, calling him "bastard," and he was cut off from sex, so began picking up hookers, leading to the rape of a 23-year old hooker and a 3-month jail sentence. When released, he kept calling Lena who was then 8 months pregnant, wanting to know whether the surviving twin was a boy or girl. Lena just said "boy" and hung up. Lewis continued to stalk Lena, often hiding in the bushes to spy on her. To remind her of his presence he set fire to her car. One time, he attempted suicide by hanging himself in an elevator at Lena's apartment complex. Then one day, upon seeing a pregnant woman walking alone at the roadside, Lewis slowed his van, hoping it was Lena; she had some of Lena's features but it wasn't her. Still, he asked if she was looking for a ride. The woman answered "Yeah, you looking for a girl?" which meant she was a prostitute. He drove with her for about 15 minutes to a wooded area, parked beside a gravel pit, made her get out, raped her as she screamed, strangled her, then raped her again. He then sliced open her stomach in a confused effort to find "his" unborn child. He then stabbed her 30 to 40 times until his hand grew tired and her hand turned cold. Lewis pled Guilty to the November 2001 murder of Peggy Lynn Grimes, 22, who was 8 months pregnant at the time of her murder in Douglas County Georgia. His known victims were:
- Kathleen Bracken, 32, abducted Highway 98, found off Highway 80, Daphne;
- Misty McGugin, 22, found off Route 66, Daphne;
- Unidentified prostitute, 23;
- Peggy Lynn Grimes, 22, (and her unborn baby), Douglas County, Georgia

--<u>Source</u>: Murderpedia

16

## McLENDON, Michael Kenneth
### ("Highway 52 Shooter," "Geneva County Massacre")

On March 10, 2009, as he drove along Highway 52 toward Geneva, Alabama, Michael McClendon, 28, shot and killed 10 people and 3 dogs during a shooting spree in 3 communities in 2 southern Alabama counties before committing suicide, making 11 total deaths. He continued to shoot from his car, wounding 6 others, leading police on a 24-mile chase, and ending up at Reliable Building Products where he had worked since 2003. Five of his 10 victims were family members and 2 were children. He first killed his own mother, Lisa White McClendon, 52, and burned down her house in the town of Kinston. He then killed Virginia E. White, 74, his maternal grandmother, James Alford White, an uncle, two cousins, and two neighbors including Andrea Meyers, 21, and her 18-month old daughter, Corrine Gracy Meyers. He then drove off, shooting strangers along the highway from his car. First to die as he approached highway onramp was Sonya Smith, 43, a gas station attendant. He then shot and killed a passing motorist, Bruce Malloy, 51. Later, on a city street, James Starling, 24, was the last to die when McClendon shot him in the back as he tried to run away. And there, using an assault rifle, he had a shootout with police, wounding Police Chief Frankie Lindsey in the arm. The shooting spree lasted about one hour until he committed suicide by shooting himself. He had fired more than 200 rounds and had more ammunition and other guns in his car, which made it evident that he intended to shoot a lot more people. McClendon's parents divorced when he was young and he was raised mostly by his aunt and uncle. He had been depressed about job issues, disappointed that he failed to qualify for the Marines or for law enforcement. Alabama officials said it was the worst mass shooting in Alabama history.
--Source: Wikipedia

## SASSER, Christopher Bruce
### ("The Highway 84 Shooter")

Christopher Sasser, 59, was charged with 5 counts of Attempted Murder and First Degree Felony Manufacturing of a Controlled Substance (methamphetamine) in the December 8, 2014 shooting on US-84 at Daleville, Alabama, that left one person with a foot wound. It was determined that Sasser, reportedly under the influence of alcohol, randomly pulled his red pickup truck up alongside and fired about 7 shots into another vehicle in which a family of 5 was traveling, including 2 teenagers and their grandmother; the female victims did not know each other. Although Sasser had a male passenger with him at the time of the shooting, it was determined that the other man had nothing to do with the shooting and could not have stopped Sasser.
--Source: WSFA-12 News, 12-8-14; Dothan Eagle, 12-10-14; Southeast Sun, 12-17-14.

# ALABAMA UNSOLVED CASES

## *"THE HIGHWAY 231 KILLER"*

Ozark, Alabama was 20 miles from Highway 231 where two girls took the wrong Interstate ending up in Ozark. Their bodies were found in the trunk of a car a mile from the Ozark convenience store pay phone where they were last known to have stopped. The girls, Tracie Hawley and "J.B." Beasley, both 17, were last seen on July 31, 1999 when they left Dotham for a party just 10 miles away to celebrate Tracie's 17th birthday. Tracie phoned her mother at 11:35 PM, 5 minutes past her curfew, telling her that they had taken a wrong turn and ended up at a pay phone in front of a closed convenience store, but they "would be home in no time." An autopsy at first determined the girls had not been raped, nor was there alcohol or drugs involved. But, later, the lab found DNA from semen on "J.B's" bra and panties, so police then investigated the murders as a sex crime. A grainy, poor quality surveillance video at the "Big / Little" convenience store caught glimpse of a small white pickup truck at the gas pumps at the time Tracie phoned from the pay phone, but the video never clearly showed the driver nor anyone getting out of the truck, and there was no record of a credit card purchase for gas. Each girl was shot once in the head. Their clothing was muddy-wet. Because the car's windows were rolled down and both girls' drivers licenses were on the dashboard, not in their purses which were still in the car, and the car keys were missing, it was speculated that they were stopped by a *police officer*, or someone pretending to be one, which could also be the profile of an unknown serial killer. The 1999 murders remain unsolved.

--<u>Source</u>: *"Ten Years, No Answers in Complex Murder Case,"* Dothan Eagle, 8-22-09

# ALASKA

### BUNDAY, Thomas Richard
### (*"The Richardson Highway Killer"*)

Thomas Bunday, 35, confessed to Alaska State Police, after 3 years and over 5,000 leads tracking him to Wichita Falls, Texas, that he strangled and shot to death 5 young women between 1979 and 1981, and dumped 4 of the bodies along the 25-mile stretch of Richardson Highway between Fairbanks and Eielsen, Alaska. His known victims were:

- Glinda Soderman, 19, of Fairbanks - 8-29-19;
- Marlene Peters, 21, of Tarana - 1-31-81;
- Wendy Wilson, 16, of Eielson - 3-5-81;
- Lori King, 18, of Fairbanks - 5-16-81;
- Doris Oehring, who was last seen June 13, 1980, never found.

Bunday denied killing Cassandra Goodwin, 22, of Anchorage, whose body was found in Hurricane Gulch off Parks Highway, 150 miles south of Fairbanks.

On March 15, 1983, 35 minutes after an arrest warrant was issued in Fairbanks, Bunday was killed when his motorcycle slammed head-on into a dump truck about 45 miles east of Wichita Falls, Texas, possibly a suicide. Born in 1948, Bunday, who had no prior criminal record, was a Technical Sergeant at Sheppard Air Force Base in Wichita Falls, Texas, and had been stationed at Eielson Air Force Base near Fairbanks until 1981.
--Source: "Man Wanted in Five Murders Dies in Texas Cycle Accident," *The Hour*, Norwalk, Connecticut, 3-17-83; *AlaskaWeb.org/blacksheep/index*

### HANSEN, Robert Christian
### (*"Butcher Baker"; "The Alaska Highway Killer"*)

Christopher Hansen admitted to a spree of at least 17 murders and 30 rapes of Alaskan women, most ages 16 to 19, from 1971 to 1983, who he abducted, raped and murdered along Alaska's highways, including Seward Highway which extends 125 miles from Seward to Anchorage, and along Glenn Highway which reaches the Canadian border. After abducting and raping women, Hansen would release them into the woods and *then hunt them down and kill them for sport* with a Ruger mini-14 and other weapons. He may have murdered as many as 30 women traveling alone on Alaska's highways. Almost all of Alaska's Interstates are rural two-lane undivided highway with at-grade "crossings," rather than Interstate-standard multilane divided controlled-access highway, and so not all of Alaska's "Interstates" are required to meet conventional Interstate standards, unlike the Interstates in the lower 48 and Hawaii, per Federal legislation enacted in 1980. Born February 15, 1939 in Estherville, Iowa, to Danish immigrant parents, Robert Hansen grew up fantasizing revenge upon girls who he believed rejected him due to his acne and stuttering about which he was also bullied. After a one-year enlistment in the Army Reserves, and a one-year stint as a drill instructor at Pocahontas, Iowa Police Academy, on December 7, 1966, Hansen burned down the Pocahontas Board of Education School Bus Garage, for which he served 20 months of his 3-year sentence. One of his victims, Cindy Paulson, 17, managed to escape after he chained her to a post in his basement in Muldoon, where he tortured and raped her, then drove her to Merrill Field Airport where he informed her he was going to take her where he had taken other women -- to his isolated "cabin in the woods" off Old Glenn Highway. He admitted to throwing one body in the river "near the new highway at Knik." While he was loading his plane, she made a run for her life, still handcuffed and barefoot, with Hansen chasing her, until she reached Sixth Avenue and managed to flag down a truck. Because Paulson was a prostitute with a record, police didn't take her seriously and the case went cold. Hansen was finally apprehended June 13, 1983, but not until several women were turning up dead or were missing around Anchorage, Seward Highway, Glenn Highway and the Matanuska-Susitna Valley area which extends to the Glenn Highway. Supported by victim Paulson's testimony, a warrant was obtained to search Hansen's plane, car and home. On October 27,1983, investigators found not only jewelry belonging to some of the still-missing women, but also an aviation map with "x" marks, which turned out to be locations where Hansen hid their bodies. His known victims were:

- Lisa Furrell, 41, body found with Hansen's help - disappeared
- 9-6-80;
- Malai Larsen, 28, body found with Hansen's help;
- Sue Luna, 23, body found with Hansen's help; disappeared 5-26-82;
- Angela Feddern, 24, body found with Hansen's help-found 3-26-84;
- Teresa Watson, body found with Hansen's help - found 4-26-84;
- DeLynn "Sugar" Frey, acknowledged; body discovered by a pilot; found 4-25-84;
- Paula Goulding, acknowledged; body found; disappeared 4-25-83- found 9-2-83;
- Andrea "Fish" Altiery, admitted; disappeared 12-22-91;
- "Eklutna Annie,"admitted, identity unknown - found on Eklutba Road 7-21-80
- Sherry Morrow, 24,admitted; disappeared 11-81,bodyfound 9-12-82;
- Joanna Messina, admitted; body found - disappeared 7-80;
- "Horseshoe Harriet,"unidentified, found with Hansen's help-disappeared 1980-83;
- Roxanne Easland, 24; acknowledged; found, disappeared 6-28-80;
- Ceilia "Beth" Van Zanten, 17 - disappeared 12-22-71
- Megan Emerick, 17, denies, a suspect "x" was on his map - disappeared 7-73;
- Tamara "Tami" Pederson, 19 - found 4-29-84;
- Mary Kathleen Thill, 23, suspect "x" on map; not found - disappeared 7-5-75;
- Cindy Paulson - escaped 6-13-83

Hansen was sentenced to a total of 467 Years in Prison (Alaska does did not have the Death Penalty) in 4 of the 17 murders, and for Kidnapping and Rape of Cindy Paulson, the only known victim who escaped. On August 21, 2014, at age 75, Hansen died at Anchorage Regional Hospital due to undisclosed, lingering health conditions.

--Source: Wikipedia; Murderpedia

## KEYES, Israel
## ("The Cross Country Killer")

Israel Keyes stated that he murdered along highways in no less than 10 states -- from Alaska to Vermont, Washington and New York -- as well as in Montreal, Canada, and Mexico -- where he drove and flew to seek out, abduct, murder and dispose of women who were prostitutes. It is likely that he abducted a victim in one state, transported the victim to another state where he or she was murdered, and potentially drove the victim to a third state to dispose of the body, sometimes committing arson in an attempt to cover up the murders or victims' identities. The FBI uncovered 2 caches of weapons in Eagle River, Alaska, one of several cross country locations including Green River, Wyoming, and Port Angeles, Washington, where Keyes stored his "killing kits" of weapons and items used to dispose of bodies. From March 1 to March 9, 2007, Keyes drove the Alaska-Canada Highway, flew back to Anchorage in 2010 and in 2011 he staked out a park at Point Woronzof in Anchorage. He admitted that, while there, he intended to shoot a couple just sitting in their car, but his plans were disrupted when a police officer, who he also then intended to shoot, drove into that parking lot. He chose to shoot neither the couple nor the police officer when a second police officer drove into the parking lot. On June 8, 2011, Keyes flew from Anchorage to Vermont where he abducted and murdered Bill and Lorraine Currier. On June 16, 2011, Keyes returned to Anchorage where he abducted and murdered Samantha Koenig and disposed of her body in Matanuska Lake near Palmer, Alaska. In February 2012, Keyes flew to New Orleans where he went on a cruise, then flew to Texas where authorities believe he committed a murder and set fire to a home in Aledo, Texas, then robbed a bank, also in Aledo, Texas.

--Source: "FBI Requests Public's Assistance on Case of Serial Killer Israel Keyes," FBI-Anchorage website, 8-12-13.

## SILKA, Michael Allen
## ("The Route 2 Tanana Spree Killer")

On May 17, 1984, Michael Silka was last seen driving along Alaska's 150-mile State Route 2, which ends at Fairbanks. He was driving a 1974 Dodge Monaco with camping equipment and an aluminum canoe on its roof when, on May 17, 1984, Silka killed 9 people from the village of Manley Hot Springs. That was also where 6 villagers who were traveling via State Route 2 to a boat landing disappeared. Bodies of 4 of Silka's victims -- Fred Burke, Lyman Klein, Dale Madajski, and Larry Joe McVey -- were recovered from the Tanana River. It is believed Silka dumped more bodies into the river hoping they would never be found because the 70 to 80 foot deep mile wide water remains near freezing and the glacier-fed river is heavily silted, so bodies are likely to remain below the surface. The motives for the murders Silka committed remains unclear. Born August 20, 1958 in Illinois, Silka, who loved the outdoors, had a history as a teenager of run-ins with the law for burglaries. He and his brother, Steve, ran away from high school to the Canadian wilderness until they ran

21

out of provisions. Still, he graduated from Hoffman Estates High School in 1977. In 1981, he was stationed at Fort Wainwright Army base north of Fairbanks, Alaska, and jumped bail when arrested for illegal possession of firearms discovered during a traffic stop. He returned to Alaska as a drifter and on April 29, 1984 police responded to a report of gunshots heard. Thinking Silka had been killed, they questioned a man about blood on a snow covered mound at his cabin, not knowing it was Silka who they were questioning. Silka alleged the blood was from a moose hide. The police later learned that on April 29, 1984, Silka's neighbor, Roger Culp, had gone missing; they returned with a warrant and found human blood after the snow had melted, but Silka was gone.

On May 19, 1984, State troopers searching by helicopter spotted Silka along Route 2 and chased his car along the Zitziana River where Silka ultimately got out about 25 miles upstream and ducked behind a tree. The troopers offered Silka a chance to surrender, but instead, he stepped out from his cover and fired on the helicopter with a high powered Ruger 30-06 caliber rifle, striking trooper Troy Duncan in the head, killing him instantly, and injuring trooper Donald Lawrence in the face. Troopers returned M16 rifle fire from the helicopter, striking Silka 5 times, killing him. Silka's victims were:

- Fred Burke, 30, Athabaskan Alaska Native, fisherman; boat was stolen by Silka;
- Albert Hagen, Jr., 27, Alaska Native, construction worker;
- Joyce Klein, about 30, who was 4 months pregnant;
- Lyman Klein, 36, husband of Joyce Klein;
- Marshall Klein, 2, son of Joyce and Lyman Klein;
- Dale Madajski, 24, a carpenter, cabin builder;
- Larry Joe McVey, 38, trapper, severely disabled Vietnam veteran;
- Roger Culp, 34, wood cutter, Silka's neighbor, possible victim;
- Troy L. Duncan, 34, Alaska State Trooper, U.S. Marine veteran

--Source: Wikipedia, and "Hunted" TV series narrated by John Walsh

# ALASKA UNSOLVED CASES

## "THE SEWARD HIGHWAY KILLER"

In January 1978, the body of 16-year old Shelley Connolly was found in a ditch off the Seward Highway (where Robert Christian Hansen also stalked his victims from 1971 to 1983). An autopsy determined she had been beaten, sexually assaulted, dragged behind a car, and then tossed down an embankment. Her broken fingernails suggested she had tried to crawl back to the highway before she died. On June 30, 2015, the Alaska Bureau of Investigation's cold case unit, which investigated cases like Shelley Connolly's, was eliminated due to budget cuts in the Department of Public Safety. Her killer was never caught.

--Source: "Family Clings to Hope in an Unsolved Murder Nearly 40 Years Old," Alaska Dispatch News, 5-4-15

# ARIZONA

## GOUDEAU, Mark
## ("The Baseline Killer")

Mark Goudeau was first dubbed "The Baseline Rapist" for sexually assaulting females as young as 12 at gunpoint near Baseline Road, a 43-mile long arterial route that runs parallel to US 60, intersects Loop 101 and then Interstate 10, on the outskirts of Phoenix, and provides ease of navigation on this long route as well as access to the significant number of municipalities that the route encompasses. In the Spring of 2006, the "Baseline Rapist" became "The Baseline Killer" when investigators began to link a series of murders and armed robberies to the rapist after momentous advances in DNA technology. In 2007, a jury returned a Guilty verdict on 67 of the 72 charges against 47-year old Goudeau, including all 9 First Degree Murder counts. He is serving a 438-year sentence
--Source: "A Chilling Look at the Baseline Killer Case," Phoenix New Times, 11-10-11.

## GREENAWALT, Randy ("The I-40 Trucker Killer")
## and GARY GENE TISON

Randy Greenawalt was sentenced to Life after the 1974 slaying of a trucker who was sleeping in his cab at an I-40 rest stop near Winslow, Arizona. Greenawalt drew an "X" on the trucker's door near his head, then fired a round through it. Greenawalt also confessed to killing another trucker in Arkansas and to killing a man in Colorado. He was sentenced to Arizona State Prison at Florence, Arizona. While in prison, he befriended Gary Tison and, together with Tison's 3 sons, Greenawalt planned and successfully executed a prison escape on July 30, 1978. Tison's sons' job was to gain access on pretext of a visit, then overpower the guards A prison employee provided the getaway vehicle that was waiting for the 5 fugitives. Their escape wasn't without its hitches, though. At one point, they had two flat tires, so they flagged down a passing car. In the car was 24-year-old John Lyons, his 23-year-old wife Donnelda, their two-year-old son Christopher, and the couple's 15-year-old niece Teresa Tyson. The 5 criminals forced their innocent victims into their car with the flat tires and drove them to the desert. There, Tison and Greenawalt opened fire with the shotguns. The bodies of John, Donnelda, and Christopher were found on August 6. Five days later, Teresa's body was found a short distance away. Later, while they were stuck in traffic in Colorado, Greenawalt and the four Tisons saw a van that suited them better. They forced their way into the van and killed the newly married couple inside. The bodies of 26-year-old James Judge and 23-year-old Margene Judge were found partially buried a few months later. On August 11, the gang was stopped by a police roadblock. Tison's oldest son, who was driving the van, was shot in the head when he tried to ram a second barricade. Tison, his remaining two sons, and Greenawalt, ran into the desert.

23

Everyone but Tison was arrested. On August 22, Tison was found dead of dehydration in the desert. Greenawalt and the two surviving Tisons were sentenced to Death. The Tisons had their sentences commuted to Life. Greenawalt was executed on January 23, 1997 for the 6 murders that he helped commit during the gang's 12 days on the run.
--Source: Robert Grimmick, "*Serial Killers Who Escaped From Custody,*" Listverse 7-15-15.

## HAUSNER, Dale Shawn and Samuel John DIETEMAN ("The Serial Shooters")

Hausner and Dieteman were a team of serial drive-by spree shooters, arsonists, and thrill killers who terrorized Phoenix and surrounding Arizona cities along the I-10, from May 27, 2005 to July 30, 2006 when 8 were killed and over 20 were attempted killings. Hausner received 6 Death sentences and committed suicide via overdose of Elavil, an anti-depressant drug, and Dieteman is serving Life Without Parole.
--Source: Wikipedia

## MERRITT, Leslie Allen ("The I-10 Phoenix Sniper")

Leslie Allen Merritt Jr, 21, was arrested for the September 2015 sniper shootings on Phoenix roadways along the I-10 which runs from Palm Springs, California, through Phoenix and southern Arizona, on through the southern United States to Florida. Arizona Police confirmed an 11th random shooting since August 29th on I-10 at Phoenix, with 8 vehicles hit by bullets and 3 by projectiles such as BB gun pellets. Categorized as "domestic terrorism," at least 2 of the gunshots hit commercial trucks, and although no deaths were reported, a 13-year old girl was cut by shattered glass. Merritt's gun was "forensically linked" to the first 4 shootings.
--Source: "*Arizona Police Confirm 11th Vehicle Attack,*" AP; KMIR.com; "*Arizona Police Quiz 2 People in Connection with Freeway Shootings,*" FOXNews.com, 9-11-15; "*Phoenix Freeway Shooter: 'I'm the Wrong Guy,*" HGN, 9-19-15

## MILLER, Brian Patrick ("The I-17 Black Canyon Freeway Killer")

In the 1990s, bodies were turning up underneath the Black Canyon Freeway, a section of the 1-17 in that runs through the Phoenix metropolitan area and becomes the Maricopa Freeway at its southern part. DNA evidence led to the arrest of Brian Patrick Miller, 42, in the murders of bike riders Angela Brosso, 21, and Melanie Bernaz, 17. Brosso's headless body was found on the outskirts of Phoenix, and, 11 days later, her head, and then Bernaz's

24

corpse was discovered in the Arizona Canal under the Black Canyon Freeway.

-Source: *"Man Arrested in 1990s Canal Murders,"* The Arizona Republic, and USAToday.com, 1-14-15

## ZAMASTIL, William Floyd (*"15-Freeway Killer"*)
(see CALIFORNIA)

# ARIZONA UNSOLVED CASES

## *"THE I-40 VALENTINE SALLY TRUCK STOP MURDER"*

On Valentine's Day, February 14, 1982, a white female, estimated age 17 to 24, was discovered face down under a tree in Williams, Coconino County, Arizona, about 25 feet from Westbound I-40. The area was a place where trucks regularly pulled over to cool their brakes. Death had occurred on or around February 1. Because of decomposition and scavenging animals, her fingerprints could not be obtained, although her DNA and dental xrays were documented. But no match was found. Because the remains were located on Valentine's Day, the victim was nicknamed "Valentine Sally."   The victim was approximately 5-feet-five-inches tall, weighed 120 pounds and had strawberry blond hair which was straight and around 10 inches long, and blue eyes. The victim, who was killed by either suffocation or strangulation, wore Seasons brand jeans with a handkerchief in her pocket and had one earring in her left ear. It is unknown if her right was pierced, as *her right ear was not recovered.* She had scars on her left foot and right thigh and moles on her right breast. A distinct white sweater with thin red stripes and a bra which may have belonged to the victim were found near the remains.  The victim may have been last seen at a truck stop in Ash Fork, Arizona, in early February of the same year. Patty Wilkins a waitress at the Monte Carlo Truck Stop remembers a young girl, age 16 or 17, who had been asking for aspirin *because of a toothache*. The girl was with two older men, one Black and one White.  The White man, age 60 to 65, wore a felt cowboy hat adorned with peacock feathers. He expressed concern over the girl's tooth pain.  The pair came in at 3 AM and left an hour later. Valentine Sally's xray appeared to have an incomplete root canal on one of her molars, which may have caused an infection that she suffered from. She had a lower molar prepared for a root canal approximately one week before her death. In 1984, the girl seen at the Monte Carlo Truck stop was misidentified as a different "runaway," who was later located.  In 2013, the federal government awarded the Arizona sheriff's office a $300,000 grant to do DNA testing on remains in unsolved homicide cases.  Valentine Sally's DNA was then placed into a national DNA database but came back negative - meaning no relatives have any DNA evidence in the system. So the case remains unsolved.

--Source:   Larry   Hendricks,   The   Arizona   Daily   Sun,   8-28-13;   Wikipedia, Wikivisuals.com

# ARKANSAS

**GREENAWALT, Randy** *("The Trucker Killer")*
**and GARY GENE TISON** (see ARIZONA)

## WARD, Ronald James
### *("The I-40 Rest Stop Killer")*

In 2007, Ronald James Ward, who was already in prison in Montana for the October 2000 murder of Craig Sheldon Petrich, 43, in a remote recreation area in the Sapphire Mountains, when he was sentenced to Life for killing Kristen Laurite, 25, of Scotch Plains, New Jersey at an I-40 rest stop in central Arkansas, linked via DNA 5 years after he raped her, stabbed her 11 times, and left to die at a rest stop near Little Rock at Morrilton, Arkansas. That rest stop, where another murder occurred 3 years earlier, was closed by the state. Laurite's parents had a billboard put up on the well-traveled I-40 with their slain daughter's photo with the plea, *"Do you know who murdered me?"* By 2005, investigators matched DNA found on Laurite's body to a sample found at the scene of the 2000 murder of Jackie Travis, 49, in Merced, California. Travis, who previously resided in Newport, Arkansas, was found beaten and strangled in her home, with symbols carved into her skin. In 2007, Ward admitted killing Laurite, claiming he was high on moonshine and heroin when he killed her. The DNA later also linked Travis' death to Shela LaRae Polly, 33, of Modesto, California, and then to a sample from Ronald James Ward. Ward is also suspected of other murders. His known victims were:

- Craig Sheldon Petrich, 43,at Sapphire Mountains, Montana - October 2000;
- Kristen Laurite, 25, at Morrilton Arkansas - 8-26-00;
- Jackie Travis, 49, of Newport, Arkansas, in Merced, California – 12-7-00;
- Shela LaRae Polly, 33, of Modesto, California - 12-30-00

Born in Hood, Oregon, Ward was married with 6 children, in April, 2014, Ward died in prison at age 48. He would have been eligible for parole in 2036.
--<u>Source</u>: John Gambrell, AP Writer, *"Murder at Arkansas Rest Stop,"* MTS Standard, 6-13-07; Chandra Johnson, *"DNA Helped ID Serial Killer Imprisoned in Montana,"* Missoulian, 6-17-08; *"Montana Inmate Serving Life for 4 Slayings Found Dead in Prison,"* Missoulian, 4-10-14.

## ARKANSAS UNSOLVED CASES

### *"THE REDHEAD MURDERS"*

*"The Redhead Murders"* are a series of unsolved homicides believed to have been committed by a single unidentified serial killer whose victims were found along Interstate highways, mostly in Arkansas but also in Tennessee, Kentucky, Mississippi and Pennsylvania, between 1978 and the 1980s, but they may have continued to 1992. The 8 to 11 victims, including many who have never been identified, had reddish hair;

their bodies were abandoned along major highways after they were hitchhiking or engaged in prostitution. The victims were:

- Unidentified. Body of a White female, 35-45, auburn hair, found naked along Route 250 in Littleton, Wetzel County,
- Virginia, 2-13-82, died 2 days before found; was sexually assaulted;
- Lisa Nichols, 28 (aka Lisa Jarvis) had strawberry blonde hair, found 9-16-84 along I-40 near West Memphis, Arkansas, after leaving a truck stop alone, and may have been hitchhiking;
- Unidentified. Skeleton of redheaded female, 31-40, found al the side I-24 on 3-31-85. Unlike other victims, she was clothed;
- Unidentified. Woman, 24-35, foot-long red hair, died by suffocation, found alongside Route 25 *inside a white Admiral Refrigerator* in Gary, Knox County, Kentucky on 4-1-85. The refrigerator had a decal on the door with the words *"Super Woman."* There were reports she may have been soliciting a ride to North Carolina via a trucker's CB radio;
- Unidentified. White female, 14-25, light brown to blonde hair with reddish highlights, found in Greene County, Tennessee;
- Unidentified. Dubbed "Rising Fawn Jane Doe," 16-25, red hair, found near I-59 in Georgia; she had been sexually assaulted;
- Unidentified. Found in Arkansas in 1978;
- Unidentified. Found in Arkansas in 1985;
- Unidentified. Found in Arkansas along I-102, Benton County;
- Unidentified. Hebron, Ohio, Jane Doe, red hair, found near the I-40 in 1990; she was sexually assaulted;
- April Lacey, murdered in 1990 and left along a road in Texas, believed to be a victim of the same Redhead Killer;
- Unidentified. Her decomposed body was found along I-75; she died in 2001, inconsistent with the other murders, but had reddish hair.

--Source: Wikipedia

## *"THE TRUCK STOP KILLER"*

An unknown serial killer was targeting prostitutes, at least 4 of whom were last seen at Arkansas truck stops. Prostitution often goes hand-in-hand with truck stops. Seven bodies, including that of Margaret Gardner, were found near highways and creeks in Arkansas, Mississippi, Oklahoma and Texas. The prostitutes were found nude, or only partially clothed, and at least 3 were strangled. The killer may be a long-haul truck driver, and the transient nature of the victims also makes it particularly difficult to solve the crimes.

--Source: CBS-TV News/AP

## "THE HIGHWAY 18 KILLER"

Amanda Tusing, 20, was last seen when she left her fiance's apartment in Jonesboro, Arkansas at 11:30 PM on June 14, 2000. Her black 1992 Pontiac Grand Am, was found parked in a well-lit area along the side of Arkansas Highway 18, about 5 miles east of the St. Francis Bridge. She was going to drive to her parents' home, 40 miles away in Dell, Arkansas. Her wallet was still in the car, and her keys were still in the ignition. The windshield wipers had stopped mid-swipe, and the radio was turned to her favorite station. There were no signs of a struggle. Three days later, on June 18, Tusing's body was found in a rain-swollen ditch, about 12 miles west from where her car was found. There were no signs of a sexual assault. She had been dead – suffocated – before she ever hit the water. After 7 years and more than 200 interviews, investigators' can only theorize what happened to Tusing. Tusing's mother, Susan, thinks she was pulled over by *either a law enforcement officer or someone impersonating a law enforcement officer,* and later killed. However, no suspects have been identified. Law enforcement officials in the area were interviewed and passed lie detector tests.
--Source:  ABC NEWS, Law and Justice Unit, June 18, 2007

## "HAUNTED HIGHWAY 365 KILLER"

On October 12, 2010, Patricia Guardado, 20, a University of Arkansas-Little Rock student, was last seen leaving home for school. Four days later, fisherman found her body floating in a pond off the I-365 in Pulaski County. Her car was found in a parking lot of a Burger King across the UALR campus.  Cause of death had not been determined and police still have no leads on a suspect. The I-365, south of Little Rock, is also home to *"Vanishing Hitchhiker"* stories.  Many witnesses over the years claimed they had picked up a young woman, usually wearing a white dress, who mysteriously "vanishes" from their cars *while* they are taking her home. It is speculated Guardado's murder was connected to such I-365 disappearances.
--Source: Alexis Rogers, *"What Happened to Patty?  The Unsolved Case of Patricia Guardado,"* ABC-7, KATV-Little Rock, 11-16-15; *"Arkansas' Haunted Highway,"* PrairieGhosts.com/hwy365.html

## "'DORA DOE KILLER"

On Oct. 23, 1994, the unidentified body of a woman was dubbed "Dora Doe" because she was discovered on the intersection of I-40 and US-64D, 2 miles south of Dora, Arkansas. The body had been carefully wrapped in landscaping material, tied up neatly with twine; her heart and left lung were missing and her head was found 15 feet away.  She was about 50 years old, 5' 3," mixed race, Caucasian and possibly Asian or American Indian. A computer reconstruction gave her a face. But DNA was too deteriorated for testing.
--Source:  Staff Reports, *"Little Known About 1994 Murder of Unknown 'Dora Doe,"* InsideFortSmith.com News online, 1-10-18.

28

# CALIFORNIA

## BIANCHI, Kenneth Allesio, and Angelo BUONO
### ("The Hillside Stranglers")

Kenneth Bianchi and his adoptive cousin, Angelo Buono, are alleged to have actually killed 25 women, ages 12 to 28, who were often hitchhiking along interstate highways - 23 women in Los Angeles and 2 women in Washington state. They abducted their victims by flashing fake police badges and alleging they were undercover police officers when they ordered their victims into Buono's car which they claimed was an unmarked police car. They would then take their victims to their home. Both men would sexually abuse their victims before strangling them to death. They also experimented with other methods of killing, such as lethal injection, electric shock, and carbon monoxide poisoning. Kenneth Bianchi was born 5-22-61 in Rochester, New York, to a prostitute who gave him up for adoption when he was 2 weeks old. He was adopted at 3 months by Frances and Nicholas Bianchi. His adopter described him in childhood as being "a compulsive liar, quick to lose his temper." At age 5 he was diagnosed with "petit mal seizures," and at age 10 as having "Passive Aggressive Disorder." Angelo Buono was born 10-5-34 in Rochester, New York, to Jenny Buono and her husband, who were first generation immigrants from San Buono, Italy. In 1939, when Angelo was 5, his parents divorced and he was informally adopted by his grandparents. Their victims were:

- Yolanda Washington, 19 - 10-17-77;
- Judith Lynn Miller, 15 - 10-31-77;
- Lissa Kastin, 21 - 11-6-77;
- Jane King, 28 - 11-10-77;
- Dolores Cepeda, 12 - 11-13-77;
- Sonja Johnson, 14 - 11-13-77;
- Kristina Weckler, 20 - 11-20-77;
- Lauren Wagner, 18, 11-29- 77;
- Kimberly Martin, 17 - 12-9-77;
- Cindy Lee Hudspeth, 20 - 2-16-78;
- Karen Mandic, 22 - 1-11-79;
- Diane Wilder, 27 - 1-11-79

Even while committing the murders, Bianchi applied for a job with the Los Angeles Police Department (LAPD) and, unbeknown to Buono, had even been taken for several "ride-alongs" with police officers while they were searching for the Hillside Stranglers. Shortly after they botched their would-be 11th murder, Bianchi revealed to Buono he had participated in the LAPD police "ride-alongs" and that he was currently being questioned about the Hillside Stranglers case. Buono flew into a rage, threatening to kill Bianchi if he did not move to Bellingham, Washington. Bianchi moved to Bellingham in May 1978. On January 11, 1979, while working as a security guard,

29

Bianchi lured two Washington University students, Karen Mandic, 22, and Diane Wilder, 27, into a house he was guarding where he raped and murdered them. The legal case against Buono was based largely upon Bianchi's testimony. Both Bianchi and Buono were convicted of Rape and Murder of 10 women. Bianchi is serving a Life sentence at Walla Walla State prison. Buono married in 1986 and died of heart failure at age 67 at Calipatria State Prison in California.

--<u>Source</u>: *"Infamous American Murders,"* Court TV; Oracle ThinkQuest website.

## BITTAKER, Lawrence Sigmund, and RAY LEWIS NORRIS
### *("The Toolbox Killers")*

For 5 months in 1979, Lawrence Bittaker, together with Ray Norris, kidnapped, tortured, raped and murdered 5 female teenage hitchhikers who they picked up while cruising California's highways and beach roads. Bittaker met Norris at California Men's Colony and Norris, an electrician, later became Bittaker's accomplice in murders and they became known as *"The Toolbox Killers"* because most of the instruments used to torture their victims were the type normally stored in a household toolbox. Lawrence Bittaker was born an only child on 9-27-40, in Pittsburgh, Pennsylvania, placed in an orphanage by his mother, and was subsequently adopted in infancy as the only child of Marie and George Bittaker. The Bittakers worked in aircraft factories that required the family to move often -- from Pennsylvania to Florida, to Ohio and to California. At age 12, and multiple times thereafter, Bittaker came to the attention of police and juvenile authorities for shoplifting and petty thefts. Although Bittaker had a tested high IQ of 138, he dropped out of high school in 1957 after further run-ins with the law and was incarcerated at California Youth Authority until age 18. That's when he discovered his adoptive parents had "disowned" him and he never saw the again. Over the next 20 years, he worked as a machinist and was in and out of prison for Auto Theft, Hit-and-Run accidents, Burglary and Parole Violations. Bittaker described his motivation to kill as follows*: "Well, it was exciting in a certain sense. Age is not relevant as long as they're young and attractive. I got a problem with women anywhere near my adopted mother's age. My adopted parents were kind of old when they adopted me, in their 40s. Having sex with a woman of that age reminds me of my mother."* He also said his crimes were the result of not being loved by his parents. During Bittaker's incarcerations, prison psychiatrists diagnosed him as being Paranoid and Borderline Psychotic. But when he stabbed a grocery store employee who caught him stealing steaks, and was once again incarcerated, a prison psychiatrist rejected the previous diagnosis and labeled him "Classic Psychotic." Another psychiatrist decided he was a "Sophisticated Psychotic," yet in 1978 he was again released. Roy Norris was born February 5, 1948 in Greeley, Colorado. Norris was conceived out of wedlock and his parents married to avoid the social stigma surrounding illegitimate birth at that time. His father worked in a scrapyard, and his mother was a housewife who is known to have suffered from a drug addiction. Although he occasionally lived with his biological parents throughout his childhood and adolescence, Norris was repeatedly placed in the care of foster families within the state of Colorado. Norris' recollections of his childhood are interspersed with memories of wrongful accusation when he lived with his biological parents, and of neglect by many of the foster families; he frequent referenced being denied sufficient food or clothing. He also states he was the victim of sexual abuse when in the care of a Hispanic family; he later stated the racism he holds towards Hispanic people originates from the neglect and abuse he endured as a child when placed in their care. At ag 16, Norris, at the time living with his birth parents, visited the home of a female relative in her early twenties and began talking in sexually suggestive terms to her. In response, this relative ordered him to leave her house. Norris' father was informed of this incident and threatened to beat his son. So Norris stole his father's car and drove into the Rocky Mountains where he attempted to commit suicide by injecting pure air into an artery in his arm. He was later apprehended as a runaway, and returned to live with his parents. When he returned home, his parents informed Norris that he and his younger sister were both unwanted, and that they had intended to divorce when both children reached adolescence. One year later, Norris dropped out of school, joined the U.S. Navy, and was stationed in San Diego between 1965 and 1969 when, at age 21, he was deployed to serve in Vietnam, although he did not see active combat during the 4 months of his deployment. He returned to the United States later the same year. Throughout his service in Vietnam, Norris experimented with both heroin and marijuana. Although he did not become addicted to heroin, he did become a regular user of marijuana. Evidence showed Bittaker and Norris drove their victims to remote mountain locations and used ice picks, vice grips, wire hangers and a sledgehammer to torment the girls. Bittaker took photographs of one of his victims and tape-recorded Shirley Ledford as he tortured her. That tape recording was played in court during trial. Their known victims were:

- Lucinda Schaefer, 16, of Torrance - 6-24-79;
- Jackie Gilliam, 15, of Long Beach - 9-3-79;
- Jacqueline Lamp, 13, Redondo Beach (with Gilliam) – 9-3-79;
- Andrea Hall, 18, of Tujunga - 7-8-79;
- Shirley Ledford, 16, of Sun Valley - 10-31-79.

Bittaker was sentenced to Death for the 5 murders on March 24, 1981, and remains on Death Row at San Quentin State Prison. Norris accepted a plea bargain whereby he agreed to testify against Bittaker and was sentenced to Life imprisonment on May 7, 1980, with possibility of parole after serving 30 years.

--Source: *"Adopted Killers,"* by Lori Carangelo; *"Redondo Beach Killer Denied Parole,"* The Daily Breeze, 9-15-09; and Wikipedia;

### BONIN, William George and Vernon Robert BUTTS ("The Freeway Killers")

William Bonin, a homosexual truck driver, was convicted of 14 murders. But he is suspected of murdering at last 30 other male hitchhikers who he picked up along Los Angeles and Orange

County freeways in his van, raping and strangling them to death and dumping their bodies along the same freeways. Born January 8, 1947 in Willimantic, Connecticut, Bonin was neglected by his alcoholic and drug addicted parents and placed in an orphanage at age 6. He was informally adopted and raised by his biological grandfather who sexually abused him from age 8. After graduating high school in 1965, he served in Vietnam, logging over 700 hours in combat and patrol time and earning a Good Conduct Medal. While in Vietnam, Bonin risked is own life to save a fellow soldier, but also later admitted to sexually assaulting 2 fellow soldiers at gunpoint. He was honorably discharged from the U.S. Air Force in 1968 and returned home to his mother in Connecticut before moving to California. On November 17, 1968, Bonin committed a sexual assault on a boy, and in late 1968 and early 1969, he kidnapped and assaulted 4 boys, ages 12 to 18. He was later sadistically raped by older boys at knifepoint in juvenile detention and was sent to Atascadero State Hospital as a Mentally Disordered Sex Offender and from there, to prison in 1971. He was diagnosed at Atascadero State Hospital as "brain damaged" in the area of the brain thought to control violent impulses, as well as being Manic Depressive. In 1974 Bonin was declared "no longer a danger to others" and was released in 1975. Within 16 months of that release, Bonin raped and attempted to strangle David McVicker, 14, but McVicker survived. Bonin also attempted to abduct another boy but was captured and imprisoned at California Institution for Men at San Luis Obispo. He was again released from the California prison system in 1978, found work as a truck driver, and began picking up male hitchhikers along Los Angeles County and Orange County freeways, as well as from city streets, into his van that he called his "murder mobile," raping, torturing, murdering and dumping their bodies along those same freeways. Bonin was known to recruit accomplices, particularly, Vernon Butts (who committed suicide by hanging while in jail), and to a lesser degree Gregory Matthew Miley, William "Billy" Ray Pugh, and James Michael Munro -- all young men ages 17 to 21. Bonin's known murder victims include:

- Thomas Glen Lundgren, 13 - 5-28-79;
- Mark Shelton, 17 - 8-4-79;
- Markus Grabs, 17 - 8-5-79;
- Donald Ray Hyden, 15 - 8-27-79;
- David Murillo, 17 - 9-79;
- Robert Wirostek, 18 - 9-17-79;
- Unidentified "John Doe," 9 to 25 - 11-29-79;
- Frank Dennis Fox, 17 - 11-30-70;
- John Frederick Kilpatrick, 15 - 12-10-79;
- Michael McDonald, 16 - 1-1-80;
- Charles Miranda, 15 - 1-3-80;
- James Michael Macabe, 12 - 2-3-80;
- Ronald Gatlin, 18 - 3-14-80;
- Glenn Norman Barker, 14 - 3-21-80;
- Russell "Rusty" Duane Rugh, 15 - 3-21-80;
- Harry Todd Turner, 15 - 3-24-80;
- Steven Wood, 16 - 4-10-80;
- Lawrence Eugene Sharp, 18 - 4-10-80;

- Darin Lee Kendrick, 19 - 4-29-80;
- Sean King, 14 - 5-19-80;
- Steven Jay Wells, 18 - 6-2-80;
- "Harry T," 15 - 6-11-80 (rescued)

Bonin was executed 2-23-96 at age 49 at San Quentin, California. David McVicker, who Bonin had raped but released, makes his objection known whenever James Munro comes up for parole, despite that Munro was not associated with Bonin at the time of McVicker's rape. Munro, who was 18 and homeless when Bonin picked him up, claims he, too, was a victim, and that, in 1980, Bonin forced him to participate in disposing of Steven Wells' body under threat of death.

--Source: Newsclips, research by Radford University Department of Psychology, Radford, VA, and correspondence with James Michael Munro for *"JAMES MUNRO – And the Freeway Killers,"* by Lori Carangelo; Wikipedia; Daily News, 3-25-08; *"Adopted Killers"* by Lori Carangelo.

## BUNDY, Theodore Robert "Ted"
*("The Coed-Killer': "The Campus Killer"; "Lady Killer")*
(see WASHINGTON)

## BUONO, Angelo and BIANCHI, Kenneth– (*The Hillside Stranglers*)
(see BIANCHI, under CALIFORNIA)

## CLARK, Michael Andrew
*(The Highway 101 Sniper)*

On early Sunday morning, April 25, 1965, Michael Andrew Clark, age 16, opened fire on cars traveling along Highway 101 just south of Orcutt, California, from a nearby hilltop, killing 3 people including a 5-year old boy and injuring 10 others before committing suicide as police closed in.
--Source: Wikipedia

## DUNCAN III, Joseph Edward, *("The I-10 Killer")*
(see IDAHO)

## EDWARDS, Mack Ray
*("The Freeway Killer")*

Born in Arkansas in 1918, Mack Ray Edwards moved to Los Angeles County in 1941. He told police that he buried all of his victims along freeways at highway construction sites where he was working, using the heavy equipment he operated as part of his job working on the early freeway construction in Los Angeles County as a heavy equipment operator for CALTRANS, starting in 1941. He confessed to murdering at least 6 children but also claimed to have actually murdered 18

33

children. The body of one of his victims was found underneath the Santa Ana Freeway and he claimed to have disposed of another beneath the Ventura Freeway. Edwards had a relationship with the family of Roger Dale Madison, 15, and had dinner in their home. On December 11, 1968, Edwards lured Roger into an orange grove, stabbed him multiple times killing him. After confessing, Edwards led police to sites where he had buried 3 more of his victims. Their bodies were recovered; he was convicted of the crimes and sentenced to Death; another 3 bodies, including Madison's, were never found. His known victims, who he was convicted of murdering, were:

- Stella Darlene Nolan, 8, of Compton - 6-20-53;
- Gary Rochet, 16, of Grenada Hills - 11-26-68;
- Donald Allen Todd, 13, of Pacoima - 5-16-69;

He also confessed to murders of:

- Donald Lee Baker, 15, of Azusa - 8-6-56;
- Brenda Jo Howell, 12, of Azusa, with Donald Baker – 8-6-56;
- Roger Dale Madison, 15, of Sylmar - disappeared -12-16-68.

Edwards was also considered a suspect in the disappearances of :

- Thomas Eldon Bowman, 8, of Pasadena - 3-23-57;
- Bruce Kremen, 6, of Grenada Hills, last seen Los Angeles Forest – 7-12-60;
- Karen Lynn Tompkins, 11, of Torrance - 8-18-61;
- Dorothy Gale Brown, 11, of Torrance - 7-3-62;
  Brown's body was recovered from the ocean, Corona del Mar, Newport Beach; molested, drowned.
- Ramona Price, 7, disappeared in 8-61 when Edwards worked in Goleta, California. In June 2011, Santa Barbara Police searched for Price's remains near a Goleta freeway overpass while it was under renovation but she was never found.

Edwards was apprehended in March 1970 was sentenced to Death. On October 30, 1971, after an unsuccessful suicide attempt, he managed to successfully commit suicide by hanging himself with an electrical TV cord in his cell at San Quentin prison. When he died, so did efforts to find his other victims' bodies.

--Source: Steve Proffitt, *"Dig Begins For Serial Killer's Victim, 40 Years Later,"* National Public Radio Inc - npr.org, 10-6-08; Wikipedia

## FAMALARO, John Joseph
### *("The Flat Tire Killer")*

John Famalaro 39, kidnapped Denise Huber, 23, after her car broke down on the Corona Del Mar Freeway 73 in Orange County on the night of June 23, 1991. He then took her to a Laguna Hills warehouse, sexually assaulted her and bludgeoned her to death. He was suspected of similar freeway abductions and killings at the time Huber was found. Born in 1950, Famalaro, a house painter, had a strict mother who forbid talk about sex and discouraged her son from dating. If there was a kissing scene in a movie, she would cover his eyes and once followed him on a date with a girl to make sure they didn't have sex. Several women who had dated him found him bewildering and sometimes frightening. He was arrested in Arizona in 1994 when police found Denise

Huber's body that he *kept in a freezer as a trophy for 3 years.* Sentenced to Death in 1997, Famalaro remains on Death Row pending further appeals, the moratorium on the Death Penalty, and the battle over lethal injection.

--<u>Source</u>: Los Angeles Times, 4-21-97; Orange County Register 7-8-11

## FORD, Wayne Adam
## *("The Long-Haul Killer")*

From 1997 to 1998, Wayne Ford, a long haul truck driver, often picked up young, White prostitutes and hitchhikers during his truck routes. He would rape and kill them in his truck, then keep their bodies for several days before disposing of them. He was found guilty of 4 counts of First Degree Murder for the brutal slayings of 3 prostitutes and a hitchhiker - women whose bodies were dumped, some dismembered, in waterways across California; he was suspected of more murders. Ford had turned himself in to police while carrying one victim's severed breast in his pocket, tearfully telling police he "didn't want to hurt people." He confessed to his crimes "because God told him to do so." Although the murders occurred in 4 counties, prosecutors were able to combine the cases under California's "Serial Killers Law." Born December 3, 1961, Ford was the son of an American father and a German immigrant mother. His parents divorced when he was 10. Ford was sentenced to Death in August 2006 and is on San Quentin's Death Row.

--<u>Source</u>: Amanda Tullos, "*12 Terrifying Truck Driver Killers Who Committed Murder While on the Road*"; Mary Curtis, Tom Gorman, Roubert Ourlian, "*Rape Victim Identifies Alleged Serial Killer As Her Attacker,*" Los Angeles Times, 11-19-98; Ranker.com; "*Jury Convicts Man of 4 Serial Killings,*" Los Angeles Times 6-28-06.

## HERNANDEZ, Alexander
## *("The I-210 Spree Shooter")*

Alexander Hernandez, 34, was already charged with 4 random fatal shootings in 5 days on the I-210, from his utility vehicle, when he was also charged in August 2014 with 3 more Attempted Murders and another random slaying of a motorist on the I-210. A separate random shooting left a teenager paralyzed while driving his girlfriend home from their high school prom on the I-210. The victims were:

- Mariana Franco, 23 - 4-17-15;
- Michael Planells, 29 - 4-17-15;
- Gilardo Morales, 48 - 4-17-15;
- Gloria Tovar, 59 - 4-21-15;
- Sergio Sanchez, 42 - 8-20-15

--<u>Source</u>: Richard Winton, "*Accused Valley Serial Killer Charged in Another Murder, More Shootings,*" Los Angeles Times, 3-26-15; "*Alleged L.A. Serial Killer Charged with More Attacks,*" The Star Advertiser, 10-5-15.

**JESPERSON, Keith Hunter** (*"The Happy Face Killer"*)
(see NEBRASKA)

## KEARNEY, Patrick Wayne
## (*"Trash Bag Murders"*; *"Freeway Killer"*)

Patrick Kearney preyed on 32 to 43 young men in the 1970s who were usually hitchhiking on California freeways, and so Kearney shared the nickname "Freeway Killer" with other independently operating "Freeway Killers" William George Bonin and Randy Kraft. Born September 23, 1949 in East Los Angeles, Kearney, a gay man, was a thin, sickly child, raised in a stable family, and a target for bullies in school. As an adult who stood only 5'5," he chose victims who were smaller than himself. He had worked as an engineer at Hughes Aircraft in Texas, sought out gay partners in Tijuana. He moved back to California where he picked up and killed his first hitchhiking victim in Orange, California, in 1965. After more killings, he moved to Redondo Beach with a younger man, David Hill, who became his lover. His first confirmed murder was in 1968, a year after moving in with David Hill in Culver City. When Kearny and Hill began to argue more often, Kearny would go out for solitary drives in his VW Beetle or truck and pick up young men hitchhiking, or in gay bars, murder them, have sex with them port-mortem, and sometimes cut open their bodies post-mortem out of curiosity. After shooting his victims in the head while driving on the freeways, he would take their corpses to a pre-determined place to copulate and dismember them, then dumped their remains back along the freeways in trash bags. His youngest victim was Ronald Dean Smith, age 5, who disappeared from Lenox, California August 24, 1974, and whose body was found in Riverside County October 12, 1974. The victim that ultimately led to Kearney's arrest was John LaMay, 17. As police were closing in, Kearney and Hill were persuaded by their families to turn themselves in. Hill was cleared of any of his partner's crimes and was released. On December 21, 1977, Kearney confessed to 28 murders -- and later to 7 more -- in plea bargain to avoid the Death Penalty. He then pled Guilty to 21 counts of Murder, and got 21 Life sentences. He was incarcerated at Mule Creek State Prison in Ione, California.
--<u>Source</u>: Wikipedia; Murderpedia

## KIBBE, Roger Reece
## (*"The I-5 Stranglers"*)
(see also RANDY WOODFIELD, CALIFORNIA-*1-5 Stranglers*)

Roger Kibbe's victims were all found in the 1980s on the I-5 and other freeways around Sacramento with scissors-cut clothes and hair, murdered by strangulation. Working Independently, Kibbe and Randy Woodfield were responsible for at least 12 confirmed I-5 killings, but that number may be 4 times higher. Kibbe and Woodfield came from different backgrounds. Randy Woodfield was born in 1950 to an upper middle class family in Salem, Oregon. Handsome and athletic, he landed a spot on the Green Bay

Packers football team in 1974 while still in college. Roger Kibbe, was born in 1941, a stutterer who was bullied at school and beaten by a mother who hated him. He became a furniture salesman but was described as "a loner." Kibbe was collared after he picked up a prostitute and started to get rough with her. She fled when her screams alerted a nearby patrolman but when he was apprehended he was charged with Assault. On May 10, 1991, Kibbe was sentenced to 25-Years-to-Life for the murder of Darcie Frackenpohl. In 2006, DNA evidence linked Kibbe to 6 more I-5 murders, dating back to 1977, and linked Woodfield to 4 others. On November 5, 2009, Kibbe received an additional 6 Life sentences for murders of Lou Ellen Burleigh, Lora Heedik, Barbara Ann Scott, Stephanie Brown, Charmaine Sabrah, and Katherine Kelly Quinones. In June 2001, Kibbe helped find the body of Lou Ellen Burleigh who had been missing 34 years. Kibbe kidnapped his victims, tied them up and silenced them with duct tape before leaving the scene of his crime. Investigators built a case for the I-5 murders from items found in Kibbe's car -- scissors, cord, paint chips, fibers and hairs. His known victims:

- Lou Ellen Burleigh, 21 - 9-11-77;
- Lora Heedick, 20 - 4-21-86;
- Barbara Ann Scott, 29 - 7-3-86;
- Stephanie Brown, 19 - 7-15-86;
- Charmaine Sabrah, 26 - 8-17- 86;
- Katherine Kelly Quinones, 25 - 11-5-86;
- Darcie Frakenpohl, 17 – 1987

--Source: *"Two Killers Leave a Trail of Bodies Along Interstate 5 in California in the 1980s,"* The New York Daily News, 3-23-14; and Wikipedia

## KEMPER III, Edmund Emil
## *("The Co-Ed Butcher")*

Between May 1972 and February 1973, Edmund Kemper, who was 6 feet, 9 inches, and weighed more than 300 pounds, embarked on a spree of murders in Northern California, picking up hitchhiking female college students and disposing of the bodies on Northern California highways. The headless, decomposed body of Mary Ann Peso, 18, who had been hitchhiking, was found in a shallow grave near the Old Santa Cruz Highway. Cynthia Ann Schall, 19, who had also been hitchhiking, was found on Highway 1 south of Monterey near Big Sur. He would stab, shoot or smother other victims and afterwards take the bodies back to his apartment where he would have sex with them and then dissect them. He would often dump the bodies in ravines or bury them in fields; on one occasion he buried *the severed head* of a 15-year-old girl *in his mother's garden* as a kind of sick joke, later remarking that his mother *"always wanted people to look up to her."* Born December 18, 1948, in Burbank, California, at age 15, Kemper shot and killed his grandparents, the Edmund Emil Kempers, who he was sent to live with, then turned himself in. He was tried in Juvenile Court, found "insane," and sent to Atascadero State Hospital. Five years later he was pronounced "sane," his records sealed, and he was released. Kemper worked a series of odd jobs before securing work with the State of California's Department of Public Works Division of

Highways in District 4, now known as California Department of Transportation (CALTRANS). Kemper killed 6 college girls, including two students from UC Santa Cruz, where his mother worked, and one from Cabrillo College. *He would often go hunting for victims after arguing with his mother.* In April 1973, Kemper battered his mother to death with a pick hammer while she slept. He decapitated her, raped her headless body and *used her head as a dartboard,* after putting her *vocal cords* in the garbage disposal, but the machine could not break the tough tissue down and regurgitated it back into the sink. *"That seemed appropriate,"* Ed said after his arrest, *"as much as she'd bitched and screamed and yelled at me over so many years."* His murderous urges not yet satiated, he then invited his mother's best friend over and killed her too, by strangulation. He then drove eastward. But when no word of his crimes hit the radio airwaves he became discouraged, stopped his car, called the police, and confessed to being the Co-ed Killer. He told them what he had done and waited for them to pick him up, seemingly unashamed as he confessed to necrophilia and cannibalism. His known victims were:

- Maude Kemper - 8-27-64;
- Ed Emil Kemper Sr - 8-27-64;
- Mary Ann Peso, 18 - 5-5-72;
- Anita Luchese, 18 - 5-5-72;
- Aiko Koo, 15 - 9-14-72;
- Cindy Schall, 19 - 1-5-73;
- Rosalind Thorpe, 22 - 2-5-73;
- Alice Lui, 21 - 2-5-73;
- Clarnell Strandberg - 4-21-73;
- Sally Hallet - 4-21-73

In 1973, after murdering his mother, he turned himself in. At his trial his plea of insanity to 8 counts of Murder enabled conviction of all 8. He asked for the Death Penalty, but with capital punishment suspended at that time, he was instead sentenced to Life Without Possibility of Parole. --Source: Hugh Stephens, "I'll Show You Where I Buried Pieces of Their Bodies," *Inside Detective, August 1973 issue.*

## KRAFT, Randy Steven
## *("The Scorecard Killer"; "Freeway Killer"; "Ortega Highway Killer")*

Between 1970 and 1983, Kraft is believed to have killed a total of 67 victims in California, Oregon, Washington and Michigan. It was in 1973 when one of Randy Kraft's victims, Wayne Joseph Dukette, 30, a bartender, was found dumped along Ortega Highway in Orange County, where he was also suspect in unsolved murders attributed to *"The Ortega Highway Killer."* Subsequently, 3 freeway murders were linked by their dismemberment and the victim's socks stuffed into their anus, with bruises or bite marks on their genitals, or complete castration. Vincent Cruz Mestas, 23, additionally had both hands missing and a pencil size object shoved into his penis. Born March 1, 1945 in Long Beach, California, to Opal Lee and Harold Herbert Kraft, Randy Kraft, a computer programmer, led a conservative life growing up. In 1968, Kraft was dismissed from military service because he had "come out" as a gay man. In March 1970, living freely via the bars along the beach cities as conduit, the first evidence of his violent behavior that would span another 13 years in the Long Beach and Seal Beach areas began when he ran into an overly confident runaway named Joey Francher, 13, who Kraft lured to his apartment, drugged and raped. Francher did not tell his parents nor police that he had been sexually assaulted, only that he had accepted the pills voluntarily and so Kraft could not be charged. On May 6, 1975, the severed head of Keith David Crotwell, 19, was found in the Long Beach Marina. Crotwell had last been seen getting into a black and white Mustang, which led police to Kraft who said he gave the boy a ride but that Crotwell was alive when he dropped him off. Due to insufficient evidence, police were unable to charge him. In January 1976, Mark Hall, 22, turned up, his body called a "map of torture"-- legs slashed repeatedly, eyes, face, chest and genitals burned with a cigarette lighter; his genitals were castrated and shoved into his anus; prior to the castration, an object was shoved into his penis with such brutality that his bladder was punctured. Several torture-slayings later, on May 14, 1983, Randy Kraft was pulled over by California Highway Patrol for erratic driving and stumbled out of the driver's side, spilling a beer. After failing a sobriety test, officers noticed a man slouched over in the passenger seat, barefoot, genitals exposed, with red marks on his neck, along with 9 different prescription drugs and a "coded list" later said to be a scorecard-like list of Kraft's victims.

In the summer of 1980, Kraft traveled to the neighboring state of Oregon as part of a contractual assignment delegated to him by his employers. Throughout the duration of his stay, Kraft resided in a town close to Portland. Before he returned to California in August, he is believed to have claimed 2 further victims—both of whom were listed on his "scorecard" with cryptic references including the word "*Portland.*" The first victim, a 17-year-old Denver youth named Michael O'Fallon, was killed on July 17. O'Fallon had been on a solo hitchhiking trip across America and Canada, prior to his enrollment at college at the time of his murder. He was plied with both alcohol and Valium before he was strangled to death, and his nude, hog-tied body discarded ten miles south of the city of Salem. O'Fallon was listed upon Kraft's "scorecard" as "Portland Denver." The following day, Kraft is believed to have killed a man estimated to be aged between 35 and 45 years old whose body was found beside a freeway in the city of Woodburn. This victim—listed as "Portland Elk" on Kraft's "scorecard"—had ingested a toxic level of Valium and Tylenol before he was strangled to death with a ligature. In late November, 1982, Brian Witcher, 26, disappeared and on December 3, 1982, a 29-year-old carpenter named Anthony Jose Silveira disappeared while hitchhiking towards Medford, Oregon. His body was found two weeks later, strangled, sodomized and bearing evidence of having been violated with foreign objects prior to his murder. At the time of the murders of both Witcher and Silveira, Kraft was again known to have been in Oregon on a business trip. The business trip concluded the day of Silveira's murder. On December 4, Kraft is known to have driven from Portland to Seattle, Washington to visit friends. Throughout this brief visit, he was observed wearing a military jacket inscribed with the name "Silveira." On December 5, Kraft flew from Seattle to Grand Rapids, Michigan—again "on business." His known victims were:

- Joey Francher, 13 - 3-70;
- Wayne Joseph Dukette, 30 - 9-20-71;

- Edward Moore, 20 - 12-24-72;
- Kevin Bailey, 17 - 4-9-73;
- Ronnie Wiebe, 20 - 7-28-73;
- Vincent Cruz Mestas, 23 - 12-29-73;
- James Reeves, 19 - 11-74;
- Malcolm Little, 20 - 11-74;
- Roger Dickerson, 18 - 11-74;
- John Leras, 17 - 1-3-75;
- Craig Jonatis, 21 - 1-17-75;
- Keith Crotwell, 18 - 5-19-75;
- Kent May - 5-19-75;
- Mark Hall, 22 - 12-31-75;
- Paul Fuchs, 19 - 12-10-76;
- Scott Michael Hughes, 19 - 4-16-78;
- Roland Young, 23 - 6-11-78;
- Richard Keith, 20 - 6-19-78;
- Keith Klingbeil, 23 - 7-6-78;
- Richard Crosby, 20 - 9-29-75;
- Michael Inderbieten, 21 - 11-18-78;
- Donald Crisel, 20 - 6-16-79;
- Unidentified/Dismembered, 18-30 - 8-29-79;
- Gregory Wallace, 15 - 11-24-79;
- Mark Alan Marsh, 19 -2-18-80;
- Michael O'Fallon, 17 - 7-17-80;
- Unidentified, 35-45 - 7-18-80;
- Robert Loggins, 19 - 9-3-80;
- Robert Avila, 16 - 7-21-82;
- Raymond Davis, 14 - 7-29-82;
- Arne Mikeal Lane, 24 - 11-1-82;
- Brian Witcher, 26 - 11-82;
- Anthony Jose Silveira, 29 - 12-3-82;
- Lance Taggs, 19 - 12-8-82;
- Dennis Alt, 24 - 12-9-82;
- Christopher Schoenborn, 20 - 12-9-82;
- Eric Church, 21 - 1-27-83;
- Rodger DeVaul, 20 - February 12, 1983;
- Geoffrey Nelson, 18 - 2-12-83;
- Terry Lee Gambrel, 25 - 5-14-83

On November 29, 1989, Kraft was sentenced to Death for 16 murders and was suspected of 67 more, making him one of the most prolific serial killers in history.

--Source: *"1970-1983: Randy Kraft, The Freeway Killer,"* The Long Beach Post, 2-21-13; *"The Highway That Crime Cruises,"* Los Angeles Times, 2-27-08; and Wikipedia.

## MARLOW, James G. & Cynthia Coffman ("California's 'Bonnie and Clyde' Spree Killers")

James Gregory Marlow, born in 1957, and Cynthia Coffman, born in 1962, met and fell in love in 1986 and became heavy drug users. Marlow had been a thief since age 10 and, as an adult wearing Nazi and Aryan Brotherhood tattoos, he committed several home invasion robberies. Marlow, a rapist and White Supremacist previously imprisoned in Kentucky, was known as *"The Folsom Wolf."* Coffman, his girlfriend, was a cocktail waitress who had *"Property of the Folsom Wolf"* tattooed on her behind. The pair, dubbed *"California's* Bonnie and Clyde," ran out of relatives to live with and steal from, and were homeless when they began traveling together, randomly killing young girls on a 5-week killing spree from California to Kentucky, including Corina Novis, 20 of Redlands. Her abandoned car was found off Highway 18 which runs from Lucerne Valley and San Bernardino to Big Bear, the part in San Bernardino is known as Waterman Avenue. Marlow got the Death Penalty, and Coffman got Life in Prison Without Parole for the November 12, 1986 for the Abduction, Rape and Strangulation Death of Lynel Murray, 19, of Huntington Beach. Both were sentenced to Death in San Bernardino County, California, for the 1989 Kidnap, Rape, and Murder of Corina Novis, 20, that had occurred 3 days Murray's murder.

--Source: Michael Newton: *"An Encyclopedia of Modern Serial Killers - Hunting Humans"*; *"People v. Marlow and Coffman,"* and *"People v. Marlow,"* Supreme Court of California 8-19-04."

## MORRISON, David Allan ("The Highway Strangler") (see VERMONT)

## MULLIN, Herbert William ("The Hitchhiker Murders")

In the early 1970s, Herbert Mullin killed 13 people, mostly hitchhikers, in California. Born April 18, 1947 in Salinas, California, and raised in Santa Cruz, his father taught him how to use a gun at an early age. In high school, he was voted "Most Likely To Succeed." Loss of one of his best friends who was killed in a car accident devastated him to the extent that he built a shrine to his friend in his bedroom. Later, he expressed fears that he was homosexual even though he had a long time girlfriend at the time. At age 21, he allowed his family to commit him to a mental hospital and other mental institutions over the next few years but they would discharge himself after short stays. He self-inflicted cigarette burns, attempted to enter the priesthood, and was evicted from his apartment for repeatedly pounding on the floor and shouting at people who weren't there. Famed FBI profiler, Robert Ressler, stated Mullin had Paranoid Schizophrenia as early as his senior year in high school which

41

could have been accelerated by his use of LSD or amphetamines. At age 25, Ressler moved back in with his parents and was "hearing voices" that were telling him an earthquake was imminent and human sacrifices could "save" California. His birthday, April 18, was the anniversary of the 1906 Great San Francisco Earthquake, which he thought was significant. On October 13, 1972, Mullin encountered Lawrence "Whitey" White, a homeless man who was hitchhiking. He tricked White into looking at his car's engine, then beat him to death with a baseball bat. The next hitchhiking victim was Mary Guilfoyle, 24, a Cabrillo College student, who he stabbed through the chest and back, then dissected her body and scattered the remains along a hillside road. Only 4 days later, his 3rd victim was a Catholic priest to whom he went to confess his sins. In a delusional state, he believed Father Henri Tomei had volunteered to be his next sacrifice to prevent the earthquake, when he beat, kicked and stabbed the priest to death. After killing Father Tomei, Mullin decided to join the Marines and passed the physical and *psychiatric* tests, but he was refused entry when his past arrests for bizarre behaviors was discovered. This rejection fueled his Paranoid Delusions of "a conspiring group of hippies." By 1973, Mullin stopped using drugs which he blamed for his problem, but on January 25, 1973, he killed Jim Gianera, who he blamed for selling him drugs, and Gianera's wife, with gun shots to their heads, then repeatedly stabbed their bodies. He then went to the home of Kathy Francis where he shot and killed her and her 2 sons, ages 4 and 9. In February 1973, Mullin was wandering around Henry Colwell Redwoods State Park when he encountered a group of teenage boys who were camping. He told the boys he was a Park Ranger, that they were polluting the Park, and ordered the to leave, stating he would be back the next day, but the boys didn't take him seriously and refused to leave. Mullin did return, shot them all, and left their bodies on the spot where they were found a week later. The final murder took place 3 days later when Mullin was driving past an elderly Hispanic man who was weeding his lawn. Mullins made a u-turn, stopped his car, got out, laid his rifle across the hood to steady his aim, and killed the man. There were a number of witnesses who gave police Mullins' license plate number and Mullins was captured a few minutes later. His known victims were:

- Lawrence "Whitey" White, 55 - 10-13-72;
- Mary Guilfoyle, 24 - 10-24-72;
- Father Henri Tomei, 64 - 11-2-72;
- Jim Ralph Gianera, 25 - 1-25-73;
- Joan Gianera, 21 - 1-25-73;
- Kathy Francis, 29 - 1-25-73;
- Daemon Francis, 4 - 1-25-73;
- David Hughes, 9 - 1-25-73;
- David Allan Oliker, 18 - 2-6-73;
- Robert Michael Spector - 18. 2-6-73;
- Brian Scott Card, 19 - 2-6-73;
- Mark John Dreibelbis, 15 - 2-6-73;
- Fred Perez, 72 - 2-13-73

Mullin was found guilty of First Degree Murder in the cases of Jim Gianera and Kathy Francis because they were premeditated, while he was found guilty of Second Degree Murder in 8 other murders because he acted more on impulse. He was sentenced in

Santa Cruz County to Life in Prison at Mule Creek State Prison in Ione, California, with Possibility of Parole in 2021
--<u>Source</u>: Wikipedia

## *"SONS OF SATAN KILLERS"* aka *"YELLOWSTONE KILLERS"*
**(Stanley Dean Baker, Steven Hurd, Arthur "Moose" Hulse, Harry Stroup)**
(see MONTANA)

### SUFF, William Lester
### *("Riverside Prostitute Killer"; "Lake Elsinore Killer")*

Beginning in 1986, Bill Suff went on a sex-murder spree, raping, stabbing, strangling to death, and sometimes mutilating 12 or more prostitutes in Riverside County, California. He dumped their bodies along highway roadsides and in orange groves. Born August 20, 1950 in Torrance, California, as Bill Lee Suff, in 1974 a Texas jury convicted him of beating his 2-month old daughter to death. He served only 10 years of his 70-year sentence before his 1994 release on parole. There had been insufficient evidence to also convict his then-second wife, Teryl, of the crime. On January 9, 1992, he was arrested in a routine traffic stop after pulling his car up to a suspected prostitute but then making an illegal u-turn. Detectives inspecting his van found rope, a bloody knife, and a sleeping bag with fibers matching those found on some of the bodies. Suff worked as a County stock clerk, allegedly delivering supplies to the task force investigating his killing spree. He liked to impersonate police officers, drive fancy cars, and do community service. His neighbors described him as a friendly man who liked to do things to help people. He cooked chili at police officers' picnics and won the "Riverside County Employee Chili Cookoff." *Subsequently it was alleged he used the breast of one of his victims in his chili.* On July 19, 1995, a Riverside County jury found him guilty of killing 12 women and attempting to kill another. He had taken photos of his victims both alive and dead in carefully posed positions. He is suspected of as many as 22 other deaths. His known victims were:

- Janet Suff, his 2-month-old daughter - 10-86;
- Michelle Yvette Gutierrez, 23 - 10-86;
- Charlotte Jean Palmer, 24 - 12-86;
- Linda Ann Ortega, 37;
- Martha Bess Young, 27;
- Linda Mae Ruiz, 37;
- Kimberly Lyttle, 28;
- Judy Lynn Angel, 36;
- Christina Tina Leal, 23;
- Daria Jane Ferguson, 27;
- Carol Lynn Miller, 35;
- Cheryl Coker, 33;
- Susan Melissa Sternfeld, 27;
- Kathleen Leslie Milne, 42;

- Cherie Michelle Payseur, 24;
- Sherry Ann Latham, 37;
- Kelly Marie Hammond, 23;
- Catherine McDonald, 30;
- Delliah Zamora Wallace, 35;
- Eleanore Ojeda Casares, 39

On August 17, 1995, he was sentenced to Death.

--Source: Murderpedia; Wikipedia

## SYED, Ali
## ("Route 55 Shooter")

Ali Syed, a 20-year old part-time student, was identified as the shooter in California State Route 55 freeway murders that occurred on the morning of February 10, 2013. Syed was believed to have first killed a woman in her Ladera Ranch home, then drove off in a stolen black SUV to Tustin near the 55-Freeway where he crashed the SUV and committed a carjacking but did not harm that motorist. But Syed shot and wounded a bystander before driving off in the carjacked Dodge pickup. He then began firing randomly at passing cars on State Route 55. When the pickup truck ran low on gas, he carjacked a BMW, executing the driver. He abandoned the BMW in a parking lot where he stole another pickup truck and shot 2 men, killing one and wounding the other. Police closed in on Syed who killed himself before he could be arrested.

--Source: Heavy.com News, 2-19-13

## WILDER, Christopher Bernard ("The Beauty Queen Killer")
(see FLORIDA)

## WOODFIELD, Randall "Randy" Brent
## ("The I-5 Stranglers")
(see also ROGER REECE KIBBE, CALIFORNIA, *The 1-5 Killer*)

The I-5 stretches nearly 1400 miles, from the Mexican border to British Columbia, except for a brief section where it is known as the San Diego Freeway, though most natives refer to it as "The 5" as well. Two serial killers who stalked women along the I-5, Randy Woodfield and Roger Kibbe, were known as "*The I-5 Stranglers*." Investigators linked Woodfield to an estimated 44 murders and 60 sexual assaults along the 1-4. But not all cases came to trial as result of his Life+ sentence." Woodfield and Kibbe were responsible for at least a dozen confirmed killings, but investigators believe that number is 4 times higher. Woodfield and Kibbe came from different backgrounds. Woodfield, born in 1950 to an upper middle class family in Salem, Oregon, was handsome and athletic. He landed a spot on the Green Bay Packers football team in 1974 while still in college. Kibbe, born in 1945, was a furniture salesman and a loner - a stutterer who was bullied at school and beaten by a mother who hated him.

Early criminal behavior was Woodfield and Kibbe's common bond. Woodfield's first offense was for Public Indecency ("flashing") which got him cut from the Green Bay Packers. Back home in Portland, he was arrested for attacking women, forcing them to perform oral sex and then stealing their purses. Sentenced to 10 years in prison in 1975, he was out in 4 years. Soon after that, young people began to die -- Cherie Ayers, a former classmate of Woodfield's in Portland on October 9, 1980, then 2 sexual assaults and shootings in January 1981 in Salem -- Shari Hull who died, and Beth Wilmot who survived. In February 1981, Woodfield left Oregon for Northern California, to the towns of Redding, Yreka and Mountain Gate, where a wave of robberies and sexual assaults were capped off by the double murder of Donna Eckard and her 14-year old daughter. Both had been shot in the head several times; the girl had been sodomized. The day after Valentine's Day, February 14, 1981, Woodfield's former girlfriend, Julie Reits of Beaverton, Oregon, was shot dead in her home. Throughout February, rapes, robberies and murders continued along the I-5. Police caught up with Woodfield in March and linked him to murders all over the region. Some of his known victims were:

- Cheri Ayers, raped, murdered, Portland, Oregon - 10-9-80;
- Darcey Renee Fix - 11-80;
- Douglas Keith Altic - 11-80;
- Shari Hull - 1-81;
- Beth Wilmot, (survived) - 1-81;
- Donna Eckard, Mountain Gate, California - 2-5-81;
- Donna Eckard's daughter, 14, Mountain Gate, California 2-81;
- Julie Reitz, Beaverton, Oregon - 2-15-81.

Woodfield went on trial in Salem for Hull's murder, June 1981, was found guilty, and sentenced to Life Plus 90 Years in prison. A month after Woodfield's conviction, more bodies were turning up along the I-5 and Roger Reece Kibbe came under suspicion. Roger Kibbe was convicted in March, 1991 and is serving his Life sentence at Mule Creek State Prison.

--<u>Source</u>: *"Two Killers Leave a Trail of Bodies Along Interstate 5 in California in the 1980s,"* The New York Daily News, 3-23-14.

## ZAMASTIL, William Floyd
## *("The I-15 Freeway Killer")*

William Zamastil may have begun killing when he was 16 in 1968 as he was a person of interest in the 1968 murder of Christine Rothschild, a University of Wisconsin student. Zamastil was a drifter believed to have trekked the Mohave Desert from Needles to Barstow, California, in the 1970s, leaving a trail of murdered young men and women victims who had been hitchhiking. Born in 1952 in Wisconsin, Zamastil had a wife and child in Barstow, had previously lived in Needles and Barstow, and returned to Wisconsin on July 17, 1978. He is described as a vagrant who traveled by hitchhiking and had criminal records in Arizona, California and Washington. In February 1978, Jaqueline Bradshaw, 18, and her brother Malcolm, 17, who were hitchhiking home from Las Vegas, were last seen being driven off from a Barstow truck stop by a man of Zamastil's description; the teenagers were taken to an area in the desert east of the I-15 Freeway and beaten to death, their bodies found a month later, partially clothed, near a truck stop where Zamastil once worked. In May 2004, Zamastil pled guilty to slaying the teenagers. In a plea bargain, Zamastil was sentenced to 25 Years to Life, to run concurrent with a 25 Years to Life sentence. He was already serving in Wisconsin for the 1978 Rape and Murder of Mary Johnson, 24, when he was 26. He abducted her in the parking lot of Copps department store in Madison, Wisconsin, and forced her at gunpoint to drive to a wooded area at Derluth Park in Sauk City where he raped and shot her in the back of her head. He then phoned Deputy Sheriff David Storely who he had befriended the year before when jailed for car theft, and told Storely he "thought he hurt a girl." Upon Storley finding the woman dead, Zamastil went on a shooting spree by forcing a woman friend to drive him with her 2 sons in the back seat, as he shot a pistol through the open car window, hitting farm buildings and road signs, but no one was injured. Authorities suspected him of committing 5 additional murders in California and Arizona, including that of Leesa Jo Shaner, a former FBI agent's daughter, whose naked body was found by soldiers on the Ft. Huachuca Army post in Arizona. She had been kidnapped, raped and murdered. DNA testing of hairs on Shaner's body linked Zamastil to the murder. On September 5, 1977, Scott Allison, 21, an Army soldier, was driving home to Bakersfield, when he became tired and pulled over in the San Bernardino Desert to camp outside and sleep. That night, his head was smashed in with a rock and his yellow 1977 Chevy Monza was stolen. Zamastil's known victims were:

- Christine Rothschild - 1968;
- Leesa Jo Shaner, Tucson, Arizona, 5-29-73 - found 9-73;
- Scott Allison, 21, San Bernardino desert - 9-5-77;
- Jaqueline Bradshaw,18 - 2-78;
- Malcolm Bradshaw, 17, with sister Jaqueline Bradshaw),
  Ft. Huachuca base  2-68;
- Mary Johnson, 24, Madison, Wisconsin - 8-1-78

--Source: "8 Unsolved Killings Get New Probe," Los Angeles Times, 6-18-03; "Murder of Former Agent's Daughter in Tucson," FBI.gov, 10-20-11; Murderpedia; "'70s Serial Killer Continues to Rack Up Murders," True Crime Report, 12-4-09; The Sun; and Inland Valley Daily Bulletin, 11-13-13; "Man Sentenced in 1973 Murder of Tucson Woman," FBI website, 6-20-11.

# CALIFORNIA UNSOLVED CASES

## "THE I-2 KILLER"

Michelle Lozano, 17, was kidnapped from Lincoln High School on April 2014 and found nude and strangled to death in a container on the I-5 Freeway a day later. Bree Anna Guzman, 22, mother of 2, went out to buy cough drops December 26, 2011 but never returned. Her partially nude body was found a month later along the Riverside Drive off-ramp at the I-5 and I-2 freeway Interchange. There were others.
--Source: "Is There A Serial Killer on he Loose in LA?" The Daily Mail, 4-8-14

## "THE LOS ANGELES 101 FREEWAY KILLER"

In October 2014, California Highway Patrol found the body of a 33-year old man on the Highway 101 Freeway near Silver Lake Boulevard off-ramp. Glendora Police also found another man's body with multiple gunshot wounds near the Sunflower Avenue off-ramp. The murders remain unsolved.

--<u>Source</u>: The Daily Mail, 4-8-14; Los Angeles Times, 10-23-14

## "THE SANTA ROSA HITCHHIKER MURDERS"; "THE HIGHWAY 101 MURDERS"

On March 16, 1971, Lisa Smith, 17, was last seen at about 7 p.m., hitchhiking along the south Santa Rosa highway. Hitchhiking was a common denominator in at least 7 of the 1970s slayings in the Santa Rosa area. Smith's age also falls squarely within the pattern of the killer's victims who were 12 to 23 years old. On March 5, 1972, two high school students discovered the nude body of Kim Wendy Allen, 19, lying in a creek bed. She had last been seen hitchhiking to school and carrying a wooden soy barrel with red Chinese characters on it. Coroners soon discovered that Allen was tortured to death before being dumped. Her wrists and ankles had been bound and she had been raped before being strangled by a cord. Investigators determined that she was strangled slowly over the course of half an hour. Allen was last seen on Enterprise Road in Santa Rosa. Her body was found 8 miles east of there. From the late 1960s through the 1970s, there was no shortage of crime, murder, and mayhem in California during this period -- the infamous "Zodiac Killer" was making headlines for several murders in the San Francisco Bay area on down, and even more bodies were left on the side of the road in Santa Rosa. On April 27, 1972, Jeannett Kamahele, 24, was last seen hitchhiking 20 miles from where Allen was found. Rumors and connections were made as officials began warning co-eds against hitchhiking to class and work. Two more bodies were discovered in an embankment northeast of Santa Rosa. Maureen Sterling and Yvonne Weber, both 12-year-old middle school students, were last seen February 4, 1972 hitchhiking on Guerneville Road. Their skeletal remains were found 6 months later. Cause of death as never determined. Lisa Smith, 17, went to a hospital Emergency after being beaten, and after leaving the hospital was picked up while hitchhiking and disappeared. Lori Lee Kursa's mother reported her 13-year-old daughter missing on November 11, 1972. Believed to have run away from home, and known to hitchhike, Lori was last seen visiting friends in Santa Rosa 10 days after her mother reported her missing. On December 14, the 8th grader's body was found down an embankment off Calistoga Road in north Santa Rosa. The cause of death was a broken neck. But with Lori's death came a potential break in the case. A witness came forward claiming to have seen 2 men force a young girl matching Lori's description into their van – that the 2 men grabbed the girl and threw her into the back of a van which was being driven by a White man with an "Afro hairstyle." Carolyn Davis, 14, from Anderson, California, 3 hours north of Santa Rosa, ran away from her home on February 6, 1973. She was last seen alive by her grandmother who dropped her off at the Garberville Post Office, 2 hours north of Santa Rosa, on July 15, 1973. Witnesses claimed to have seen a young girl matching Carolyn Davis' description hitchhiking down Highway 101 heading toward Santa Rosa. Davis' body was discovered one year after Maureen Sterling and Yvonne Weber vanished and only 3 feet from the exact spot where their bodies were discovered. The cause of death was strychnine poisoning. Theresa Walsh, 23, was last seen on December 22, 1973 at Zuma Beach in Malibu, California, 460 miles from Santa Rosa. Friends said she was intent on hitchhiking north to Garberville so she could spend the holidays with her family. She never made it home. On December 28, 1973, boaters discovered Walsh's body partially submerged in Mark West Creek just west of Santa Rosa. She was the 6th victim found in Sonoma County in just 2 years. In 1975 the 6 Santa Rosa victims, as well as the Jeanett Kamahele disappearance, were linked to the same killer, as were 8 other killings. And in 1979, unidentified skeletal remains were found 100 yards from where Lori Lee Kursa's body discovered. The victims were:

- Lisa Smith, 17, never found, Santa Rosa - 3-16-71;
- Kim Wendy Allen, 19, raped, tortured, strangled to death, Santa Rosa - 3-5-72;
- Jeanett Kamahele, 24, body never found, last seen in Santa Rosa – 4-27-72;
- Maureen Sterling, 12, skeletal remains, cause unknown, Santa Rosa - 2-4-72;
- Yvonne Weber, 12, skeletal remains, cause of death unknown – 2-4-72;
- Laura Lee Kursa, 13, broken neck, Santa Rosa - 11-11-72;
- Carolyn Davis, 14, strychnine poisoning, Santa Rosa - 7-15-73;
- Theresa Walsh, 23, partially submerged in creek, Santa Rosa, 23 - 12-28-73;
- Rosa Vasquez, 20, strangled at Golden Gate Park, San Francisco – 5-29-73;
- Yvonne Quilantang, 15, strangled, Bayview area, San Francisco – 6-10-73;
- Angela Thomas, 16, smothered to death, school playground, Dale City - 7-2-73;
- Nancy Patricia Gidley, 24, strangled behind a school, San Francisco - 7-12-73;
- Nancy Feusi, 22, stabbed to death, Redding - 7-22-73;
- Laura O'Dell, 21, beaten to death behind boathouse, Golden Gate Park - 11-7-73;
- Brenda Merchant, 19, stabbed to death, Marysville - 2-1-74;
- Donna Braun, 14, strangled in the Salinas River near Monterey – 9-29-74;
- Unidentified remains, Santa Rosa - found in 1979

By the 1980s the cases had gone cold and have remained that way ever since. The young woman found in 1979 has never been identified, Lisa Smith and Jeanett Kamahele have still never been found.

--Source: David Ian McKendry, "*The Disturbing Unsolved Santa Rosa Hitchhiker Murders*," 13thFloor.tv, 11-22-16.

# WANTED

## "THE ZODIAC KILLER"
(major suspects as of 2017: Ross Sullivan and Lawrence Kane)

On September 27, 1969, Pacific Union College students Bryan Hartnell and Cecelia Shepard were picnicking at Lake Berryessa on a small island connected by a sandspit to Twin Oak Ridge. A white man, about 5'11" weighing more than 170 lbs with

48

combed greasy brown hair, approached them wearing a black executioner's-type hood with clip-on sunglasses over the eye holes and a bib-like device on his chest that had a white 3"x3" cross-circle symbol on it. He approached them with a gun, which Hartnell believed to be a .45. The hooded man claimed to be an escaped convict from a jail with a two-word name, in either Colorado or Montana (a police officer later inferred he had been referring to a jail in Deer Lodge, Montana), where he had killed a guard and subsequently stolen a car, explaining that he now needed their car and money to go to Mexico, as the vehicle he had been driving was "too hot." He had brought pre-cut lengths of plastic clothesline and told Shepard to tie up Hartnell, before he tied her up. The killer checked and tightened Hartnell's bonds after discovering Shepard had bound Hartnell's hands loosely. Hartnell initially believed this event to be a weird robbery, but the man drew a knife and stabbed them both repeatedly, Hartnell suffering 6 and Shepard 10 wounds in the process. The killer then hiked 500 yards to Knoxville Road, drew the cross-circle symbol on Hartnell's car door with a black felt-tip pen, and wrote beneath it: "*Vallejo/12-20-68/7-4-69/Sept 27–69–6:30/by knife.*" At 7:40 p.m., the killer called the Napa County Sheriff's office from a pay phone to report this latest crime, first stating to the Operator that he wished to "*report a murder - no, a double murder,*" and that he had been the perpetrator. The phone was found, still off the hook, minutes later at the Napa Car Wash in Napa by KVON radio reporter Pat Stanley, a few blocks from the sheriff's office, yet 27 miles from the crime scene. Detectives were able to lift a still-wet palm print from the phone but were never able to match it to any suspect. Meanwhile, a man and his son who were fishing in a nearby cove heard screams, discovered the victims, and summoned park rangers. Sheriff's deputies Dave Collins and Ray Land were the first law enforcement officers to arrive at the crime scene. Cecelia Shepard was conscious when Collins arrived, *providing him with a detailed description of the attacker.* Hartnell and Shepard were taken to Queen of the Valley Hospital in Napa by ambulance. Shepard lapsed into a coma and died two days later, but Hartnell survived to recount his tale to the press. Sheriff Detective Ken Narlow, who was assigned to the case from the outset, worked on trying to solve the crime until his retirement in 1987. From December 1960 to October 1969, many suspects were thought to be the unidentified "Zodiac Killer" who left a trail of random killings, mostly of young couples parked in cars at lovers' lanes, in the San Francisco area of Northern California, and also murder of a woman in Riverside, in Southern California, which indicated a similar "signature." Zodiac gained notoriety by writing several coded letters to police and newspapers boasting of the slayings. On August 8, 1969, the

"408 cipher" was cracked by Donald Gene and Bettye June of Salinas, California, used homophonic substitution to identify the solution, after spending over 20 hours on it. But the translated cipher turned out to be the killer's thoughts and ramblings, containing numerous spelling errors, yet it failed to reveal his identity as the killer had promised. Harden's "408 cipher" results were also confrmed by the FBI. Zodiac's confirmed victims were:

- David Farrady, 17, Benicia, California - 10-2-68;
- Betty Lou Jensen, 16, Benicia, California (with Farrady) - 10-68;
- Darlene Elizabeth Ferrin, 22 - Vallejo, California - 7-4-69;
- Michael Renault Magean, 19 (with Ferrin), Vallejo, California (survived) - 7-4-69;
- Cecilia Shepard, 22;

- Bryan Calvin Hartnell, 20, Napa Valley, California (survived) - 9-27-69;
- Cecelia Ann Shepard, 22, Napa Valley, California - 9-27-69;
- Paul Lee Stine, 29, Presidio Heights, San Francisco - 10-11-69

Other suspected victims were:
- Robert Domingos, 18, Gaviota Beach, California - 6-4-63;
- Linda Edwards, 17, Gaviota Beach (with Domingos) – 6-4-63;
- Cheri Jo Bates, 18, Riverside (survived) - 10-30-66;
- Donna Lass, 25, Stateline, Nevada - 9-6-70;
- Kathleen Johns, 22, abducted with infant daughter, Highway 132 near I-180, Modesto, California (escaped) - 3-22-70
- Two others survived and described their attacker.

There have even been multiple confessions, but their stories have not panned out. Author Lyndon Lafferty, in *"The Zodiac Killer Coverup,"* claimed Zodiac's identity has been known to police since March 15, 1971, but the book did not reveal the name. Gary Stewart, in *"The Most Dangerous Animal of All"* (as the Zodiac Killer called his human prey) said the Zodiac was his own biological father, Earl Van Best, Jr., who died in 1984. In April, 2018, the Paramount TV Network aired a series, *"It Was Him: The Many Murders of Ed Edwards"* in which investigators noted that convicted serial killer Edwards (*"The Sweetheart Murders"*) lived in Northern California at the time of each of the Zodiac's murders in the 1960s, and would have closely resembled Zodiac's description. Even Edwards (who died in prison in 2011) and his children claimed he was responsible for Zodiac's murders and many others, but that claim was discredited. In 2017, half a century after the Zodiac case went cold, in The History Channel series, *"The Hunt for the Zodiac Killer,"* 3 experts presented new evidence narrowing Zodiac suspects to **Ross Sullivan** or **Lawrence Kane.** The experts were Kenneth Mains, world class detective and cold case specialist, and Sal LaBarbera, now retired as one of the most decorated homicide detectives in the country, known as "the LA Murder Cop," and Kevin Knight, professor of computer science at the University of Southern California (USC) and code breaker. They utilized a "super computer" dubbed "CARMEL" which was fed Zodiac's writings so it could "think like the killer." Additionally, "Touch DNA" was found in the form of two bloody handprints found on the pants of victim Darlene Ferrin. Ross Sullivan was questioned by police in the murder of Cheri Jo Bates. Detective Mains noted that Bates' killer sent a letter to police and newspapers confessing to the crime that was very similar to letters the Zodiac sent -- so much so, that he misused and *misspelled the same letters.* Lawrence Kane also has some red flags that jump out. Kane, who died in 2010, was a Navy veteran who studied *cryptology.* In the Zodiac's own words (including his *misspellings*): *"I like killing people because it is so much fun it is more fun than killing wild game in the forest because man is the most dangerous animal of all to kill something gives me the most thrilling experience it is even better than getting your rocks off with a girl the best part of it is that when I die I will be reborn in paradise and thei have killed will become my slaves I will not give you my name because you will try to sloi down or atop my collecting of slaves for my afterlife ebeorietemethhpiti"*-- allegedly the solution to Zodiac's "408 symbol" cipher. The meaning, if any, of the final eighteen letters has not been determined." As of 2018, Ross Sullivan and Lawrence Kane remain the best suspects.

--Source: *"The Hunt for the Zodiac Killer,"* History Channel, January 2018; and Wikipedia.

# COLORADO

## BUNDY, Theodore Robert "Ted"
*("The Co-Ed Killer;" "The Campus Killer;" "Lady Killer")*
(see WASHINGTON)

## GROVES, Vincent Darrell
### *("The Prostitute Murders")*

Vincent Groves was convicted of murder in the strangulation death of Diane Mancera, whose body was found dumped at the Surrey Ridge exit off of I-25 on July 25, 1988. Groves is probably the most prolific serial killer in Colorado history, making his mark between 1979 and 1988. Though he was only convicted of four murders, Groves had been linked to 24 homicides. At a hulking 6 foot 5 inches tall, his focus was on strangulation of young women; some prostitutes who worked on Colfax Ave, others just acquaintances.
--Source: Murderpedia

## LUCAS, Henry Lee and Otis Elwood TOOLE
*("The Orange Socks Killer")*
(see TEXAS)

## LUTHER, Thomas Edward
### *("The Highway 285 Killer")*

While in jail awaiting trial for the 1982 rape of a Denver woman in Summit County, Colorado, Thomas Luther boasted to other inmates that he had killed 2 other Colorado women - Bobbi Jo Oberholtzer, whose blood stained wool glove was found on a barbed wire fence along Highway 285, and Annette Schnee, 21, whose body was found face down in Sacramento Creek, 10 miles south of Oberholtzer's body. Both women had been known to hitchhike rides from their jobs in Breckenridge. Schnee's backpack had been found near Oberholtzer's body. Evidence suggested Oberholtzer had been picked up hitchhiking and fought her way out of a car parked at Hoosier Pass, causing her attacker to bleed as evidenced by the blood stained glove, and apparently ran 100 yards downhill before she was shot with a grazing bullet that struck her right breast. A second Winchester hollow-point copper bullet struck her in the chest. Her tracks show backtracking near the spot where she was shot in the back from a distance of only a foot or two. Her body was found fully clothed but her clothes were in disarray, which seemed to indicate that someone raped her and then re-dressed her. *Oberholtzer was wearing one striped sock and one orange sock. Schnee was wearing the mate to the orange sock.* In 1993, Luther was charged with the murder of Cher Elder, who was shot in the head and dumped. He broke her ring finger, although folklore alleges he cut off her ring finger and lips, because she threatened to expose an illegal sports-card ring connected to him. In 1994, Luther was convicted in West Virginia for the rape of a 30-year old Virginia woman. Born on June 23, 1957 in Hardwick, Vermont, Luther was the first of 5 children born in his family. In each of Luther's rape and murder convictions, he had attacked women who, prosecutors have said, "resembled his mother who abused him." It is believed that Luther began drinking at the age of 9 and was using drugs by the age of 12. He also claimed that at age of 12 he was having sexual intercourse with his aunt. Prior to and throughout his murder series, Luther had a criminal record for Rape, Sexual Assault, Assault and Attempted Murder.

--Source: Kirk Mitchell, *"Breckenridge: Two Young Female Hitchhikers Kidnapped and Murdered."* The Denver Post, 12-6-14.

# COLORADO UNSOLVED CASES

## *"THE I-25 SERIAL SHOOTER"*

On April 22, 2015, Cori Romero was shot in the neck while driving along I-25 near Fort Collins, Colorado. In May, 2015, the FBI joined the local investigation into a possible serial shooter on the loose in rural Colorado, after John Jacoby, 48, was fatally shot while biking. Police found Jacoby dead on a stretch of road near his bike in Windsor, Colorado - the first homicide in Windsor in 8 years. Jacoby, a part-time parks worker and grocery bagger, rode his bike everywhere and was known and loved by all.

--Source: *"Colorado Town on Edge as Authorities Consider Serial Shooter Angle,"* ABC News, 5-21-15

## *THE I-70/US-6 COLORADO SERIAL KILLER*

Stephanie Ann Bauman's face was battered. The 15-year-old runaway was raped on the hard ground in subfreezing temperatures. It happened on a remote farm near a windmill south of Interstate 70 in Arapahoe County. She took off running in the darkness, barefoot and nude, sometimes falling and scraping her knees. Her rapist jumped in a vehicle and charged after her, staying close behind her heels, pushing her on and on as she became exhausted and confused, crisscrossing barren wheat fields, running along a gravel road and into a ditch — for 4 miles. The temperature had dipped to 27 degrees that night. Authorities believe whoever killed Stephanie Bauman also killed Kimberly Jean Grabin, 16, a year earlier, as well as Donna Wayne, 18, in 1986, and Karolyn Walker, 18, in 1987, and that he "posed" the bodies of the four victims within a mile of I-70 in Arapahoe County, east of the metro area. Their killer had manipulated their bodies as if they were mannequins, spreading their legs wide apart. It was the killer's "signature." From 1975 to 1995, and since then, the Denver area almost always had more than 100 homicides a year. As was common at the time, detectives with each sheriff's office or police department investigated their own cases, and there often wasn't much communication with counterparts in other jurisdictions. It seemed unlikely to investigators that any of these were victims of Vincent Groves, a serial killer who dumped his victims out of cars like trash, their arms and legs bent in unnatural positions. But there were at least 20 victims who, for one reason or another, didn't seem to match Groves' pattern. And then witnesses identified a White suspect in 2 of these cases, whereas Groves is African-American. The task force's inner workings, was outlined in a memorandum that was drafted before it was disbanded in the 1990s, and the ongoing work of a new generation of detectives have not been revealed until now. A report concluded a "pattern" existed in which victims shared 13 common characteristics. *"During the past 20 years, 20 women have been murdered and deposited in rural settings around the Denver metro area,"* the report said. It was apparent the victims had been killed *in other locations and driven long distances on busy roads. The suspect is brazen enough to actually transport a deceased corpse far enough in a vehicle to be in a somewhat rural or isolated area,"* the report said. The task force concluded, after much analysis, that it was only logical that at least some of the murders were committed by the same serial killer. Task force members met for years to come, but made no additional arrests, and the group eventually disbanded after they exhausted all of their leads without linking anyone new to the crimes. A decade passed. Then, in 2005, Cheryl Moore, the Jefferson County detective, was working independently when she broke one of the cases. It started with the case of a Jane Doe, whose body was found in March 1989 by sightseers on Lookout Mountain, Moore said. In October of the same year Jane Doe's body was found; the case was very similar to that of another 1989 murder, that of Lanell Williams, a Denver prostitute whose slaying had been investigated by the homicide task force. But Williams' strangled body was found nearly a mile west of Golden *on US-6*. Moore took a fresh look at the two cases and eventually concluded the cases were related. But in order to solve both cases, she needed to first identify Jane Doe. She scoured the case files of the two women and found an investigative gap. Sixteen years earlier, detectives had taken fingerprints from the Jane Doe corpse. Moore had a lab technician run the fingerprints in different ways. The third time, a match was made to a Denver prostitute, 33-year-old Lisa Kay Kelly. DNA evidence — a science that was in its infancy in the 1980s — identified a suspect in The Lanell Williams' case -- Billy Edwin Reid, 52, who was convicted of murdering both women and sentenced to Life in prison in 2008. A witness statement and a letter also linked him to the murder of a third woman, Queena Sanders, whose body was found in Denver on Feb. 14, 1988. Her case, like Lisa Kay Kelly's, hadn't been identified by the task force. Denver police have presented the Sanders case twice for prosecution, but the evidence wasn't sufficient to prove Billy Reid murdered Sanders beyond a reasonable doubt. Still, Moore suspects that Reid committed other murders but Moore had been working the cold cases alone.

Then, a group of cold-case investigators began looking at the multi-county cases *together*. Their work convinced them that the same killer who posed the bodies of 4 teens within a mile of I-70, between 1979 and 1986 – Those victims were:
- Karolyn Walker, 18;
- Kimberly Grabin, 16;
- Stephanie Bauman, 15; and
- Donna Wayne, 18

He may have also killed 7 others. Additionally, Moore said she found similarities between those cases and as many as 5 in Jefferson County and one in Larimer County. The total of 17 cases — identified by detectives and investigators in Arapahoe and Jefferson counties — are linked by similar circumstances. Most of the victims were pretty, petite, in their teens or early 20s. Most were killed after hitchhiking or visiting bars. In recent years, investigators from Aurora and Larimer, Weld, Jefferson and Arapahoe counties have all submitted evidence to the Colorado Bureau of Investigation for DNA testing, but because of agency backlogs, they have already waited more a year for results in some instances or the evidence has been returned without new DNA hits. Although Denver was involved in the task force initially, its lab, which has helped solve scores of cold-case rapes and murders, has not processed evidence linked to the serial cases, even though the victims were mostly Denver residents… and it's a jurisdictional issue. Although the victims may have come from Denver, they were dumped in other counties. Just because they come from Denver doesn't mean they were killed in Denver, as it's accepted police practice that the jurisdiction where the body is discovered leads the case. It is believed that Karolyn Walker was kidnapped in the city which could be the key to solving it and as many as 16 others.

--Source: Kirk Mitchell. *"Serial Killers Worked Denver Streets from '75 to '95, Police Say,"* The Denver Post, 9-1-12; Kirk Mitchell, *"Colorado Investigators Suspect Serial Killings in Unsolved Cases,"* Denver Post, 4-28-16

# CONNECTICUT

### CARR III, Robert Frederick
*("The Hitchhiker Killer")*

As an adult in Connecticut, Robert Carr, a soft spoken redhead, probably began picking up hitchhikers in Connecticut before 1972. That was when the skeletal remains of Rhonda Holloway, 21, were found in a remote area in Connecticut, and before he kidnapped and raped Tammy Ruth Huntley, 16, when she was hitchhiking in North Miami. Born in 1943, Carr described his troubled childhood, killing baby chickens with a stick, being paid by men for sex when he was 11, stealing cars when a teen. Robert Carr was married, but said that while he would having sex with his wife, he would fantasize *raping* someone else. From 1973 to 1975, Carr, a TV repairman and house painter, had been imprisoned for a rape in Connecticut and paroled. He later confessed to raping and killing more than a dozen young boys and girls in the 1970s, and was caught while trying to rape a housewife. In 1976, Carr was also convicted and imprisoned for Kidnapping, Rape and Murder of Todd Payton and Mark Wilson, both 11, who were hitchhiking together. He tortured, strangled and buried their bodies in Mississippi and Louisiana. Carr also assaulted a woman named Sari, repeatedly raping her at knifepoint over a 36-hour period before she escaped. A series of unsolved rapes in Dade County, Florida, ended when Carr was arrested at the end of May 1976. His victims were:

- Tammy Ruth Huntley, 16;
- Todd Payton, 11 - 1972;
- Mark Wilson, (hitchhiking with Payton), 11-72;
- Woman named Sari;
- Rhonda Holloway, 21

Carr was sentenced to 3 Life Terms Plus 360 Years. On July 6, 2007, Carr died at Florida's Union County Correctional prison at age 63.

--Source: *"1400 Years Added to Sentence of Killer Rapist in Florida,"* Miami Herald, 6-8-00; and 7-22-07; David Ovalle, *"Serial Killer Provided a Glimpse Into Warped Mind,"* The Miami Herald, 7-21-07.

### DELAGE, Richard Tobias
*(The Taconic Parkway Killer)*

Richard Delage was only 14 in 1960 when he committed his first highway abduction with intent to kill. Driving his father's pickup truck and carrying a gun he purchased from another student, he randomly selected and abducted Julia Rosa, 30, in Stamford, Connecticut, by slowing down to wait for her to pass

55

him, then jumping from the truck, gun in hand, grabbed her arm and ordered her into his vehicle. But she screamed and panicked as he fired 2 shots. He told Stamford Police he had planned for 2 months to seek out a girl -- any girl -- at gunpoint if necessary. Rosa suffered bullet wounds to her neck and head but survived. Delage was again arrested on October 3, 1976, while at a Norwich, Connecticut mental hospital and charged with kidnapping and threatening a female hitchhiker. He had gone to the hospital to talk to a psychiatrist after calling the doctor and saying be had done "something bad." A psychiatrist who examined Delage found him to be "normal." But Delage had a long history of mental problems and was confined several times in mental hospitals. More than 15-1/2 years after Carole Elaine Segretta, a school teacher, was found shot to death in her car, a Westchester County grand jury indicted Delage, charging him with her murder. Delage, a 1971 University of Connecticut graduate, was also held in Connecticut on a charge of First Degree Murder when he killed Paget Weatherly, 23, a St. Lawrence University student -- the charge carried a maximum sentence of Death. Information was developed connecting Delage with both the Weatherly and Segretta slayings. The Segretta case came to the attention of authorities when a motorist observed a tall, thin man wearing a cowboy hat, lifting a limp body in the front seat of a car parked in a roadside area just off the heavily traveled Taconic State Parkway. Thinking that an accident had occurred, the motorist stopped and called through his open passenger window offering help. When the Delage turned, the motorist noticed a gun butt in his waistband and blood on the front of his shirt, and he sped off to call police. When state troopers arrived, the Delage was gone and Miss Segretta was dead. She had been shot four times. The resulting investigation included the questioning of more than 2,000 persons before Delage was named in the arrest warrant. At the time of the Weatherly and Segretta's murders, Delage was just under 15 years old and lived in the Cos Cob section of Greenwich, Conn. Under the 1960 murder statute a 15-year old could be prosecuted for Premeditated Murder and there was no statute of limitations in a murder case. Both women were shot with a .32-caliber pistol. Miss Weatherly was shot three times in the chest. During questioning following his arrest in the Connecticut kidnapping, Delage "admitted certain facts about the death of the school teacher, Segretta," troopers said.

--Source: "*Connecticut Man Indicted in Death of Teacher 15 Years Later*," Watertown Daily Times, and AP, 2-11-76; "*Teenager Attacks, Shoots Woman, 30*," Sunday Herald, 11-20-60; and subsequent cases reported by Murderpedia

### HOWELL, William Devin
*("The 'Murder Mobile' Killer"; "The Sick Ripper")*

On January 14, 1991, April Marie Stone, 21, disappeared after she was seen walking along the I-414 at South Apopka, Florida. Stone, 21, was found two days later, wrapped in a blanket off a dirt road in nearby Sanford, Florida. Her killer would have had to travel with her, or her body, from the I-414 along the I-4 and then turn onto the I-17 to reach Sanford. Born February 11, 1970 in Hampton, Virginia, William Howell, at age 45, was believed to be Connecticut's most prolific serial killer He was 5'10", 230 pounds, a former landscaper and drifter who lived in Connecticut, North Carolina, and

Virginia in the early 2000s. He was described by a former girlfriend's daughter as "*a kind hearted giant, who was really funny... always smiling and laughing.*" Howell nicknamed himself "*The Sick Ripper*" as result of his criminal convictions in several states from Connecticut to Florida for serial murders of 5 women and one man, while already behind bars for the murder of a 6th woman, Nilsa Arizmeni, who disappeared in 2003. Before being caught, he had planned to continue his killing spree on a cross country journey in his 1985 Ford Econoline van that he referred to as his "*murder mobile*" – the same term California's "*Freeway Killer,*" William Bonin, used to describe his van. Howell was apprehended in May 2005 and sentenced to 15 years for Arizmendi's murder before additional bodies were found. Law enforcement officials identified 7 prostitutes who he killed in 2003 while living with his girlfriend. Bodies of 6 of them were discovered buried in a marshy, wooded, 15-acre site behind West Farms Shopping Mall, in New Britain, Connecticut, which Howell called his "garden," after a hunter found human bones there in 2007. Three of the women had been raped, one with a foreign object (shock absorber); some were mutilated. One woman who he raped and strangled in the back of his van "wouldn't die," so he smashed her face and head with a hammer, and, because it was too cold at the time to bury her, for 2 weeks, he slept in his van next to her body which he called his "baby." He later cut off her fingertip, removed her jaw, and got rid of those body parts somewhere in Virginia, according to his prison confession. His known victims were:

- April Marie Stone, 21, missing in South Apopka, Florida - 1-14-91;
- Nilsa Arizmendi, 33, Wethersfield, CT, found at New Britain burial site - 2003;
- Janice Roberts aka Danny Lee Whistnant, 44, a transgender female, found buried, New Britain - 6-25-03;
- Diane Cusack, 53, of New Britain, Connecticut, found buried in New Britain;
- Joyvaline Martinez, 24, East Hartford, CT found buried in New Britain;
- Mary Jane Menard, 40, New Britain, CT, found buried in New Britain;
- Melanie Ruth Camilini, 29, disappeared from Waterbury, Connecticut - 1-03;
- Marilyn Gonzalez, 26, Waterbury, Connecticut

On November 17, 2017, he was sentenced to 6 consecutive Life terms after pleading guilty to the murders of Cusack, Martinez, Menard, Gonzalez, Camilini and Whistnant. --Source: "*Serial Killer Suspect Is Drifter With Criminal Record,*" The Hartford Courant, 3-14-15; Dave Altimari and Ailaine Griffin, "*Suspected Serial Killer Arraigned in 6 More Slayings; Records Give Crime Details,*" The Hartford Courant, 9-18-15; Jonathan Vankin, "*William Howell: Serial Killer 'Sick Ripper' Gave Horrifying Details of Sex Killings Records Say,*" Inquisitr, 9-18-15.

**LUPINACCI, Robert F.,** (actual killer; no photo available), and
**MILLER, Benjamin Franklin** (photo; wrongfully convicted)
*("The Bra Murders"; "Merritt Parkway Killer")*

Between 1967 and 1971, in Stamford, Connecticut, there was a string of murders of Black female prostitutes, 4 of whom were strangled with their own bras and dumped near the Merritt Parkway in Stamford. The bodies were all found within a quarter mile radius of the Riverbank-Roxbury Road freeway overpass;

4 of the 5 were from Stamford; one was from Mt. Vernon, New York. Tire tracks found backing into the crime scene indicated the killer carried the bodies in his trunk before dumping them in the same area. The victims were:

- Rose Ellen Pazda, 29, missing 8-4-67; skeletal remains found – 4-69;
- Donna Roberts, 22, missing 5-3-68, found next day - 5-4-68;
- Gloria Conn, 21, strangled, found next day, 200 feet from Roberts – 9-7-68;
- Gail Thompson, 19, 3 years after the previous killing - 7-10-71;
- Alma Henry, 34 - 8-22-71.

Alleged evidence led investigators to Bejamin Franklin Miller, a Darien, Connecticut post office clerk and self-ordained street preacher with a history of mental illness who joined Black congregations after his own church expelled him. Arrested March 8, 1972, Miller was charged with all 5 "Bra Murders," signed a confession he later claimed was signed under duress. He was found "Not Guilty by Reason of Insanity," and was committed to the custody of the State Mental Health Commissioner. But 4 months after Miller was charged with the Bra Murders, during a nationally televised news conference, Lupinacci, a Stamford electrician, was discovered trying to strangle a young Black woman by the Merritt Parkway. In the trunk of Lupinacci's car police found hairs from a Black person and a deck of pornographic playing cards with a missing Queen of Hearts. Such a card had been found beside the body of one of the victims a year earlier. Lupinacci was known to patronize Black prostitutes, and witnesses placed his car near the murder scenes as well as at the bars and hotels frequented by the victims. Only Lupinacci knew that not all the murders involved the victims' bras. But no one wanted to take a closer look at Lupinacci. After the attempted strangulation by the Merritt Parkway, Lupinacci was convicted of assault and served 3 years in prison. After release, he moved to Norwalk and remarried. Lupinacci claimed the crime for which he served time was unrelated to the Bra Murders for which Miller spent 16 years in a state institution for the criminally insane before a federal court set him free. Ten years later, a New Haven attorney, John Williams, looked at the case of Benjamin Franklin Miller, the man who went to prison for Lupnacci's killings, and his claim of innocence. Williams argued it in court for 7 years.

Miller was 80 when he died in February 2010, a free man.

Lupinacci died in prison in 2014 at age 79.

--Source: *"Will the Truth Ever Be Known About the Bra Murders?"* The Stamford Advocate, 11-24-14

### ROSS, Michael Bruce
### *("The Roadside Strangler")*

Between 1981 and 1985, Michael Ross abducted and murdered 8 girls and women, ages 14 to 21, most killed or dumped near I-84 in Connecticut and NewYork; he had raped 7 of them. Born July 26, 1959, in Putnam, Connecticut, to parents who were unhappily married after his mother discovered she was pregnant, Michael Ross grew up on his parents' chicken farm in Brooklyn, Connecticut. His mother, who hated farm life, had 4 kids and 2 abortions and beat all 4 of her children, but perhaps beat Michael the worst. She abandoned him and was institutionalized. His parents later divorced and sold the farm. Some family members

58

and friends say Ross was sexually molested by a teenaged uncle who committed suicide when Michael was age 6, after which the job of killing sick and malformed chickens was imposed on Michael at age 8. He would strangle them with his hands. Yet he was a good student with a high IQ of 122, graduated high school, and in 1977, Ross entered Cornell University and studied agricultural economics, graduating in May 1981. He began dating a woman who was in ROTC and dreamed of someday marrying her. When the woman became pregnant and had an abortion, the relationship began to falter. After she decided to sign up for a four-year service commitment, the relationship ended. In retrospect, Ross says the relationship became more troubled when he began to have fantasies that were sexually violent. By his sophomore year he was stalking women. In his senior year at college, despite being engaged to another woman, Ross' fantasies were consuming him and he committed his first rape. In that same year, he also committed his first rape-*murder* by strangulation. Ross said afterward that he hated himself for what he did and had tried but failed to commit suicide. Instead, he promised himself he would never hurt anyone again. His victims were:

- Dzung Ngoc Tu, 25, a Cornell University student – 5-12-81;
- Tammy Williams, 17, Brooklyn, Connecticut -1-5-82;
- Paula Perrera, 16, Walkill, New York - 3-1-82;
- Debra Smith Taylor, 23, Griswold, Connecticut - 10-23-83;
- Robin Dawn Stavinsky, 19, Norwich, Connecticut – 11-16-83;
- April Brunais, 14, Griswold, Connecticut - 4-22-84;
- Leslie Shelley, 14, Griswold, Connecticut - 4-22-84;
- Wendy Baribeault, 17, Griswold, Connecticut - 6-13-84.

Ross was apprehended June 29, 1984 and was executed by lethal injection by the State of Connecticut May 13, 2005, the first execution in New England since 1960.

--Source: *"Profile of a Serial Killer: Michael Ross,"* About.com; Wikipedia

# CONNECTICUT UNSOLVED CASES

## *"THE I-84 VERNON MURDERS"*

There have been at least 5 unsolved disappearances in a 10-year time frame in the 1-84 Vernon area.

- July 24, 1968 - Debra Spickler, 13, vanished from Henry Park in Vernon.
- July 26th of 1973 - Janice Pockett, 7, disappeared just blocks from her home in the neighboring town of Tolland.
- March 1, 1971 - Irene Larosa, 17, was last seen by family members in Ellington around March 1, 1971. At first it was believed she had run away but it looks like she may have been a victim of foul play.
- November 1, 1974 - Lisa White, 13, after leaving her home in Vernon and visiting a friend in the Rockville section of town. After visiting her friend, she left to go home and was last seen on Prospect Street. She has not been heard from since. She was described at the time as having blonde hair, blue eyes, 5 feet tall and 110 pounds.
- 1975 - Susan Larosa, 20, of Vernon, was reported as missing and found

deceased years later in a wooded area just miles from her home, a few hundred yards from I-84.

- July 21, 1975 - Stephanie Olisky, 15, suspicious death happened 2 towns away from where Lisa White disappeared. She had been found near death on Route 5 in East Windsor. She died days later from complications of serious head trauma, the manner of death undetermined.
- March 26, 1976 - Dawn Peterson, 13, was found murdered a block away from her home in North Windham. She had been bludgeoned to death. A teenaged neighbor named Andrew Carr was tried for her murder but acquitted. Her homicide occurred just a few towns away from the disappearances in Vernon and Tolland. Her murder is still unsolved.
- July of 1978 - Patricia Luce; 18, disappeared in after a trip to a convenience store in Vernon, she was found deceased years later in a wooded area of Marlborough, several towns away. It was thought that many of these cases could have been linked yet no strong evidence has ever proved that.

Over the years arrests were made in other sexual assaults. Two individuals particularly stand out -- one a former volunteer firefighter, the other a former metal shop teacher. Both men are alive and still live in state.

--<u>Source</u>: *"40 Years Later and Still No Trace. Is her Disappearance Linked To Several Others?"* Connecticut Cold Cases, ctcoldcases.com website.

## *"THE 1-91 CONNECTICUT KILLER"*

On June 30, 1985, right under the I-91 overpass, near the Connecticut River, lay the 98 pound body of Raquel Ramirez, 29. The mother of 3 had been beaten and strangled. She had last been seen alive at the Amigo Cafe on Park Street in Hartford. Witnesses allege that she was involved in an argument with a man who slapped her and shoved her into a car. At the time of her disappearance, she wore bluejeans, a blouse with a dragon print, and shoes. The State of Connecticut is offering a $20,000 reward for any information leading to the arrest and conviction of the person(s) responsible for the homicide or Raquel Ramirez.

--<u>Source</u>: *"Family Searches for Justice,"* Connecticut Cold Cases, ctcoldcases.com website.

## *"THE I-95 CONNECTICUT KILLER"*

On August 16, 1975 the body of an unidentified woman, age estimated to be between 18 to 29, was found behind an old department store on Frontage Road, not far from I-95 in East Haven. She had been bound and gagged and Police estimate she had been killed days earlier. Her identity and murderer are still unknown. In April of 2002 the decomposed remains of Philip Scaplen, 43, of Niantic was found and his death was never determined. (See also I-95 Killer Rhode Island.)

--<u>Source</u>: *"Questions Surround Rhode Island Man's Death Weeks After Disappearance,"* Connecticut Cold Cases, ctcoldcases.com website.

## "THE ROUTE 2 KILLER"

On St. Patrick's Day of 1982 the partially naked body of Leslie St. Laurent was found off of an embankment on Route 2 in Glastonbury. She was found strangled near the Wassuc Road Exit, almost 3 weeks after she had been reported missing. It is possible that she was murdered the day she went missing due to her being found in the same clothes she had last been seen in. Police do not believe that robbery or sexual assault were the reason for her homicide.
--Source: *"Two Different Glastonbury Murders over 25 Years Ago May Have a Common Link,"* Connecticut Cold Cases, ctcoldcases.com website

## "THE ROUTE 8 and NEW BEDFORD MURDERS"
(see also MASSACHUSETTS)

Beginning in the summer of 1988 until 1989, the New Bedford Massachusetts serial killings occurred approximately 150 miles from discovery of 9 bodies of prostitutes and/or drug addicts strangled and dumped along the portion of the multi-state "New England Route 8" within Connecticut, running north–south from Bridgeport, through Waterbury, to the Massachusetts state line where it continues as "Massachusetts Route 8." There appeared to be 2 serial killers at work. The "Route 8 Killer" did not seem as well organized as the "New Bedford Killer." Differences in their profiles partly involve regional locations and visibility of the bodies from the view of the road itself. However, the New Bedford killings ceased in September 1988 and the Route 8 killings then began in October 1988. The only suspect indicted for the New Bedford serial murders was **Ken Ponte**, an attorney with a taste for illegal drugs and pornography, but he was later cleared of all charges. He died on 2006. The only other suspect in the New Bedford Murders was **Tony "Flat Nose" DeGrazia**, who, as a young boy, had his nose bashed in by his abusive mother and thereafter carried a strong rage against women. Due to lack of evidence, no charges were filed and DeGrazia allegedly committed suicide in July 1991. (See also Massachusetts: *"The New Bedford Highway Killer"*)
--Source: *"The Route 8 Murders" rte8murders.blogspot.com*, 2-22-15

## "THE ROUTE 16 KILLER"

August 27, 1978, Janette Reynolds, 17, vanished while hitchhiking from Middletown, Connecticut, to her hometown of Griswold. She had been last seen at Four Corners in Colchester, allegedly getting into an International Scout vehicle that was believed to be blue with a white top. The car had been seen heading eastward on Route 16. Nearly a year later on March 25, 1979, Reynolds was found deceased in Groton under the Gold Star Memorial Bridge. Her murder still has not been solved.
--Source: *"40 Years Later and Still No Trace. Is her Disappearance Linked To Several Others,"* Connecticut Cold Cases, ccoldcases.com website

## "THE ROUTE 244 SHOOTER"

On August 22, 1988 around 9:15 in the morning on Route 244 in Pomfret Connecticut, a woman was shot for no apparent reason while at a stop sign. The suspect was described as a 28-32 year old white male with hair that covered his ears. He had been driving a dark colored, relatively new, full size Ford step-side pickup truck which was in good condition. The woman survived and the case eventually made it's way to the popular TV show, "Unsolved Mysteries." Despite the publicity, Connecticut State Police have never named a suspect.

--Source: *"Random Daytime Shooting Still A Cold Case,"* Connecticut Cold Cases, ctcoldcases.com website

# DELAWARE

## PENNELL, Steven Brian
## *("The US-13/Route 40 Corridor Killer")*

Steven Brian Pennell, a 31-year old married father and Delaware's first convicted highway serial killer, was already serving a Life sentence in 1989 for the 1987-1988 Rape-Torture-Mutilation Murders of 2 women along the US-13/Route 40 Corridor, when he was indicted on charges of killing 2 others about which he pled "No Contest." Psychiatric evaluations never diagnosed him with any mental issues. Shirley Anne Ellis, 23, was Pennell's first victim on November 29, 1987. Ellis, a former streetwalker who was planning to attend nursing school, knew the best way to catch a ride into the city was to hitchhike along Route 40, the area just south of Wilmington where she had plied her trade and where a car pulled up and offered her a ride that day. Her body was discovered partially clothed, her legs spread apart. The autopsy told a macabre story of torture and mutilation. She had been bound at her feet and ankles. Black duct tape, likely used to prevent her from screaming, was still attached to strands of her hair. No evidence of sexual assault was uncovered but the autopsy did reveal that Ellis was tortured with work tools before she died. The killer then wrapped a ligature around her neck and repeatedly struck over her head with a hammer.

On June 28, 1988, it happened again when Catherine DiMauro, 31, was walking along Route 40 around 11:30 PM. She accepted a ride from a stranger in a blue van. Construction workers found her body at 6:25 the next morning. She was completely naked and, like Ellis, her wrists and ankles were bound and she was silenced with duct tape. Again, there were no signs of sexual assault but she, too, had been tortured and mutilated with work tools, strangled with a ligature, and bludgeoned with a hammer. But also, DiMauro was covered head to toe in *blue carpet fiber*. Undercover female officers dressed as prostitutes began walking the I-40 looking for clues. On August 22, a prostitute named Margaret Lynn Finner who had been working the streets along US-13 went missing. Witnesses last saw her leave in a blue Ford panel van with round headlights, driven by a White male. About 3 months later, Finner was found dead near the Chesapeake and Delaware Canal. Her body was in such an advanced state of decay that a cause of death could not be determined. On September 14, 1988, New Castle County undercover Police Officer Renee Taschner, 23, had been walking Route 40 when a blue Ford van stopped and demanded that she get in. Taschner refused but immediately saw the *blue carpet* covering the van's interior and pretending to playfully run her fingers over the carpet, puling out some blue fibers. Taschner's partner ran the van's license plate. It was registered to Steven Brian Pennell, a Delaware electrician. On September 16, 1988 Pennell struck again when a known prostitute, Michelle Gordon, 22, from New Castle, last seen on Route 40, disappeared. Gordon's body washed up on the banks of the Chesapeake and Delaware Canal on September 20th. Three days later,

Kathleen Meyer, 25, from Brookmont Farms, was last seen hitchhiking along Route 40 and accepting a ride from a stranger in a blue van. Meyer's body was never found. The body of a 5th woman Pennell is suspected of killing has never been found.

Inside Pennell's van, police found a so-called "rape kit" that contained devices with which to torture his victims - pliers, a whip, handcuffs, knives, restraints. Sometimes he would just bind his victims by the hands and ankles while he raped them and beat their buttocks with his whip. Other times, he would beat them with a hammer until they were battered and bloody but still alive, or use the pliers to squeeze the victim's breasts and cut off their nipples, then strangling and/or in their skulls with a blunt object. He then dumped their bodies alongside Route 40 and I-13. Not much is known about Steven Pennell's childhood, although he appeared to have a normal and stable upbringing. He had completed several semesters studying *Criminology* at the University of Delaware and applied for numerous positions with the State *Police* Department but was *rejected* for various reasons, so became an electrician, got married, but had no children. Pennelle was finally captured when an undercover female State Police officer, Renee C. Lano, posing as a prostitute on Route 40, was able to gather fibers from Pennell's van and submit them to the FBI for testing. The fibers were an exact match to *blue carpet fibers* from the vehicle of one of his victims. The victims were:

- Shirley Ellis, 23 - 11-29-87;
- Catherine DiMauro, 32 - 11-87;
- Kathleen Meyer, 25 - 9-10-88;
- Michelle Gordon, 22 - 9-20-88;
- Margaret Lynn Finner, 27 (suspected of murdering) - 8-88

Convicted as result of DNA evidence for the murders of Ellis and DiMauro, Pennell was sentenced in 1990 to 2 Life terms. Subsequently he was indicted in the murders of Meyer and Gordon, pled "No Contest," and asked the Superior Court to sentence him to Death. On Halloween 1991, Pennell got his Death sentence. His wife, Kathy Pennell, and her 14-year-old daughter pleaded for Penell's life, and, with the two children from her marriage with Pennell -- a daughter, 4, and a son, 6 -- moved out of the mobile home that police had been watching. On March 15, 1992, Parnell was the first person executed in Delaware since reinstatement of the Death Penalty.

--<u>Source</u>: Jeff Mordock, "*Route 40 Killer Remains an Enigma After Being Convicted 25 Years Ago*," Delaware Today, November 2014.

# DELAWARE UNSOLVED CASES

## *"THE HIGHWAY 13 MURDERS"*

In New Castle County, northern Delaware, the murder of 4 women and the disappearance of another along U.S. Highway 13, near St. Georges, 1987 and '88 remains unsolved. The 4th confirmed victim of Delaware's serial slayer was found by deer hunters on November 12, 1988. A 5th victim remains missing and presumed dead, while police have no leads to the killer's identity.

--<u>Source</u>: "*'D'" Serial Killers,*" Crimezzz.net

# FLORIDA

### BOLIN Jr, Oscar Ray
### *("The Highway Killer")*

In 1986, Oscar Ray Bolin murdered at least 3 Florida women in the Tampa Bay area, while working as a long-haul trucker. He was convicted of murdering Teri Lynn Matthews, 26, Natalie Blanche Holley, 25, and Stephanie Collins, 17. He was arrested in 1987 after he and 2 other men kidnapped and brutally raped a 20-year-old truck stop cashier. After raping her for hours in his truck, the men let her go. She went to the police and Bolin was subsequently arrested. Bolin's cousin, Douglas Tedrow, told detectives that the woman he and Bolin kidnapped and raped in 1987 was Deborah Diane Stowe in Greenville, Texas; Bolin choked her to death. Texas authorities let Florida indict Bolin. Other homicide cases were scrutinized, including the April 1985 killings of college students Lisa Eisman and Kim Vaccaro, both 20, who were found in the Hillsborough River near I-75. Each had hitchhiked to Florida. Detectives also looked at Bolin in the case of Connie Louise Collins Jones, 22, who was found dead in the same spot by the river on November 19, 1984; and for Sharon Joan Hopper, 25, an exotic dancer found dead a year later in Lutz. Those cases are still unsolved. Bolin was sentenced to Death and executed by lethal injection, January 2016.
--<u>Source</u>: Amanda Tullos, *"12 Terrifying Truck Driver Killers Who Committed Murder While on the Road,"* Ranker.com/list/truck-driver-crimes/amandatullos

### BUNDY, Theodore Robert "Ted"
### *("The Co-Ed Killer;" "The Campus Killer;" "Lady Killer")*
(see WASHINGTON)

### CARR III, Robert Frederick  *("The Hitchhiker Killer")*
(see CONNECTICUT)

### CONDE, Rory Enrique
### *("Tamiani Trail Strangler" ; "Highway 41 Strangler")*

"Tamiami Trail" is the nickname given to the final section of Highway 41 from Tampa through to Miami. It was also the dumping ground of Rory Conde, dubbed *"The Tamiami Strangler."* His 6 victims were:
- Lazaro Comesana, cross-dressing male prostitute, strangled – 9-16-94;
- Elisa Martinez, found strangled to death - 10-8-94;
- Charity Nava, found dead just off the Tamiani Trail - 11-20-94;
  Charity's killer had written several taunting phrases on her back, including

*"Third"* and *"if you can catch me."*

- Wanda Crawford was found - 11-26- 94;
- Nicole Schneider, found strangled - 12-17-94;
- Rhonda Dunn, found strangled - 1-12-95;
- Gloria Maestre, (survived) - 6-19-95

After Rhonda Dunn's discovery, Miami police had connected the 6 victims to one unknown suspect via DNA analysis. The case took a dramatic turn when on June 19, 1995, frantic banging could be heard from a house belonging to Rory Conde. Inside, officers found the gagged and bound Gloria Maestre. Gloria pointed out her attacker via photos found in the house. Conde was arrested on June 24, 1995 at his Grandmother's house in Hialeah. During questioning, Conde confessed to the 6 murders and blamed his split from his wife, Carla, as being the catalyst for the killings. He explained that he killed Lazaro after discovering, during sex, that the prostitute was a man. In each of the murders, at his house, Conde strangled his victim from behind, then performed anal sex on the dead body before dumping their bodies on the Tamiami Trail. On July 12, 1995, Conde was charged with 6 counts of First Degree Murder. In April 2001, as part of a plea bargain, Conde pleaded guilty to the remaining 5 murders, and in return he was sentenced to 5 consecutive Life sentences. Conde returned to court on September 4, 2003 to find that he had failed to get his Death sentence overturned for the murder of Rhonda Dunn.

--Source: Murderpedia

## EVANS, Donald Leroy  *("The Rest Stop Killer")*
(see MISSISSIPPI)

## GORE, David Allen, and FRED WATERFIELD
*("The Killing Cousins")*

Born August 21, 1952 in Florida, David Gore, 29, an Auxiliary Deputy at the Indian River County Sheriff's Office, while on probation for Trespassing, together with his cousin, Fred Waterfield, 30, a mechanic, in July, 1983, picked up 2 girls -- Lynn Elliott, 17, and Regan Martin, 14. The girls were hitchhiking on US-1 from Vero Beach to Wabasso Beach, Florida. Gore and Waterford, handcuffed the girls and drove them to Gore's parents' house on the outskirts of Vero Beach where he and Waterfield raped them. Elliott was chased down and shot as she tried to escape, as witnessed by a 15-year old Vero Beach boy who phoned 911 and which led to Martin's rescue and an end to the "Killing Cousins" reign of terror. Their crimes included the rape of 7 women, murder of 6 -- some tortured, some dismembered and buried in citrus groves along Vero Beach, between 1981 and 1983. Their victims were:

- Lynn Elliot, 17;
- Regan Martin, 14 (with Elliott), escaped;
- Angela Hammel (raped, released);
- Barbara Ann Byer, 14;

66

- Angelica LaVallee, 14;
- Judy Kay Daley; 35;
- Hsiang Huang Ling, 48;
- Ling's daughter, Ying Hua Ling, 17

Gore might have provided a clue as to what makes a serial killer tick when he wrote this passage:     "...*I don't think a serial killer really has a choice. They may be able to suppress their desire and urges, but if genes play a part, how do you change your genes? Even people who know it's wrong are powerless against it... I've never tried to hide from who I am. I've always known there was something inside of me that made me different... I'd be at a friend's house sometimes and I'd be seeing his wife and I'd be thinking Damn, I'd like to [rape and kill] her — and immediately after thinking that, I'd say to myself - Why am I thinking this? - you see, I'd knew it wasn't right, but it was there lurking just beneath the surface, always on my mind...*"

He "couldn't help himself." Waterfield received 2 Life sentences for his role, while Gore was convicted and sentenced to Death in addition to 5 consecutive Life terms, and was executed by Lethal Injection at Florida State Prison on 4-12-12.

--<u>Source</u>: Steve Bousquest, "*Florida Executes Serial Killer David Allen Gore After 28 Years*," Tampa Bay Times, 4-12-12; Pete Easley, "*A Serial Killer Talks Too Much, May Speed Up His Own Execution*," Huffpost, 1-23-12; "*First Murder in 1980s Led 'Killing Cousins' Gore and Waterfield on Crime Spree*," TCPalm.com, 11-28-10

## JESPERSON, Keith Hunter (*"The Happy Face Killer"*)
(see NEBRASKA)

## KNOWLES, Paul John (*"The Casanova Killer"*)

Born April 17, 1946, in Orlando, Florida, Paul Knowles' was given up to foster homes and reformatories by his father after his father was convicted of a petty crime. First incarcerated at age 19, Paul continued to spend time in Florida prisons, including Raiford State Prison where, in 1974, he began a correspondence with Angela Covic, a San Francisco divorcee, who visited him in prison, accepted his marriage proposal, and paid his legal fees. Upon his release, he flew to California to be with her. After a psychic warned her of a dangerous man entering her life, Covic broke off the relationship and called off the wedding. Knowles claimed that, devastated by the rejection, he killed 3 people on the streets of San Francisco that night, before returning to Florida where he was soon arrested for stabbing a bartender during a fight. But on July 26, 1974, he picked the lock in his detention cell and escaped. Knowles then went on a murder spree ending after a chase and hostage taking. The victims were:
- Alice Curtis, 65, Florida, choked to death on a gag while he robbed her;
- Lillian Anderson, 11 - 8-74;
- Mylette Anderson, 7; Lillian and Mylette Anderson strangled to death - 8-74;
- Marjorie Howe, strangled with a nylon stocking during theft of TV in Florida;
- Ima Jean Sanders, 13, Tecas runaway, hitchhiking in Georgia, raped, strangled;
- Kathy Pierce, strangled with a cord - 8-23-74;
- William Bates, Ohio, murdered, his car, cash, credit cards taken –9-3-74;

67

- Emmett Johnson - 8-74;
- Lois Johnson, Emmet's wife - both murdered in Nevada - 9-18-74;
- Charlynn Hicks, Texas, motorcycle broke down; raped, strangled – 9-21-74;
- Ann Dawson, Alabama, traveled with Knowles 9-23-74, never found - 9-29-74;
- Karen Wine - 10-16-71;
- Wine's daughter, 16, both raped, strangled, tape recorder missing -10-16-74,;
- Doris Hovey, 53, Virginia, shot to death with her husband's rifle – 10-19-74;
- Carswell Carr, stabbed,
- daughter strangled, necrophilia attempt, Georgia - 11-6-74;
- Edward Hilliard - 11-2-74;
- Debbie Griffin, never found, was hitchhiking with Hilliard, Georgia - 11-2-74;
- Charles Eugene Campbell, Highway Patrol, abducted in Florida, shot to death;
- James Meyer, taken hostage with Campbell, shot with Campbell's gun.

On 12-18-74, Sheriff Earl Lee and Georgia Bureau of Investigation (GBI) Agent, Ronnie Angel. were traveling down the I-20 with Knowles handcuffed in the back seat. on their way to Georgia. Knowles grabbed Lee's handgun, discharging it through the holster while Lee was struggling with Knowles; Angel fired 3 shots into Knowles killing him instantly.

--Source: Wikipedia

## SCHAEFER, Gerard John
### ("The Hitchhiker Murders")

Gerard Schaefer claimed to have started murdering women as early as 1965, when he was 19. Two young school girls, Peggy Rahn, 9, Wendy Stevenson, 8, vanished in late 1970 after being seen in the company of a man fitting Schaefer's description. Schaefer denied being involved when he was publicly accused of that crime, but in 1989 in a letter to his former girlfriend, true crime writer, Sandra London, he boasted of killing and cannibalizing the two children. Schaefer was convicted for murders he committed while a Sheriff's Deputy. He boasted verbally and in writing of killing over 30 women and girls from 1969 to 1973, after picking up 2 girls, 17 and 18, who had been hitchhiking. He took them into a secluded wooded area where he threatened to kill them or sell them into prostitution. But when he got a call on his police radio, he left the girls tied up and with a noose around the neck of each that would hang them if they could not maintain their balance on tip toes, and stated he would return. While he was gone, the girls managed to escape their bonds and went to the nearest police station, which was Schaefer's station. When Schaefer returned to the woods and found the girls were gone, he radioed his station reporting that he had "done something foolish" by "pretending" to threaten to the girls "to scare them from hitchhiking." Schaefer's boss didn't believe him, stripped him of his badge, and charged him with False Imprisonment and Assault. While out on bail, on September 27, 1972, Schaefer abducted, tortured and murdered 2 hitchhiking girls, Susan Place, 17, and Georgia Jessup, 16, and buried them on Hutchinson Island. Authorities did not know about Place and Jessup when Schaefer agreed to a plea bargain in the first case, and he served one year on a charge of Aggravated Assault.

In April 1973, 6 months after Place and Jessup disappeared, their remains were found tied to a tree. In the bedroom of his mother's house, police found lurid stories he had written describing rape, torture and murder of women, along with personal possessions of his victims such as jewelry and diaries -- and in one case, teeth -- from at least 8 young women and girls who had gone missing, including items from Leigh Hainline (Bonadies), who had lived next door to him when they were teenagers and who vanished in 1969 after leaving a note for her husband saying she was driving from their Fort Lauderdale home to Miami but would be back in time to play tennis with him. Her remains went undiscovered until construction workers were working on the site 5 years later in 1978. Her skull was found to have multiple bullet holes. Schaefer received 2 Life sentences for Place and Jessup's murders. but was never charged in the murder of Hainline. His known victims were:

- Leigh Hainline (Bonadies), disappeared 4-69, Ft. Lauderdale - found 4-78;
- Susan Place, 17 - 9-27-72;
- Georgia Jessup, 16 - 9-27-72;
- Mary Briscolina, 14 - 10-23-72;
- Elsie Farmer, 15, (with Briscoline) - 10-23-72;
- Nancy Leichner, 20, who vanished - 10-2-66;
- Pamela Ann Nater, 20, who vanished - 10-2-66;
- Deborah Sue Lowe, 13, known to Schaefer and who vanished – 2-29-72;
- Carmen Marie Hallock, 22, who vanished - 12-18-69.

On December 3, 1995, Schaefer was found stabbed to death in his prison cell, killed by fellow inmate, Vincent Rivera. At the time of Schaefer's death, a homicide detective had been preparing to charge Schaefer with 2 additional murders, that of Nancy Leichner and Pamela Nater.

--Source: Wikipedia

## STANO, Gerald Eugene
## ("The Serial Confessor")

Born September 12, 1951 in Schenectady, New York, as Paul Zeininger, his natural mother neglected him to such an extent that she finally gave him up for adoption when he was six months old. County doctors declared him "unadoptable" because he was functioning at what they described as "an animalistic level," even ingesting his own feces to survive. Still, he was eventually adopted by Norma Stano, a nurse, who renamed him Gerald Eugene Stano. Stano murdered an estimated 80 young women, from Pennsylvania to Florida – 41 were prostitutes, runaways, hitchhiking teenagers; the youngest was age 12 - before his arrest at age 27 in 1980. Prior to killing, he had sought help from 3 psychiatrists who never raised the issue of adoption and so didn't treat him. Stano said "*Adopted kids like me seek out rejection, and believe on some level that no one will keep them.*" Stano was executed March 23, 1998.

--Source: Denise Lang, "*Dark Son,*" Avon, 1995.

## WILDER, Christopher Bernard
## ("The Beauty Queen Killer")

Christopher Wilder was charismatic, well dressed, and had learned how to display empathy and show concern -- even though he abducted and raped at least 12 women, killing at least 8 of them, during a 6-week cross country spree that began in Florida on February 26, 1984 and continued, through Texas, Oklahoma, Nevada, California and New York. Between February and April 1984, he was linked to murders and disappearances of many other women, some found in areas of Florida that he was known to frequent. Born March 13, 1945 in Australia, the son of an American Naval Officer and Australian National, Wilder was a rare breed of American serial killer, a "Successful Psychopath." In 1962 or 1963, he pleaded guilty to a gang rape at a beach in Sydney and was sentenced to probation, during which he received electroshock therapy. There is evidence to suggest that this treatment exacerbated his violent sexual tendencies. He married in 1968 but his wife left him after one week complaining of sexual abuse and finding photos of naked women and underwear that wasn't hers in his briefcase. Wilder then emigrated from Australia to the Florida in 1969. From about 1971 to 1975, he faced various charges of sexual misconduct, eventually for Rape of a young woman who he lured into his truck on the pretext of photographing her for a modeling contract, which became his modus operandi. Despite several convictions, Wilder was never jailed for those crimes, nor for sexual offenses against two 15-year old girls while visiting his parents in Australia in 1982. His parents posted his bail and he was allowed to return to Florida while awaiting trial. The first murder attributed to Wilder upon his return to Florida was that of Rosario Gonzales, 20, who was last seen February 26, 1984 at the Miami Grand Prix where she was employed as a model and where he was racing in a Porsche 911. Soon after, Wilder's girlfriend, "Miss Florida" finalist, Elizabeth Kenyon, went missing. Neither woman was ever found but were linked to Wilder by a detective who Kenyon's parents hired following the disappearance of Colleen Osborn, 15. She was last seen a few blocks from a Daytona Beach motel where Wilder was staying. Wilder fled Daytona Beach before her body was found near a lake in Orange County a few weeks later but she was not identified until 2007.

On March 18, he lured Theresa Wait Ferguson, 21, away from Merritt Square Mall in Merritt Island and murdered her, dumping her body at Canaveral Groves, where it was discovered March 23. He abducted his next victim, Linda Grover, 19, from Florida State University in Tallahassee, Florida, by offering to photograph her for a modeling agency, which she declined, after which he assaulted her in a mall parking lot, bound her hands, wrapped her in a blanket, and put her in the truck of his car. and transported her to Bainbridge, Georgia on March 20. That night, in Room 30 of the Glen Oaks Motel, he raped her, using super glue heated by a blow dryer to blind her. He further tortured her by applying copper wires to her feet and passing electric current through them. He beat her when she attempted to escape, but she did escape by locking herself in the bathroom and pounding on the walls. Hotel guests and employees who heard screams for help thought the incident was a case of domestic violence and did not want to get involved. Wilder fled in his car with all his belongings to Texas. The next day, March 21, he approached Terry Walden, 23, a wife, mother, and nursing student at Lamar University in Beaumont, Texas, about posing as a model. She turned him down, then disappeared on March 23. Wilder had stabbed her to death and dumped her body in a canal along Waldon Road where it was found March 26. Wilder then fled to Oklahoma in Walden's 1981 Mercury Cougar and on March 25 abducted Susan Logan, 21, at Penn Square Mall in Oklahoma City. He took her 180 miles north to a motel on the I-35 at Newton, Kansas; the next morning, he had breakfast, then drove her 90 miles to Newton Reservoir where he stabbed her to death and dumped her body under a cedar tree. In March, he took 18-year old Sheryl Bonaventura captive, at Grand Junction, Colorado, shot and stabbed her to death around March 31 near Kanab River, Utah; her body was not found until May 3. Michele Korfman, 17, an aspiring model, disappeared from a Seventeen Magazine cover competition at Meadows Mall in Las Vegas on April 1. Her body remained undiscovered at a Torrance, California, rest stop until May 11 and not identified until June. Wilder photographed Tina Marie Rosico, 16, before abducting her and driving her to El Centro where he assaulted her but kept her alive to be of use in helping him lure other victims as he traveled through Prescott, Arizona, Joplin, Missouri, and Chicago, Illinois.

In Merrillville, Indiana, Rosico was forced to help him abduct Dawnette Wilt, 16, at the Southdale Mall at Penn Yam and he attempted to suffocate her before stabbing her and leaving her for dead but Wilt survived and told police Wilder was headed for Canada. At Eastview Mall in Victor, New York, Wilder forced Elizabeth Dodge, 33, into his car and had Rosico follow him in Dodge's Pontiac Firebird. A short drive away, Wilder shot Dodge and dumped her body behind a high mound of gravel. He and Rosico then drove the Firebird to Logan Airport in Boston where he bought her a ticket to Los Angeles. On April 13, he attempted to abduct Carol Hilbert, 19, in Beverly, Massachusetts, but she managed to escape. Wilder's victims were:

- Rosario Gonzales, 20, Miami, Florida - 2-26-84;
- Elizabeth Kenyon, Florida - 1984;
- Colleen Osborn, 15, Daytona Beach, Florida - 3-84;
- Theresa Wait Ferguson, 21, Merritt Island, Florida – 3-18-84;
- Linda Grover, 19, Tallassee, Florida, taken to Bainbridge, Georgia– 3-18-84;
- Terry Walden, 23, Beaumont, Texas - 3-23-84;
- Susan Logan, 21, abducted in Oklahoma City, taken to Newton, Kansas - 3-25-84;
- Cheryl Bonaventura, 18, Grand Junction, CO, taken to Kanab River, UT - 3-31-84;
- Michele Korfman, 17, Las Vegas, Nevada - 4-1-84;
- Tina Marie Rosico, 16, El Centro, California (released) -  4-84;
- Dawnette Wilt, 16, Pen Yam, (survived) - 4-84;
- Elizabeth Dodge, 33, Victor, New York - 4-84;
- Carol Hilbert, 19, Beverly, Massachusetts (escaped) – 4-13-84

On April 13, 1984, after Hilbert escaped, Wilder stopped at a gas station in Colebrook, New Hampshire, and was noticed by two New Hampshire State Troopers. Wilder retreated to his car and pulled out a .357 Magnum. A scuffle ensued and as the Troopers attempted to grab and disarm him, Wilder was struck by two bullets in his chest, one piercing his heart, and he died. Wilder was cremated in Florida, leaving an estate worth $2-million.

--Source: Michael Robtham, "*The Beauty Queen Killer*," MulhollandBook.com, 9-25-12

## WUORNOS, Aileen Carol Pittman
## (*"Damsel of Death"*; *"Hitchhiker Killer"*)

Between 1989 and 1990, Aileen Wuornos shot and killed 7 men who she had picked up for their money along the I-95 that runs from north to south Florida. Born 2-29-56 in Rochester, Michigan, to Diane Pittman, Aileen never knew her father, Leo Dale Pittman, a child molester and sociopath who was strangled to death in prison in 1969. Her mother abandoned her and her brother, Keith. By age 10, she and her brother experimented sexually with each other, and by 11 she was having sex with neighborhood boys for money when she was raped by an older man. Pregnant at 14, Aileen claimed her brother was the father of her baby. Her grandparents sent her to a home for unwed mothers to adopt out her baby boy. It was not so much the adoption that she objected to but that her baby was taken without her ever seeing him or having any say. By 15, Aileen and her brother went their separate ways. Aileen, living on the road hitchhiking and prostituting in Florida, slept on the beach. There, a 70-year old retiree, Louis Feld, picked her up and married her, but because she would strike him when he didn't give her money, the marriage lasted only 9 weeks. In 1978 at 22, she shot herself in the abdomen and told emergency room doctors it was not the first time she attempted suicide, but she received minimal psychiatric care. She then spent 3 years in prison for Robbery and was released in 1983 to a life of alcohol and prostitution. At 33, desperate for love and acceptance, Aileen turned to lesbianism at a biker bar with Tyria Banks. They were an inseparable couple from then on, Tyria calling Aileen "her wife" and sharing a nomadic lifestyle, Aileen still prostituting, Tyria cleaning motel rooms. In 1991, Aileen pleaded "No Contest" to the murders of 6 men, claiming "self defense" and was sentenced to Death in 1992. Her victims were:

- Richard Malloy, Clearwater, Florida - 11-30-89;
- Tony Burress, 50, , body found along State Road 19 – 7-31-90;
- David Spears, 43, Winter Garden - 6-1-90;
- Walter Gino Antonio, 62 - 11-19-90;
- Peter Siems, 65, Pasco, Florida (never found) - 7-4-90;
- Charles Carskeddon, 40, Paso County - 6-16-90;
- Charles "Dick" Humphrey, 56 - 9-12-90.

Arlene Pralle, 44, and Pralle's husband, born-again Christians, befriended Aileen in prison but were not allowed to visit her because prison rules restricted visits to "family members." So the Pralles legally *adopted* Aileen to have access to her. At 45, Aileen asked the state to stop all automatic appeals and proceed with her execution, by confessing she had not killed in self-defense. On 10-9-02, Aileen Wuornos was executed by lethal injection.

--Source: Biography Channel telecast video at Biography.com; Clark County Prosecutor at clarkprosecutor.org; Biography.com; New York Times, 12-30-03

# FLORIDA UNSOLVED CASES

## *"THE DAYTONA BEACH TRUCKER KILLER"*

From late 2005 to early 2008, 4 women were found shot dead in the head, execution style, in Daytona Beach, Florida. The FBI investigated 24 other murders that also occurred beside highways in the same time frame, attributed to long-haul truckers. The victims were:

- Laquetta Gunther, 45, a prostitute;
- Julie Green, 34, found in a ditch on a construction site;
- Iwana Patton, 35, discovered on a dirt road;
- Nelita Ramos, kidnapped, led at gunpoint to alley, begged for life and released;
- Charlene Gage, 30, last known victim in 2008.

--Source: FBI website

## *"THE FORT LAUDERDALE KILLER";*
## *"THE FEDERAL HIGHWAY KILLER"*

The severed body of Delia Lorna Mendez was found in a dumpster along Federal Highway (US-1) in Hollywood, Florida, after 4 prostitutes, 3 with similar physical appearance who were last known to be strolling the same US-1, were also found mutilated and dumped near a Palm Beach highway. Boston Police were looking for a connection between the Mendez case and that of Karina Holmer, an Austrian nanny also found strangled, similarly cut in half with surgical precision, and left in a dumpster.

--Source: Mayhem.net

# GEORGIA

## DAUGHTREY Jr., Earl Lewellyn
## ("The Double Knot Strangler")

Earl Daughtrey had a long history of serial crimes against women that does not include a murder conviction despite that the FBI publicly declared him a suspect in at least 3 serial slayings. Born in 1949 in Berrien County, Georgia, Daughtrey's first hint of violence was in the late 1960s when a female classmate accused him of trying to choke her. No charges were filed and he dropped out of high school in his senior year. In March 1971, he married and they moved to Anniston, Alabama where he worked on a local construction crew. Daughtrey's crew was working on the landscaping of the home of Harvie and Betty Renfroe when Harvie found his wife dead on the kitchen floor, partially clothed and strangled with one of his own shirts double knotted around her neck. Although Harvie Renfroe was convicted of the murder, based on the testimony of the local sheriff, the sheriff was later impeached and removed from office. It was shown that a report from state investigators had named Earl Daughtrey as a "possible suspect" in the slaying of Betty Renfroe, but prosecutors suppressed the document and Harvie Renfroe, convicted again in 1980, served 17 months of a 5-year prison term; he emerged embittered and determined to clear his name. In September 1971, Daughtrey moved back to Ray City, Georgia. That same month, Daughtrey was charged with Assault after choking Jo Ann Peters in her Ray City home. In lieu of prosecution, Daughtrey was sent to a state mental hospital, diagnosed as a "hysterical neurotic" with "good prognosis" and released as "cured" on April 29, 1972. Harvie Renfroe then won his appeal for a new trial in 1972. In 1973, Emma Rogers, 27, was forced off the highway and shot 6 times while driving through Madison County, Florida, just over the Georgia state line. She survived and described her assailant. Earl Daughtrey was named as suspect but no charges were filed.

Four months later, Doris Register was chased down in her car in Cook County, Georgia, and was wounded by a shotgun blast to her head. She, too, survived after facing the gunman who peered through her car window and laughed in her face. She was able to provide the license number which was traced to Daughtrey. Paint samples from Daughtrey's car helped convict him for the Rogers case in Florida. In the Florida case, he was sentenced to Life Plus for Robbery and Aggravated Assault with Intent to Kill; his trial in Georgia added 10 more years to run consecutively with his sentence in Florida. In 1980, he was transferred to a Georgia prison. In Georgia, he served only 3-1/2 years when the Georgia Parole Board that "honestly believed he had gotten his act together." On January 7, 1984, police caught Daughtrey trying to strangle Brenda Debruhal, 34, at a public park in Tift, Georgia. Police captured him after he rammed two police cars in a high speed chase. He was charged with Aggravated Assault, Reckless Driving and Attempting to Evade Arrest. Florida revoked his parole and when back in prison in Florida, he was convicted of Simple Assault in the Debruhal case, receiving a one-year term of probation.

On October 29, 1985, Cheryl Fletcher, after advertising some items for sale, was found dead in her home in Ocilla, Georgia, strangled with a lamp cord tied with double knots around her neck. On March 12, 1987 Beverly Kaster was killed in her Lennox, Georgia home, strangled with a blouse double-knotted around her neck after advertising her home for sale in the same shopper newspaper as in the Debruhal case. Two months later in 1987, Louise Spotanski grew suspicious of the man who phoned in response to her Shopper ad offering a pair of recliner chairs for sale. Officers arrived to find Daughtrey advancing on the woman in a menacing fashion, a towel wrapped around his fists. Sentenced to 30 days in jail, he served only a week and was released. The double knots employed in 3 known murders rang a bell with state investigators who filed an affidavit citing FBI profiling of Daughtrey as exhibiting the behavioral traits and tendencies of a serial killer. The victims were:

- Betty Renfroe, Anniston, Alabama - 3-71 ;
- Jo Ann Peters, Ray City, Georgia - 9-71;
- Emma Rogers, 27, Madison County, Florida - survived;
- Doris Register, Cook County, Georgia - survived;
- Brenda Debruhal, 34, Tift, Georgia - survived;
- Cheryl Fletcher, Ocilla, Georgia - 10-29-85;
- Beverly Kaster, Lennox, Georgia - 3-87;
- Louise Spotanski – survived

In December 1987, Harvie Renfroe filed a civil suit against Daughtrey in the 1971 Wrongful Death of Betty Renfroe, seeking $32.5-million in punitive damages. Daughtrey responded with a counter suit in January 1988 asserting that Alabama's statute of limitations had run out on the charge and that Harvie's suit was frivolous and harassment. Investigation of the three "Double Knot Murders" continues.
--<u>Source</u>: Michael Newton, *An Encyclopedia of Modern Serial Killers,*" Murderpedia

## KNOWLES, Paul John  (*"The Casanova Killer"*)
(see FLORIDA)

## LEWIS, Gerald Patrick (*"The Highway 80 Killer"; "The Twilite Killer"*)
(See GEORGIA)

## MENDENHALL, Bruce D.  (*"The Truck Stop Killer"*)
(see TENNESSEE)

# GEORGIA UNSOLVED CASES

## *"THE I-95 GEORGIA KILLER"*

The body of Melissa McCarthy Comiskey, 27, was found in the woods off the I-95 exit at Woodbine, Georgia. She had been killed by a single gunshot to the head.
--<u>Source</u>: *"Woman's Body Found by I-95 Off Ramp Identified,"* St. Mary's First Coast News, 12-7-11

# HAWAII

### WILSON, Waldorf "Wally"
### ("The West Side Serial Killer")

Wally Wilson was a person of interest in the wake of the unsolved murders of Amber Jackson in June 2000, and tourist Nola Rebecca "Becky" Thompson whose body was found a week after she went missing on September 10, 2010, near Highway 50. Wilson's criminal history included a conviction on July 26, 1983 of First Degree Rape, First Degree Sex Abuse and Kidnapping; he paroled January 9, 1999. In January 2000 he moved to Kahua'i, Hawaii. In Spring and Summer of 2000, on Kaua'i's west side, 3 white women were stabbed and sexually assaulted; 2 died; the 3rd who had been left for dead survived. Kaua'i Police Department (KDP) quickly identified Wilson as a prime suspect, but they could not gather enough evidence to charge him. Some KPD officers believed Wilson was the *"West Side Serial Killer"* (*"KPD Blue"* by Anthony Sommer). When Wilson was kept off the streets, there were no more attacks. Amber Johnson and Rebecca Thompson's murders occurred in 2010 after Wilson's release.

--Source: *"Alleged Westside Serial Killer Wilson Said to be Out of Jail and Back on Island"* parxnewsdaily.blogspot.com

## HAWAII UNSOLVED CASES

### "THE HONOLULU STRANGLER"

From 1985 to 1986, 5 Honolulu women were found raped and strangled to death near water. Police set up roadblocks at the Nimitz Highway viaduct to the H-1 Freeway near the airport, Six days later, police arrested and booked a 43-year-old Ewa Beach man in connection with Linda Pesce's murder. Police and prosecutors believed they knew the man who killed the 5 women, but could never prove it. The victims were:

- Vicki Gail Purdy, 25 - 5-29-85;
- Regina Sakamoto, 17 - 1-14-86;
- Denise Hughes, 21 - 1-30-86;
- Louise Medeiros, 25 - 3-26-86;
- Linda Pesce, 36, the last known victim - 4-29-86.

In 2015, Honolulu police hoped to get access to the DNA of a man who died in 1980 to see if they can finally link him to the killings that gripped Oahu 20 years prior. Law enforcement sources told KITV 4 News they've received conflicting reports that the suspect died in California or Tennessee.

--Source: *"Detectives Hope DNA Can Link Man To Oahu's Serial Killings,"* Yahoo News, 5-19-05; *"Serial Killer Case Still a Mystery,"* Hawaii News Now, KGMB and KHNI; KITV-4 News; and Wikipedia

# IDAHO

**BRAAE, Michael**
*("Cowboy Mike," "Barefoot Cowboy"; The I-84 Killer")*
(see WASHINGTON)

**BUNDY, Theodore Robert "Ted"**
*("The Co-Ed Killer;" "The Campus Killer;" "Lady Killer")*
(see WASHINGTON)

### DUNCAN III, Joseph Edward
*("The I-10 Killer")*

After Joseph Duncan his first two killings, in 1997 that were close to his home, Duncan had started killing quite a distance from where he lived. Duncan's criminal history dates to when, at age 15, he committed his first recorded sex crime in 1978 in his hometown of Tacoma, Washington. In that incident, he raped a 9-year-old boy at gunpoint. The following year, he was arrested driving a stolen car. He was sentenced as a juvenile and sent to Dyslin's Boys' ranch in Tacoma, where he told a therapist who was assigned to his case that he had bound and sexually assaulted 6 boys, according to a report by the Associated Press. Surveillance cameras revealed that Joseph Duncan was at a truck stop hours after Russell Turcotte, age 19, a Turtle Mountain Chippewa Indian, had been hitchhiking on a desolate stretch of Highway 2 west of Grand Forks at around 2 AM, on July 12, 2002. Turcotte was allegedly picked up by Duncan and taken to a side road near Grand Forks Air Force Base where he was probably raped and killed. He was then taken to Devils Lake, 90 miles west of Grand Forks, where his partially nude body was dumped and covered with brush. His skull had been crushed. Months later, in November 2002, his skeleton was discovered by a rancher in a clump of trees.

His victims include:
- Unnamed boy, 9, Tacoma, Washington, abducted 1978 - found 11-02;
- Unnamed boy, 5;
- 6 Unnamed boys, Tacoma, Washington;
- Deborah Palmer, 7, Oak Harbor, Washington;
- Anthony Michael Martinez, 10, abducted 4-4-97, Beaumont, CA, found 4-19-97;
- Steven Earl Kraft Jr,. 12;
- Unnamed boy, 14, Tacoma, Washington - 1980;
- Slade Groene, 13, Coeur d'Alene, Idaho;
- Brenda Groene, 30, (Slade's mother) - 5-16-05;

- Mark McKenzie, 37 (Slade's stepfather);
- Dylan Groene, 9, (Slade's brother), who he tortured and murdered;


- Shasta Gorene (Dylan Griene's sister), 8, sexually molested - rescued 7-2-05;
- Sammiejo White, 11, taken Seattle, 7-6-06, found Bothell, Washington - 2-10-98;
- Carmen Cubias, taken Seattle 7-6-06, found Bothell, Washington – 2-10-98;
- Russell Turquet, 19, Highway 2, Grand Forks, Idaho.

Suspected Victim:

- Dalton Mesarchik, 7, of Streator, Illinois, disappeared 3-25-03; skull alleged crushed by hammer, found in creek next day -  3-26-03

During his incarceration, authorities connected Duncan with the unsolved murders of Anthony Martinez in California, and Carmen Cubias, and Sammijeo White, of Seattle, whose remains were found in Bothell, Washington -- all of which occurred during Duncan's parole from 1994–1997.  Duncan was convicted in Idaho for Kidnapping and Murdering the 3 victims in Coeur d'Alene, and given 6 Life sentences; and in federal court for Kidnapping Shasta and Dylan Groene and Murder of  Dylan given 3 Death sentences and 3 Life sentences; and California for Kidnapping and Murder of Martinez, for which he was given 2 Life sentences.

--Source: Robert A. Lindsay, "*Joseph Edward Duncan III*," for WordPress, 3-13-09
https://beyondhighbrow.com/2009/05/13/joseph-edward-duncan-iii/ ;
and Wikipedia

# ILLINOIS

## BIERBODT, Lonnie
### ("The I-80 Killer")

On August 23, 1992, Tammy Jo Zywicki, 21, was driving on I-80 from Illinois to Grinell, Iowa, where she was to begin a job at Grinell College. She was on a rural stretch of I-80 at Mile Marker 83, in central Illinois, when her 1985 Pontiac, which had previously overheated and was thought to be repaired, again broke down. She was last seen standing by her car at about 3:30 PM. Witnesses reported seeing a tractor-trailer in that vicinity and time frame. In Iowa, 16 carloads of college students joined the search for her. On September 1, 1992, her body, sexually assaulted, stabbed 8 times, and wrapped in a red blanket bound with duct tape, was found along I-44 in rural Lawrence County, Missouri, between Springfield and Joplin. In January 1993, an unnamed witness reported she'd seen Zywicki pull to the side of the road and that a man -- a White male 35-40, over 6 feet tall with dark, bushy hair -- was with Zywicki, watching as the young girl struggled to fix her car. The eyewitness also reported that she worked at a medical facility where the wife of a truck driver who fit the description of the suspect came in for a routine blood test and was wearing a musical watch that she said her husband had given her -- It matched the description of a musical watch that Zywicki had in her possession when she went missing but was never recovered. Officials of an FBI task force identified the trucker as Lonnie Bierbodt. The blanket in which Zywicki's body had been wrapped bore the Kenworth logo--the same type of truck Bierbodt drove--and he lived in the vicinity of where Zywicki's body was found. Lonnie Bierbodt submitted to questioning and provided a blood test and hair sample for testing, before being released. But DNA testing had not yet been used by the FBI for forensics in criminal cases. A few weeks later, the investigative task force was disbanded and again the case went cold. In 2007, Lonnie Bierbodt died at age 41. At the time, authorities questioned Bruce Mendenhall who eventually confessed to the serial slayings of 6 women in Tennessee, Indiana, Alabama, and Georgia, but denied killing Tammy Jo Zywicki.
--Source: *Chicago Tribune*, 8-27-92; *"Iowa Cold Cases,"* CBS Denver, Iowacoldcases.org/case-summaries/tammy-zywicki; 2-25-14

## EYLER, Larry
### ("The Interstate Killer"; "Hoosier Highway Killer")

After becoming part of the Indianapolis gay community in 1982-3, Larry Eyler was believed to have killed from 20 to 23 victims in 5 states, who he repeatedly stabbed, dismembered, placed in trash bags and threw into dumpsters or dumped along US-40. From March 22, 1982 to May 7, 1984, his victims were found in Illinois, Indiana, Kentucky, Wisconsin and Eyler is suspected of similar killings along US-40 in Ohio. Born December 21, 1952 in Indiana, Larry Eyler taught Library Science during college. In childhood, he was abandoned by his mother, teased and beaten by stepfathers who, along with several other families, raised him. At age 10 he was sent to the Riley Child Guidance Clinic at Indiana University Medical Center in Indianapolis, where psychological tests revealed normal intelligence, extreme insecurity, *and great fear of separation and abandonment.* Clinic staff decided Eyler's home environment was unstable and chaotic, so at age 12 he was sent to a Catholic boys' home where he lived for 5 months. On August 4, 1978, he was arrested for stabbing Craig Long who survived the attack. Eyler pled guilty to Aggravated Battery, fined $43, and released. When the gay community became suspicious of him, the gay newspaper, "*The Works,*" set up a hot-line and published a profile of the suspected serial killer. On September 30, 1983, an Indiana Highway Patrol Officer spotted Eyler's truck parked on the side of I-65, and 2 men, one of them bound, who accused Eyler of making homosexual advances; the officer searched Eyler's vehicle and found surgical tape, nylon clothesline, and a hunting knife stained with blood that would later match Ralph Calise's; Eyler's tire tracks and boot prints matched those found where Calise's body was dumped. On November 21, 1990, while on Death Row in Illinois, his plea offer of 60 years plus disclosure as to other murders in order to avoid the Death Penalty was rejected. His victims were:

- Delvoyd Baker, 14, Indiana - 10-2-82;
- Steven Crockett, 19, Indiana -10-23-82;
- Craig Townsend, 21, drugged, beaten, survived - 11-4-82;
- Robert Foley, Illinois - 11-4-82;
- John Johnson, 25, Indiana - 12-25-82;
- John Roach, 21, Indiana - 12-28-82;
- Steven Agan, 23, Indiana - 12-28-82;
- Edgar Underkofler, 27, Illinois - 3-4-83;
- Jay Reynolds, 31, Kentucky - 3-21-83;
- Gustavo Herrera, 28, Illinois - 4-8-83;
- Erwin Dwayne, Gibson, 16, Illinois - 4-15-83;
- Jimmy T. Roberts, 18, Illinois - 5-9-83;
- Scott McNeive, 21, Indiana - 4-15-83;
- Unidentified Male, Illinois - 7-2-83;
- Derrick Hansen, 18, sexually assaulted, dismembered, Wisconsin – 10-4-83;
- Unidentified Male, Indiana - 10-15-83;
- Michael Bouer, 22;
- John Bartlett, & 2 other skeletons, pants down, 1 decapitated, Indiana- 10-19-83;
- Unidentified Male, Illinois - 12-5-83;
- Richard Wayne, and an Unidentified Male, Illinois - 12-7-93;
- David M. Block, 22, Illinois - 5-7-84;
- Danny Bridges, 16, found in trash bag at Eyler's home, Indiana – 8-21-84

When Eyeler was sentenced to Death for the murder of 16-year old Danny Bridges, a boy prostitute from Uptown, Indiana, police and prosecutors thought they had brought an end to a long series of gruesome homosexual murders. But the killings continued.

In May 1985, eight months after Eyler's arrest, the body of Eric Allen Roettger, 17, turned up off rural road US-40 in the small town of Preble County, Ohio. In 1986, when a second body was found there, the county prosecutor's sole investigator, David Lindloff, took notice. In 1987, another body was found in Shelby County, Indiana, just across the border from Preble County. By April 1992, 11 bodies had turned up in rural counties in Ohio and Indiana, 4 in Preble County. The dead men, ages 15 to 32, all had links to the gay community in Indianapolis. On March 6, 1994, Eyler died of an AIDS-related complication at Pontiac Prison in Illinois. Upon his death, his attorney, Kathleen Zellner, released his signed confession to having killed 21 people.
--Source: John Conroy, "*The Return of Larry Eyler*," ChicagoReader.com; Bahr, Suffer and Wrights, Radford University Dept. of Psychology, Radford, Virginia.

### KRAJCIR, Timothy Wayne
*("The Highway 3 Rest Stop Killer")*

Timothy Krajcir was born November 28, 1944, as Timothy Wayne McBride, in West Mahanoy Township, Pennsylvania to Charles McBride and Fern Yost, his father abandoned the family when Timothy was one year old. Fern remarried when Timothy was 5 or 6 and he was adopted by her new husband, Bernie Krajcir. At age 10, Timothy had begun developing an unhealthy sexual and emotional obsession with his mother. By age 13 he was a voyeur and exhibitionist. In 1963 he was dishonorably discharged from the Navy for Sexual Assault, and in 1963 in Illinois he was in prison on a Rape conviction. As a condition of his parole, he enrolled at Southern Illinois University at Carbondale, earning a degree in Administrative Justice with a minor in Psychology. He confessed to killing 9 women - 5 in Missouri and 4 in Illinois and Pennsylvania. And the body of another of his victims, Sheila Cole, was found November 17, 1977 at a State Highway 3 rest stop near Mclure, Illinois. The 21-year old's car was later located in a Walmart parking lot in Cape Girardeau, Florida. Krajcir also traveled from Paducah, Kentucky where he murdered Joyce Tharp, 29, taking her to Southern Illinois University where he murdered Myrtle Rupp, 51, then returned to Paducah, Kentucky with Joyce Tharp's body. From then on, he spent most of his life in prison for sex crimes, Most of his victims had been raped and forced to perform sex acts. Some were tied up in their beds; others were transported *across state lines*. On December 10, 2007, Krajcir was convicted and sentenced to 40 years in prison for the 1982 killing of an SIU-Carbondale student, and also charged with 5 counts of Murder and 3 counts of Rape against women in Cape Girardeau from 1977 to 1982. On January 19, 2008, he pled Guilty to the 1978 killing of Virginia Lee Witte, in Marion, Connecticut, and received an additional 40-year sentence. On April 4, 2008, he pled Guilty to 7 other Sexual Assaults and was sentenced to 13 consecutive Life terms in a plea deal which took the Death Penalty off the table. He is in prison at Pontiac, Illinois. His known and suspected victims were:
- Sheila Cole, 21, Mclure, Illinois -11-7-77;
- Joyce Tharp, 29, Illinois, Kentucky - 1977;
- Myrtle Rupp, 51 - 1977;

- Virginia Lee Witte, 51;
- Deborah Sheppard, 23;
- Mary Parsh, 58;
- Brenda Parsh, 27;
- Mildred Wallace, 65;
- Margie Call, 57

--<u>Source</u>: *"Adopted Killers"* by Lori Carangelo

## SELLS, Tommy Lynn *("The Cross Country Killer")*
(see MISSOURI)

# INDIANA

### BAUMEISTER, Herbert Richard "Herb"
### *("The Interstate Strangler")*

Herb Beaumeister's wife, Julie, informed authorities that her husband traveled the I-70 to Ohio as many as 100 times on what he said was "store business." She didn't know he had been living a double life using the alias, Brian Smart. Whenever she took the children to their vacation home on weekends, Herb prowled the gay bars for clandestine affairs with gay men from Indiana and Ohio who became his prey between 1980 and 1990. His victims were:

- Johnny Bayer, 20;
- Allen Wayne Broussard, 28;
- Roger A, Goodlet, 33;
- Richard D. Hamilton, 31;
- Steven S. Hale, 26;
- Jeff Allen Jones, 31;
- Michael Kiern, 46;
- Manueal Resendez, 31;
- Johnny Bayer, 20;
- Allen Wayne Broussard, 28

Born April 7, 1947 in Indiana, Herb Baumeister was said to have begun life as a normal child. But in adolescence he displayed anti-social behaviors, playing with dead animals and urinating on his teacher's desk. As a teenager, he was diagnosed with Schizophrenia but did not receive further psychiatric treatment. He attended Indiana University off and on, then drifted through a series of jobs and increasingly bizarre behavior. He married in 1971, had 3 children after a commitment to a psychiatric hospital, and founded 2 successful Sav-A-Lot thrift stores in Indianapolis. In the early 1990s, police began investigating disappearances of gay men in the Indianapolis area for which Baumeister was suspected. Baumeister and his wife, Julie, refused to permit police to search their home on their 18-acre estate called Fox Hollow Farm, but later

Julie admitted that she and Herb engaged in sex only 6 times in their 25 year marriage, and that she became frightened of his mood swings, filed for divorce, and allowed the police to search; that was when they found remains of 11 men; 8 were identified. Baumeister was suspected of killing 9 others. Baumeister fled to Ontario, Canada, where, on July 3, 1996, at age 49, he committed suicide with a gunshot to his head at Pinery Provincial Park, Ontario, Canada, His suicide note claimed the reason he took his own life was his failing marriage and business, but he never mentioned the 11 gay men he had buried in his yard.

--<u>Source</u>: Investigation Discovery (ID) TV Network, 11-13-15; Wikipedia

**EYLER, Larry** (*"The Interstate Killer"*)
(see ILLINOIS)

**WILLIAMS, John Robert** (*"The Truck Stop Killer"*)
(see MISSISSIPPI)

# IOWA

### BIGGS, Benjamin "Ben"

### *("The Highway 34 Killer")*

On March 17, 2012, children riding their bikes along Old Highway 34, 10 miles west of Mount Pleasant, Iowa, discovered a human skull in a ditch. Police found the rest of the skeletal remains after a search of the surrounding area, and, based on possessions found with the remains, Jackie Liegh Douthart was identified. Douthart, 24, mother of a young child, had been reported missing to the Mount Pleasant Police Department on May 21, 2011. Biggs had been a person of interest as he was the last person to see her alive and he already had a record for drugs and assaulting a police officer. On June 29, 2011, after a high speed chase and standoff with law enforcement, Biggs fatally shot himself in the head.

--Source: *"Iowa Cold Cases,"* www.Iowacoldcases.org/case-summaries/jackie-douthart

## IOWA UNSOLVED CASES

### *"THE I-80 KILLER"*

On September 7, 1992, Rhonda Annette Knutson, 22, was murdered while working the 9 PM to 2 AM shift at the Phillips 66 gas station convenience store on US-83, a quarter mile north of Junctions 63, 18 and 346, in Williamstown, Iowa. She had suffered traumatic head injuries from being bludgeoned to death with a blunt object, but there were no signs of sexual assault nor was robbery considered to be the motive. Investigation included hundreds of interviews by deputies and agents from the Iowa Bureau of Criminal Investigation (DCI), along with private investigators and several psychics. Composite drawings were circulated of two truckers seen in the convenience store the morning Knutson was found dead, but the case remains unsolved.

--Source: *"Iowa Cold Cases,"* www.Iowacoldcases.org/case-summaries/rhonda-knutson

# KANSAS

## NEMECHEK, Francis Donald
## ("The I-70 Kansas Killer")

On December 13, 1974, Francis Nemecheck shot out the tire of a car traveling on I-70 west of Hays, Kansas, and abducted the car's occupants - Cheryl Young, 21, her 2-year old son, Guy, and Diane Lovett, 19. He drove them to a farm house where he shot and killed the women after raping Lovett, but left the boy who was found frozen to death outside the farmhouse a month later. On 6-30-76, Nemechek abducted Paula Fabrizius, 16, who was at a "Rangerette" station at the Cedar Bluff Reservoir in western Kansas, raped her, stabbed her to death, and threw her nude body and clothes over a 25-foot bluff. In Nemechek's confession, he also detailed his abduction and murder of Carla Baker, 20, who he passed riding on her bicycle and exposed himself to her. When Baker rode by and said *"You stupid bastard, you think you're funny?"* he was angry, grabbed her, pushed her into his truck and drove her to the south side of the reservoir about 50 miles away, intending to rape her but the girl kicked him between his legs. When he went to the back of his truck to get his knife, Baker attempted to flee but he caught her and stabbed her to death. In February 1977, he was found him Guilty of 5 First Degree Murders.
--Source: *"Serial Murderers,"* Murderpedia, 2-8-15.

## KANSAS UNSOLVED CASES

*"THE I-70 MUTLI-STATE KILLER"*

The I-70 runs from Baltimore, Maryland, to Cove Fort, Utah. In April 1992, there were 6 murders of store clerks within a few miles of I-70 in several Midwestern states and one witness saw the suspect climb a hill to the I-70 and vanish. The victims were:
- Robin Fuldauer, 26, at a Payless ShoeSource, Indianapolis, Indiana – 4-8-92;
- Patricia Magers, 32, Patricia Smith, 23, at a Wichita, Kansas bridal shop - 4-11-92;
- Michael McCown, clerk, Terre Haute, IN, possibly mistaken for a woman- 4-27-92;
- Nancy Kitzmiller, 24, at a Western boot shop in St. Charles, Missouri - 5-3-92;
- Sarah Lynn Blessing 37, at gift shop at a local mall in Raytown, Kansas - 5-7-92.

An auctioneer saw a mysterious unidentified man walk in and out of his store suspiciously. Minutes later, another store owner, Tim Hickman saw a man walk past his store and enter the gift shop where he heard a "pop." He found Sarah Blessing's body minutes later. A grocery clerk collecting shopping carts saw a man walk out of a store and head for the I-70. Ballistics test confirmed that all the victims were killed by the same person, and the gun was linked to another victim. There are also possible links to 4 deaths along I-35 and 45 in Texas.
–Source: *" America's Most Wanted; Dark Minds,"* Unsolved Mysteries, May 4, 1994.

# KENTUCKY

## COLEMAN, Alton, and Debra BROWN

Born 11-6-55 in Illinois, Alton Coleman began his criminal career committing 6 sex crimes from 1973 to 1983. In 1983 he met Debra Brown, who was diagnosed as being Borderline Intellectually Disabled, and the couple embarked on a crime spree across 6 states - Kentucky, Wisconsin, Illinois, Indiana, Michigan and Ohio - where 8 people were murdered between May and July 1984. Marlene Walters's Plymouth Reliant vehicle was found abandoned in Kentucky, where Coleman and Brown had also kidnapped Oline Carmical, Jr., a college professor from Williamsburg, Kentucky, then drove back to Dayton, Ohio, with Carmical locked in the trunk of Carmical's car. On July 17, they abandoned this stolen vehicle in Dayton, and Carmical, who was still locked in the trunk, was rescued by authorities. Coleman and Brown later received 20-year sentences for a Federal kidnapping charge for bringing Carmical across a state line. Coleman and Brown returned to the home of Reverend Millard Gay and his wife, Kathryn, in Dayton. Gay recognized Coleman, who at this time was the subject of a huge nationwide manhunt, and Coleman accosted Millard and Kathryn with guns. Gay asked Coleman, *"Why you want to do us like that, like this?"* and according to Gay, Coleman responded: *"I'm not going to kill you, but we generally kill them where we go."* Coleman and Brown took Gay's car and headed back toward Evanston, Ilinois. Along the way, they stole another car in Indianapolis and killed its owner, 75-year-old Eugene Scott. On July 17, 1984, Alton Coleman became the 388th fugitive listed by the FBI on its Ten Most Wanted list. Coleman was apprehended 7-20-84, received Death sentences from 3 states, and was executed in Ohio by Lethal Injection 4-26-03 at age 46. In 1991, Debra Brown's Death sentence was commuted to Life Without Parole.
Source: Wikipedia

## EYLER, Larry *("The Interstate Killer")*
(see ILLINOIS)

## MARLOW, James Gregory & Cynthia Coffman
*("California's Bonnie and Clyde Spree Killers")*
(see CALIFORNIA)

## MENDENHALL, Bruce *("The Truck Stop Killer")*
(see TENNESSEE)

**SELLS, Tommy Lynn** (*"The Cross Country Killer"*)

(See MISSOURI)

# KENTUCKY UNSOLVED CASES

## *"THE I-65 SERIAL KILLER"*

Police say a serial killer traveled up and down I-65 killing women, and, for 25 years, had not been caught. On February 21, 1987, Vicki Heath, 41 was sexually assaulted and shot to death where she worked as an overnight desk clerk at a Super 8 Motel in Elizabethtown, Kentucky. Vicki's body was found out back in a dumpster. DNA evidence linked Heath's death to 3 other attacks in Indiana. In 1989, Mary Gill, and Jeanne Gilbert, were both killed on the same night in the same way that Vicki Heath was murdered and they were both desk clerks at Days Inn Motels. In 1990, a hotel clerk was attacked but escaped and gave police a description that formed a police sketch. Police fear there may be even more victims connected to this killer who they think may have been a truck driver or salesman traveling I-65 in the late 1980s and early '90s.

--<u>Source</u>: Rachel Collier, *"I-65 Serial Killer Still on the Run,"* WDRB.com, 2-19-11

## *"THE BLUEGRASS PARKWAY DISAPPEARANCES"*

On July 3, 2015, Crystal Rogers, a 35-year old mother of 5 from Bardstown, Kentucky, disappeared. She was last seen that afternoon by her boyfriend, Brooks Houck. The next day, authorities found Rogers' 2007 maroon Chevrolet abandoned *with a flat tire* along Bluegrass Parkway. The keys were still in the ignition and her purse and cell phone were still inside the car. Authorities stated they are "sure she is dead." But extensive searches for Crystal Rogers have not turned up and leads.

--<u>Source</u>: *"Search for Missing Mom,"* Huffington Post, AP, 7-14-15

## *"THE READHEAD MURDERS"*

(See ARKANSAS)

# LOUISIANA

**CARR III, Robert Frederick** (*"The Hitchhiker Killer"*)
(see CONNECTICUT)

**EVANS, Donald Leroy** (*"The Rest Stop Killer"*)
(see MISSISSIPPI)

### DOMINIQUE, Ronald
(*"The I-182 Killer" "The Bayou Killer"*)

Allegedly homosexual, Ronald Dominque targeted his victims along Louisiana's I-182 near low budget motels known for drugs and prostitutes where he randomly chose 23 men who he raped and murdered, then disposed of them at dark locations. Ricky Wallace was the only victim who escaped Dominque who he said had driven past him several times in his truck before offering him a ride. On 9-29-08, Dominique was sentenced to 8 consecutive Life sentences and imprisoned at Louisiana Penitentiary, Angola.
--Source: Channing Parfait, *"'Bayou Blue' Recalls Serial Killer,"* The Times Houma, LA 4-8-14

### LEE, Derrick Todd
(*"The Baton Rouge Killer"*)

Several of Derrick Todd Lee's victims' bodies were dumped on the I-10 Whiskey Bay exit approximately 30 miles west of Baton Rouge, after being murdered at other locations. One of those victims, Pamela Kinnamore, 44, a mother, wife and business owner, was kidnapped from her home, beaten, raped and her throat cut. Her body was discovered four days after she went missing, concealed under bushes about 20 miles from Baton Rouge just off the I-10 in an area called Whiskey Bay. A small silver toe ring that she almost always wore was missing. Police believe it was taken by Derrick Lee as a trophy. On March 3, 2003, Carrie Lynn Yoder was living in Baton Rouge, Louisiana when she was kidnapped from her LSU apartment, beaten, raped and strangled to death. On March 13, 2003, her decomposing body was found just off the I-10 in Whiskey Bay near the same location to where Pam Kinnamore's body had been found. Unlike Kinamore's body which seemed to be carefully placed and hidden, Carrie's body appeared to have been tossed from the bridge. DNA evidence linked Derrick Lee to her murder. Highway 1 was the main road Lee traveled to and from work at the Dow Chemical Plant in Brusly, Louisiana. Highway 1 was also where Geralyn DeSoto, 21, in Addis, Louisiana, was murdered. DeSoto was found dead by her husband inside their home on Highway 1. She had been raped, brutally beaten and stabbed to death. Lee's methods varied with nearly each murder. Similarities between the crimes included the removal of cell phones from the victim's belongings, and a lack of any visible signs of forced entry into the location where the victim was attacked. His known victims were:

- Geralyn DeSoto, 21, stabbed to death - 1-14-02;
- Gina Wilson Green, 40, Baton Rouge, raped, strangled - 3-4-01;
- Charlotte Murray Pace, 22, Baton Rouge, raped, stabbed 80+ times - 5-31-02;
- Dianne Alexander, Breaux Bridge, raped, beaten, strangled (survived) - 7-9-02;
- Pamela Kinnamore, 44, Baton Rouge, raped, beaten, throat cut – 7-12-02;
- Trineisha Dene Colomb, 23, Grand Coteau, LA, raped, beaten to death - 11-24-02;
- Carrie Lynn Yoder, 26, Baton Rouge, raped, beaten, strangled – 3-3-03

In 2004, Lee was convicted of 2 of the 5 linked murders -- those of DeSoto and Pace -- and was sentenced to Death. Lee died on January 21, 2016, at age 47, of heart disease at a hospital in Louisiana, where he was transported for treatment from Louisiana State Penitentiary, Angola, where he had been awaiting execution.

--<u>Source</u>: Kevin Dupuy, *"Timeline of Events: Serial Killer Derrick Lee Todd,"* ABC, WBRZ-2 News, 1-21-16; Charles Montaldo, *"The Victims of Serial Killer Derrick Todd Lee,"* ThoughtCo.com, 3-17-17; Wikipedia

# LOUISIANA UNSOLVED CASES

Between 1991 and 1995, 27 bodies were discovered near Interstate and local highways. Most were strangled or drowned, their bodies dumped in bayous or canals along highways bordering the western banks of Lake Pontchartrain. Most of the victims, police said, were African-American women involved in drugs and prostitution; 5 of the victims were men, but some of them were reportedly transgender. The majority of the victims' tended to be in advanced states of decomposition by the time they were found, leaving evidence destroyed and some victims unidentified. The victims were:

- "Brenda," abducted near Memorial Park Drive and Nevada Street in Algiers, strangled and left for dead, described the suspect as a clean cut, well-dressed black male with a muscular build - July 1991;
- Danielle Britton, 17, Gretna, found nude in a ditch along Nevada Street in Algiers; beaten and strangled; no prior arrests for drugs or prostitution - 8-4-91;
- Tiera Tassin, 21, mother of 3 found in Harvey; prior drug arrest – 9-3-91;
- Charlene Price, 28, New Orleans: in Behrman Park in Algiers; beaten and strangled; she had a history of drug abuse - 9-21-91;
- Regina Okoh, 37, mother of 3, Algiers, found St. Joseph St, Harvey; strangled; acute cocaine intoxication; several arrests for prostitution - 11-21-91;
- Unidentified female, approximately 20, found in Algiers near Behrman Highway not far from where Danielle Britton's body was discovered. At autopsy, it was revealed she was 5'2", 125 pounds, protruding front teeth; strangled - 12-14-91;
- Lydia Madison, 29, New Orleans found beneath South Claiborne overpass near Earhart Boulevard, near police headquarters; prior drug and prostitution arrests; strangled- 1-4-92;
- George Williams, 25, New Orleans found floating in LaBranche Wetlands; asphyxiation by strangling or smothering. Williams was reportedly a

transvestite, who worked as an exotic dancer in the French Quarter, possibly mistaken for a woman, had prior arrests for drugs and burglary - 6-2-92;

- Noah Philson, 33, aka Brenda Bewitch, found floating naked in a canal off I-55, north of LaPlace; exotic dancer in the French Quarter – 7-25-93;
- Regetter Martin, 29, mother of 3, New Orleans, found near interstate in Botte; prior arrests for prostitution - 9-21-92;
- Cheryl Lewis, 30, mother of 4, Bridge City, found in a canal along Louisiana 3160, in Hahnville; strangled; prior drugs and prostitution. Witnesses saw a man drag her into a car and drive off - 2-20-93;
- Delores Mack, 42, found in a canal along Louisiana 3160, 782 feet of where Cheryl Lewis' body was found the previous day, strangled – 2-21-93;
- Jane Doe, 25 to 35, raped, strangled to death, St. John the Baptist Parish - 2-5-95;
- Jane Doe, 15 to 17, near Airline Highway-Gramercy, burned, asphyxiation - 2-10-94;
- Stephanie Murray, 25, Bridge City, found in Bonnet Carre Spillway - 2-13-94;
- Jane Doe, 25 to 35, found dead. No further details are available – 2-15-94;
- Jane and John Doe were found dead. No further details are available - 4-2-94;
- Michelle Foster, 32, of New Orleans, found dead, 7-3-94;
- Stephaney Brown, 28, New Orleans, found at US 90 near Bridge City - 10-19-94;
- Wanda Ford, 29, mother of 3, New Orleans, found in swamp along I-55 in LaPlace; prior drugs, theft and possession of stolen property arrests - 1-22-95;
- Sandra Warner, New Orleans, 39, found in St. John the Baptist Parish - 1-23-95;
- Henry Calvin, of New Orleans, 24, found in Gretna, Louisiana – 1-25-95;
- Jane Doe, 25 to 35, found beneath Tangipahoa highway overpass – 3-24-95 (On 3-22-98, authorities said they lost the remains);
- Karen Ivester, 30, strangled - 4-30-95;
- Sharon Robinson, 28, found along I-55 near LaPlace, drowned – 4-30-95;
- Sandra Williams, 39, New Orleans, found Crowder Boulevard; strangled - 5-6-95;
- Lola Porter, 39, disappeared 1992, found S. Kenner Road in Waggaman - 4-8-96.

--Source: David Lohr, Websleuths, 11-4-16

## "THE I-10 LOUISIANA KILLER"

Kaylan Ward, 16, was found dead on an I-10 overpass at Metairie, Louisiana on June 4, 2015. Jasilis Wright, 19, was found on June 10, 2015, her remains scattered on the northbound side of the I-10 at Metairie. FOX News reported the *speculation* that Ward had been killed when trying to walk across the I-10. Local residents are not so sure there's not a killer waiting to abduct his next teenage victim.

--Source: *"No Ties Surface Between 2 Female Victims Found Dead on I-10 Overpasses, Police Say,"* NOLA.com, 6-10-15; FOX2 News, 6-11-15; and *"There's No I-10 Serial Killer in New Orleans, But Don't Relax,"* NOLA.com, 8-15-15

# MAINE

**CRUZ, Akeem** ( *"The Long Island Serial Killer"*)
(see NEW YORK)

## JOUBERT IV , John Joseph
*("The I-295 Murders;" "Nebraska Boy Snatcher")*

John Joseph Joubert IV preyed on young boys in Maine and Nebraska. His first known victim, Richard "Ricky" Stetson, 11, was found at the side of the I-295 Freeway in Maine. Joubert attempted to undress him, then stabbed and strangled him. Bite marks on the boy's body were later matched to Joubert who also murdered 2 boys in Nebraska -- Danny Joe Eberle and Christopher Walden. He had approached Eberle with a knife, kidnapped him, made him strip down to his underwear, bound his hands and feet, and taped his mouth before stabbing him 9 times. Walden's body was found 3 miles from Eberle's. When Joubert ordered Walden to strip to his underwear, the boy complied but refused to lie down and was not bound when found; they struggled and Joubert cut Walden's throat so deeply that he was almost decapitated. Joubert, born July 2, 1963 in Massachusetts, Joubert began having sadistic fantasies, at age 6, that included the desire to murder and cannibalize a neighborhood girl who babysat him. He said it was *"nothing personal against the girl, just someone to kill."* He hated his mother and was bullied for his homosexual tendencies at age 12. At 13, he stabbed a 9-year old girl with a pencil and felt sexually stimulated when she cried out in pain. The next day he slashed a girl with a razor blade as she rode her bike past him, then beat and nearly strangled a boy. At 16, he beat and nearly killed Chris Day, 8, slashed and badly cut a 9-year old boy, and a male teacher, 20. Each offense gradually increased in intensity until he was caught. Joubert was sentenced to Life in Prison for the Murder of Ricky Stetson, Maine did not have the Death Penalty. But in Nebraska, he was sentenced to Death, for "exceptional depravity" and sadistic behavior by torturing Eberle and Walden. On July 17, 1996, Nebraska executed Joubert in the electric chair which generated an appeal to the U.S. Supreme Court over whether the electric chair is cruel and unusual punishment when Joubert suffered brain blisters on the top and sides of his head.
Source: Wikipedia

**KEYES, Israel** *("The Cross Country Killer")*
(see ALASKA)

# MARYLAND

### REES, Melvin Davis
### *("The Sex Beast")*

Born in 1933, Melvin Rees, a jazz musician known in the Washington, DC area, committed 5 or more murders in Maryland and Virginia between 1957 and 1959. On June 26, 1957, in an encounter on State Highway 178, known as The General's Highway, near Annapolis, Maryland, Melvin Rees murdered Margaret Harold by forcing her and her boyfriend, Army Sergeant Roy D. Hudson, off the road, gesturing to them to roll down their window and displaying a gun and demanding cigarettes and money. Refused, he shot the woman in the face. Her horrified boyfriend fled across several rural fields before reaching a farmhouse where he called police. In 1955, Rees was arrested on charges of assaulting an unidentified 36 woman, age 36; he tried to force her into his car but she escaped. The victim did not press charges and the case against Rees was dropped. On January 11, 1959, Carroll Jackson, his wife Mildred, and their infant daughters disappeared. Two months later, the decomposing body of Carroll Jackson was found in a ditch; he had been shot twice in the head, his hands tied behind his back and was dumped on top of his 18-month old daughter, Janet, while she was alive and suffocated under his weight. On March 21, the bodies of Mildred and Susan Jackson were discovered in a forest near Annapolis, showing signs of torture and pre-mortem sexual assault. Rees, under the influence of Benzedrine, confided to a friend, Glenn Moser, that he *"considered murder to just be another part of the human experience"* and *"You can't say it's wrong to kill, but only individual standards make it right or wrong."* Upon hearing of their murders months later, Moser suspected Rees of killing the family. On Moser's tip, Rees was arrested, June 24, 1960, convicted, and sentenced by in Maryland to "Life" in Prison for Murder of Margaret Harold. Virginia added a Death sentence for the other 4 murders, though it was changed to "Life" in 1972. Investigators suspected him of 4 other murders - of Maryland teenagers, Mary Shomette, Ann Ryan, Mary Fellers, and Shelby Venable, who were found raped and killed. Rees was never charged in those murders and was cleared of the murders of Shomette and Ryan whose murders were linked to a 15-year old boy who stalked them, but Rees remains the suspect in the murders of Fellers and Venable. His known and suspected victims were:

- Unidentified woman, 36;
- Margaret Harold - 6-26-57;
- Carroll Jackson - 1-11-59;
- Mildred Jackson (with Jackson family) - 1-11-59;
- Susan Jackson (with Jackson family) - 1-11-59;
- Janet Jackson, 18 months (with Jackson family) - 1-11-59;
- Mary Fellers; Shelby Venable

Rees died in prison in 1995.

--<u>Source</u>: Wikipedia

## SCOTT, Jason Thomas
## ("The Mothers and Daughters Killer")

On July 27, 2010, Jason Thomas Scott, 27, was charged in the murder of Delores and Ebony Dewitt, a mother and daughter who were found in a burning car near State Route 202 at Largo, Maryland, in March 2009. A year later, a federal judge in Greenbelt decided a 97-year prison sentence wasn't enough, and put him away for an even century. Law enforcement believes Scott also killed. Karen Lofton, 45, and her daughter, Karissa, 16, was repeatedly shot as she frantically dialed 911 from her bed. The Loftons resided less than a mile from where the Dewitts were found. There were similarities -- two mother-daughter pairs; two nurses in their 40s -- but also stark differences. Authorities suspect that Scott also killed Vilma Artis Butler, who was found dead in her burning home in Bowie, Md., in June 2008. Police said he used information in a database he got from working at UPS to track down his victims; he also stole guns and sold them on the street. Jason Scott, had a degree in computer science at the University of Maryland and had worked at UPS. It all started around when he was 10 years old... a Peeping Tom, recording people when they were sleep or undressing. He was arrested in July 2009 in a UPS parking lot after the Bureau of Alcohol, Tobacco, Firearms and Explosives got a tip that he was selling weapons out of the trunk of his vehicle. He was charged with selling 14 stolen guns including pistols, assault weapons, silencers and a machine gun. He remains jailed on Weapons and Carjacking charges.

--Source: Pierre Thomas and Enjoli Francis, *"Maryland: Suspect Named in Possible Serial Mother-Daughter Killings,"* ABC News, 7-27-10; Peter Hermann, *"Man Sentenced to 100 Years in Prison Also Suspect in Killings,"* Baltimore Sun, 1-11-12.

# MARYLAND UNSOLVED CASES

## *"THE MARYLAND TRUCK STOP UNKNOWN CHILD KILLER"*

On July 31, 1991, the remains of a female, age 16 to 25, known as *"Maryland's Unknown Child,"* were found located beneath a State Highway 76 underpass near a truck stop in Frederick County, Maryland. A trucker who had been convicted of murdering a woman in Tennessee may have been involved. At his house, authorities discovered shoes and underwear -- two types of clothing that the Frederick County Jane Doe was *not* wearing.

--Source: Wikipedia

# MASSACHUSETTS

### MAYRAND JR., Edward H.
### ("The Route 10 Strangler")

In 2014, DNA of an interstate highway drifter and serial killer, Edward Mayrand, was found on the ligature used to strangle Kathleen M. Deneault, 25, of Gardner, Massachusetts. Mayrand was also linked to the 1987 strangulation death of Judith Whitney, 43, in Winchester New Hampshire who was last seen alive on July 2, 1987 and whose body was found near the State Route 10 highway sheds. That testing and other evidence also led investigators to conclude that Mayrand had also been responsible for the murder of Patricia Paquette whose dismembered body was found in Providence, Rhode Island. Born in 1947, Mayrand had a history of violence toward women including prior convictions for Rape, Assault with Intent to Rape, and being a Felon in Possession of a Firearm. On January 23, 2014, Maynard died in prison of metastatic lung cancer while serving time for Murder of Patricia Paquette, of Providence, Rhode Island, so he could not be prosecuted for the murders of Deneault and Whitney. Authorities are also looking into 50 or 60 unresolved cases in Worcester County to see if any can be linked to Mayrand.
--Source: News Telegram and Gazette, 12-23-14; WCVB.com/news, 12-23-14

### SAMPSON, Gary Lee
### ("The Hitchhiking Carjack Killer")

Unlike serial killers who picked up hitchhikers, it was Gary Sampson who was hitchhiking on September 8, 2003, when Phillip McCloskey, 69, made the mistake of offering Sampson a ride. McCloskey's body was found stabbed to death and dumped in the woods between Main Street and Old Main Street in Mansfield, his car missing. Three days after stabbing McCloskey multiple times to death, Jonathan Rizzo gave Sampson a ride at the Plymouth waterfront. Sampson drove Rizzo's car to New Hampshire where Robert Whitney, 58, a former City Council member in Concord, was found strangled in a cottage at Lake Winnepasauke in Meredith, New Hampshire, with Rizzo's car parked outside. Rizzo's body was also subsequently found nearby, tied to a tree behind the Abingdon Ale House, stabbed 24 times. Next, William Gregory, 41, picked up Sampson at the side of a road in Vermont, whereupon Sampson put a knife to Gregory's throat, but Gregory escaped by skidding the car onto the shoulder and jumping out of the driver's side while the car was still in Drive. Sampson ditched the car and surrendered to police without a fight. Born September 29, 1959 in Weymouth, Sampson resided in Abington, Massachusetts. He had a long record of petty to felony crimes from 1974 to 1998. They included burglaries

and a bank robbery for which he attempted to surrender himself to the FBI by calling their office in Boston on July 23, 2001. But the FBI Clerk accidentally disconnected the call and no one showed up to arrest Sampson. Sampson became the focus of pre-and anti-Death Penalty factions even before his 12-23-03 Death sentence in Massachusetts, transforming himself from unremorseful to remorseful and back again. Gary Lee Sampson, 55, had been on Death Row for over a year when he threatened to kill Death Row officials and bragged about the killings he was convicted for, while spending donation money on cappuccinos. In 2011, his Death sentence was thrown out and he was set to receive another penalty trial in Fall of 2015.
--Source: Murderpedia; Wikipedia; and The Daily Mail, 5-18-15.

## SELLS, Tommy Lynn *("The Cross Country Killer")*
(See MISSOURI)

# MASSACHUSETTS UNSOLVED CASES

## *"THE NEW BEDFORD HIGHWAY KILLER"*
(see CONNECTICUT)

All of the victims were known prostitutes.
- The body of Debra Madieros, 30, found MA Route 140 exit ramp – 5-27-88;
- Nancy Paiva, 36, disappeared 7-11-88, found at I-195 exit ramp – 7-30-88;
- Deborah DeMelio, 34, found close to Pavia dump site – 11-8-88;
- Dawn Mendes, 25, missing for a wee, found on I-195 - 11-11-88;
- Deborah McConnell, 25, missing in May, found at Route 1-40 – 12-1-88;
- Rochelle Clifford Dopierala, 28, found in a rock quarry - 12-10-88;
- Robin Rhodes, 28, found off Route 140, across from Madieros dump site, 4-88;
- Mary Rose Santos, 26, found off Route 88 -7-16-88;
- Sandy Botelho, 24, mother of 2 boys, found along the I-195;
- Christine Montiero, 19, missing in 5-88, was never found;
- Marilyn Roberts, 34 went missing in 6-88, was never found.

Suspects were a rapist, Anthony DeGrazia, drug user Kenneth C. Ponte, and Daniel Tavares Jr. who claimed responsibility for the Bedford Highway Murders and had knowledge of where another woman, named Gayle, had been buried; he was also convicted of murdering Brian and Bev Muack. It was also theorized that a serial killer in Portugal, known as "The Lisbon Ripper," who disemboweled his female victims, might also be the New Bedford Highway Killer, as New Bedford had a sizable Portuguese community and many of the New Bedford Highway victims were of Portuguese ancestry. Tony "Flat Nose" DeGrazia, who as a young boy had his nose bashed in by his abusive mother, carried a strong rage against women. Due to lack of evidence, no charges were filed and DeGrazia allegedly committed suicide in July 1991.
--Source: *"The Route 8 Murders,"* rte8murders.blogspot.com, 2-22-15; *"Adopted Killers"* (under "Tavares,") by Lori Carangelo.

# MICHIGAN

**COLLINS, John Norman**
*("The Michigan Murders"; "The Ypsilanti Ripper ";
"The Co-Ed Killer")*

John Collins murdered at least 7 women were abducted while out walking or hitchhiking along highways in the highly publicized "Michigan Murders" that were committed between 1967 and 1969 in the Ann Arbor/Ypsilanti area of Southeastern Michigan. The victims were between the ages of 13 and 21. They were raped, beaten and murdered, typically by stabbing or strangulation—some of the bodies mutilated after death--and were found with a piece of their clothing tied around their necks. The known victims were:

- May Terese Fleszar, 19, raped, stabbed 30 times, feet, fingers, arm severed- 1967;
- Joan Elspeth Schell, 20, raped, throat slashed, stabbed 47 times, mutilated - 1968;
- Jane Louise Mixer, 23, garroted, shot in head, "Catch 22" by her side - 1969;
- Maralyn Skelton, 16, beaten, tortured, tree branch in her vagina - 1969;
- Dawn Basom, 13, stabbed, slashed, strangled - 1969;
- Alice Elizabeth Kalom, 21, raped, stabbed, slashed, shot in head, neck cut - 1969;
- Karen Beineman, 18, beaten, raped, burned, strangled, panties in vagina - 1969;
- Roxie Ann Philips, disappeared 6-30-69, found 2 weeks later; strangled

California and Michigan agreed that enough similarities existed between the murder of Roxie Ann Philips and the Michigan Murders to establish a definite connection between the cases. A formal indictment would later be served against Collins for First Degree Murder of Roxie Ann Philips in April 1970. Born June 17, 1947 in Windsor, Ontario, Canada, John Collins, a known motorcycle enthusiast, held a part-time job as an inspector of drum brakes, had been an honor student, a football co-captain at his high school, and was majoring in elementary education at Eastern Michigan University. Collins had a reputation among his peers at EMU as a habitual thief, and although casual acquaintances harked to his politeness around women, close female acquaintances who had dated Collins described him as an aggressive short-tempered, oversexed individual who had occasionally engaged in violence against women, including one instance of rape. Several female acquaintances divulged that Collins became enraged upon learning a woman was menstruating. Investigators established that each victim had been menstruating at the time of her death, and theorized this was a factor in the sexual violence exhibited upon the victims. Collins was arrested July 30, 1969 and sentenced to Life in prison for the final murder on August 19, 1970 and is incarcerated at Marquette Branch Prison. Although never tried for the remaining 5 murders attributed to the *"The Ypsilanti Ripper,"* nor for the murder of Roxie Ann Phillips, in California whose death has been linked to the series, investigators believe Collins is responsible for all 7 murders.
--Source: Wikipedia, Murderpedia

97

**KRAFT, Randy** (*"The Freeway Killer"*)
(see CALIFORNIA)

# MICHIGAN UNSOLVED CASES

## *"THE BLUE GREMLIN KILLER,""THE OAKLAND COUNTY CHILD KILLER," "THE I-75 CHILD KILLER,"*

On March 27, 1977, the last known victim of *"The Blue Gremlin Killer"* was placed on the I-75 northbound Exit 69, *facing the Troy Police Department building.* Construction workers who were digging a basement unearthed a 1970s blue AMC Gremlin vehicle that had been buried. The killer was suspected to have driven a car matching the description of the buried car during a late 1970s killing spree. The same serial killer, also known as *"The Oakland County Child Killer"* is an "unknown," responsible for the unsolved murders of 4 or more children, including 2 girls and 2 boys, in Oakland County, Michigan, in 1976 and 1977. Of those 4 confirmed victims, as young as 10 years old, 3 were strangled or smothered. All 4 children were kidnapped, held for up to 19 days, and then murdered. The killer would then dress them in their freshly pressed clothing, and leave their bodies carefully positioned on blankets of snow or laying in full sight next to a road. On February 15, 1976, Mark Stebbins, 12, of Ferndale, Michigan, disappeared after leaving the American Legion Hall to go home to watch TV; 4 days later, his body was found 12 miles from his home, laying in a snow bank in a parking lot in Southfield. He was dressed in the same clothes that he had was wearing on the day that he was abducted, but they were cleaned and pressed. An autopsy determined that he had been raped with an object and strangled to death. Rope burns were discovered on his wrists, indicating that his hands had been tightly bound. On December 22, 1976, Jill Robinson, 12, of Royal Oak, got into an argument with her mother and decided to pack a bag and run away from home. The next day, her bicycle was discovered behind a store located on Main Street in Royal Oak. Three days later, her body was found lying on the side of I-75 near Troy *within full sight of the Troy police station,* dead from a shotgun blast to her face. Like Mark Stebbins, she was fully clothed and her body appeared to be carefully placed on a pile of snow. On January 2, 1977, Kristine Mihelich, 10, of Berkley, went to the nearby 7-Eleven and bought some magazines. Her body was discovered 19 days later, fully dressed and her body positioned in the snow. On March 16, 1977, the body of Timothy King, 11, was found in a ditch alongside a road in Livonia, fully clothed, but it was obvious that his clothes had been cleaned and pressed. He had been sexually assaulted with an object and smothered to death. A witness had seen Timothy talking to a man with *a blue AMC Gremlin with white stripes on the side.* With her help, a police sketch artist was able to do a composite drawing of the older man and of the car. I tipster identified the killer as a pedophile named "Allen" who was never found
--Source: *"Buried Blue Gremlin Could Lead to Arrest of Child Serial Killer,"* Jalopnik.com, 8-20-13; Charles Montaldo, *"The Unsolved Case of the Oakland County Child Killer,"* Thoughtco.com, 3-12-17.

# MINNESOTA

### CARIGNAN, Harvey Louis
### ("The Want Ad Killer"; "Harv The Hammer")

Born May 18, 1927, in Fargo, North Dakota, Harvey Carignan, was a serial killer whose victims were often hitchhikers he picked up along highways in Minnesota and Washington, described himself as *"an instrument of God, one who was acting under His personal instructions. Murder, rape and mutilation are all part of a Grand Plan. God is a figure with a large hood and you can't see his face."* Under so-called *"Orders from God,"* he killed at least 5 and possibly as many as 18 women. His weapon of choice was a claw hammer which he used to rape and bludgeon his victims, earning him the nickname of "Harv the Hammer." On September 8, 1974, Carignan picked up Lisa King and June Lynch, both 16, while they were hitching rides in Minneapolis. He offered money if the girls would help him fetch another car that he claimed had been stranded in a rural area. Once out of town, however, he stopped the car and started beating June about the head and face. When Lisa ran for help, he sped away and left his latest victim bleeding on the roadside. September 9, 1974, Jewry Billings, 13, was hitching rides in Minneapolis to reach her boyfriend's house, when Carignan pulled up and offered her a ride. Inside the car, he threatened Billings with a hammer, forced her to fellate him while he rammed the hammer's handle in and out of her vagina. When he finished with her, Carignan released his battered captive, but the incident was so humiliating that the girl kept it a closely-guarded secret for several months. That was after Carignan had been sentenced in Alaska to be hanged for murdering a woman in 1949, but an appeals court reversed his sentence in 1951. And after serving 9 more years on a separate conviction for Attempted Rape, he was paroled in 1960. In 1965, Carignan was sentenced to a term of 15 years in Washington, but with time off for good behavior he hit the streets again in 1969, consumed with an abiding rage against society in general and women in particular. Carignan married a Seattle widow shortly after his 1969 parole. Sullen, uncommunicative, Carignan would frequently get up at night and drive long distances, "to be alone and think." When he refused to share his thoughts or name his destinations on the long nocturnal drives, the marriage fell apart. In 1972 marrying another widow showed no improvement. His lascivious attentions to his teenaged step-daughter finally forced the girl to run away from home, and he was faced with yet another failed marriage in the Spring of 1973. In May 1974, young Kathy Miller answered Carignan's advertisement for employees at a service station that he leased. The girl was missing for a month before two boys discovered her remains while hiking on an Indian reservation north of Everett, Washington. Nude and bundled in a sheet of plastic, Miller had been bludgeoned with a hammer, knocking holes the size of nickels in her skull. Detectives in Seattle were aware of Harvey's record, and they hounded him with such intensity that he departed from their city shortly after Miller's body was retrieved. On June 20, 1974, Carignan was placed in the vicinity where 6 women had been murdered in the past 2 years, but there was nothing solid to connect him to the crimes, and he was on his way, cross-country, seeking sanctuary in his old, familiar haunts around Minneapolis. On June 28, 1974, Marlys Townsend was assaulted at a bus stop in that city, clubbed unconscious from behind. She awoke in Harvey's car, still groggy from the blow, but when he tried to make her masturbate him, she found enough strength to save herself by leaping from the speeding vehicle. On August 10, 1974, another romance ended for Carignan, no less tragically for his intended. Eileen Hunley was a woman of the church who had looked for good in Carignan when they began to date but there was nothing to be found. She informed her friends of her intent to terminate the sour relationship and then Hunley disappeared. When she was found in Sherbourne County 5 weeks later, she was a rotting corpse, her skull imploded by the force of savage hammer blows. On September 14, 1974, an engine failure almost cost Gwen Burton her life when Carignan offered her a ride. Once alone, he ripped her clothing, choked her into semi-consciousness, and raped her with the handle of his hammer, finally slamming her across the skull with brutal force before he dumped her in a field off the highway to die. Miraculously, she survived and crawled to the highway where a passing motorist arrived in time to save her life. On September 18, the same day Hunley's body was recovered, Carignan picked up Sally Versoi and Diane Flynn, then began to make lewd propositions, assaulting both girls when they failed to respond on command. The girls escaped when he ran short of gas and was forced to stop at a rural service station. Two days later, Kathy Schultz, 18, did not return from her college classes. Next day, her corpse was found by hunters in a corn field 40 miles from Minneapolis; her skull had been destroyed by crushing hammer blows. By then, police in Minneapolis were talking to their counterparts in Washington and, within days, survivors started picking Carignan out of lineups as being the man who had abducted and assaulted them over the past 2 years. A search of Carignan's possessions turned up maps with 181 red circles drawn in isolated areas of the United States and Canada. His known victims were:

- Unidentified woman, Alaska - 1949;
- Unidentified girl, Medora, North Dakota - 4-73;
- Lisa King, 16, Minneapolis, Minnesota - 9-8-74;
- June Lynch, 16, (with Lisa King), Minneapolis, Minnesota - 9-8-74;
- Jewry Billings, 13, Minneapolis, Minnesota - 9-9-74;
- Kathy Miller, remains found in Everett Washington - 5-74;
- 6 women murdered in Carignan's vicinity - 6-20-74;
- Marlys Townsend - 6-28-74;
- Gwen Burton, (survived) - 9-14-74;
- Sally Versoi, (escaped) 9-18-74;
- Diane Flynn (escaped, with Sally Versoi) - 9-18-74;
- Kathy Schultz, 18, Minneapolis, Minnesota - 9-28-74;
- Laura Brock, Coupeville, Washington;
- Unidentified woman, Vancouver, Washington

In 1975, Carignan was sentenced to a maximum of only 40 years in prison. Minnesota term limits meant his convictions and sentences for the other assaults and murders would have no effect on his eligibility for release in 40 years. His 40 years was up and he was released May 5, 2015.

--Source: Michael Newton - "*An Encyclopedia of Modern Serial Killers-Hunting Humans.*"

## STEPHANI, Paul Michael
## ("The Weepy Voice Killer")

On August 2, 1982, a hitchhiker, Denise Williams, 21, accepted a ride from Paul Stephani, who stabbed her several times with a screwdriver. During the attack, which she survived, Williams managed to hit Stephani on the head with a soft drink bottle which caused him to be bleeding badly and he sought medical help. Born September 8, 1944, in Austin, Minnesota, where his stepfather worked as a meat packer, Stephani began his crimes on New Year's Eve, 1980. That's when he viciously attacked Karen Potack with a tire iron as she was walking home from a New Year's Eve party in Hudson, Wisconsin, and raped her. She survived, but with life-threatening injuries to her face, head and throat and brain trauma. Stephani was known as *"The Weepy Voice Killer"* for his emotional, anonymous phone calls to police that began right after the attack on Potack. On June 3, 1981, after stabbing 18-year old Kimberly Compton 61 times with an ice pick, Stephani again contacted police in his "weepy voice," pleading: *"God damn, will you find me? I just stabbed somebody with an ice pick. I can't stop myself. I keep killing somebody."* Two days later, he called police saying he was sorry for stabbing Compton and would turn himself in, but never did. Instead, on June 6, he called to say newspaper accounts of some of the murders were "inaccurate." His next call, on June 11, in a whimpering, barely coherent voice, cried: *"I'm sorry for what I did to Compton."* There was no call after he drowned Kathleen Greening, 33, in her bathtub, but he contacted police about the stabbing murder of Barbara Simons, 40, both murders occurring in 1982, stating: *"Please don't talk. Listen. I'm sorry I killed that girl. I stabbed her 40 times. Kimberly Compton was the first one over in St. Paul."* His last call linked him to Denise Williams' murder and to Barbara Simons' murder. On June 12, 1998 at age 53, after 40 years in prison, Stephani died of skin cancer at Oak Park Heights Prison.
--Source: Wikipedia, and Crimezzz.net

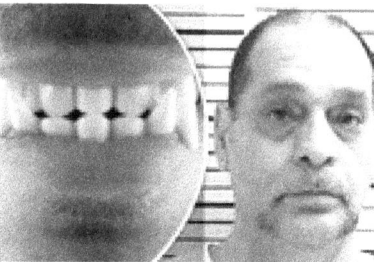

## VALFEADES, Timothy Jay
## ("The Vampire Trucker")

Timothy Vafeades was a truck driver who kidnapped young women in Minnesota and Utah and kept them in a torture room inside his truck, which he called *"the Twilight Express."* He wore fangs and forced his victims to wear fake fangs before drilling their teeth down into actual fangs. Vafeades was arrested during a routine truck stop inspection and was found with a 19-year-old girl, who he had kept in his truck for 6 months. He pled guilty to Transporting for Sexual Activity and Kidnapping of 2 Utah women he sexually assaulted and kept in his truck.
--Source: Pamela Manson, *"'Vampire' Trucker Pleads Guilty in Utah Kidnapping Case,"* Salt Lake City Tribune, 6-30-06; Amanda Tullos, *"12 Terrifying Truck Driver Killers Who Committed Murder While on the Road,"* Ranker.com/list/truck-driver-crimes/

# MINNESOTA'S UNSOLVED CASES

## *"THE 1-90 MINNESOTA KILLER"*

What remained of a body found wrapped in a tarp and tucked into trees and brush along a fence near I-90 was only bones ..... but it had a 10-karat class ring with a large red stone. It was hoped that the ring, and the man's Mario De Girard shoes, may offer clues but that case has not yet been solved.
--Source: *"Skeletal Remains Along I-90 Near Albert Lea Offer Few Clues,"* The WestCentral Tribune, 4-10-15

## *"THE I-95 MINNESOTA KILLER"*

The body of Heather Lamperd of Minneapolis was found at 10 A.M. Friday, November 3, 1989 in the shallow water of the Sunrise River off State Highway 95, in Chicago County. It appears that her body was thrown into the river from a small bridge on Highway 95. Lamperd was last seen alive leaving work at 3:30 p.m. on Thursday, November 2, 1989 from the main office of NSP (now known as Excel Energy), in downtown Minneapolis. It is not known whether she first went home, or was on her way, on this evening.
--Source: Crime Stoppers of Minnesota, 5-20-11

# MISSISSIPPI

**CARR III, Robert Frederick** *("The Hitchhiker Killer")*
(see CONNECTICUT)

### EVANS, Donald Leroy
### *("The Rest Stop Killer")*

In 1991, Donald Evans was arrested in Louisiana for Kidnapping 10-year old Beatrice Routh but escaped jail. Recaptured in 1993, he was then convicted and sentenced to Death for Kidnapping, Rape, and Strangulation Murder of Routh, who he had abducted at a Gulfport park, killed her in Louisiana, then dumped her body in *Mississippi*. Evans was also convicted of killing 3 people from 1985 to 1991, and additionally confessed to killing more than 70 people *at highway rest stops* and public parks *across 20 states*. Authorities were originally skeptical of Evans' claims, but some of his descriptions were perfect matches to unsolved cases across Florida. His known victims included:

- Ira Jean Smith, Black, female, Florida, 38 - 3-7-85;
- Janet Movich, White, female, 38 - 4-14-85;
- Beatrice Louise Routh, 10, White, female, *Mississippi*, 10 - 8-1-91

Born in Michigan in 1957, Evans displayed odd behavior as a young boy. He attempted suicide at the age of 16, which led to his first time being locked up – the first of many. He was later kicked out of the Marine Corps for having a "paranoid personality." In 1984, Evans was released from another stint in a psychiatric facility, even though a doctor said, "He shouldn't be on the street" because "he would hurt somebody." In 1995, Florida authorities also convicted him for the Strangulation Murder of Ira Jean Smith. On January 5, 1999 Donald Evans was stabbed to death at the Mississippi State Penitentiary by Jimmie Mack, a fellow inmate.
--<u>Source</u>: Amarillo News, 10-5-99; and Wikipedia

### WILLIAMS, John Robert and
### Rachel CUMBERLAND
### *("The Long-Haul Truck Stop Killers")*

John Williams, a long-haul trucker, admitted that he killed more than 30 women, stating that *"truck stop prostitutes are easy to kill."* In 2005 Williams, 28, was arrested, together with Rachel Cumberland, 35, in Mississippi, and charged with the fatal shooting of Nikki Hill, 28, of Shuqualak, Mississippi who the couple met at a casino. Hill's body was found July 18, 2004 off a county road near Philadelphia, Mississippi, with shotgun wounds to the back of her head and back.

Williams pled guilty to the Kidnapping and Murder of Hill and received a Life sentence. Cumberland pled guilty to Manslaughter and received 20 years in prison. On March 24, 2004, the body of Buffie Rae Brawley, 27, was found partially clothed about 10 miles outside of Indianapolis on the I-70, her head bashed and strangled after she had encountered Williams at a truck stop. Williams remembered Brawley had a rose tattoo on her leg with her daughter's name, "Ebony." Casey Jo Pipestem, 19, was last seen at a truck stop in Oklahoma City, 3 days before her nude body was dropped from a Texas-360 bridge. Williams and Cumberland were also suspects the slaying of Jennifer Hyman, found August 20, 2003 below a railroad bridge near Oxford, Mississippi, and the murder of Samantha Patrick in Yukon, Oklahoma.

--Source: Anya Pham, "10 Serial-Killing, Long-Haul Truckers," ListVerse, 10-31-15; and Murderpedia

### WILLIE, James D.
### ("The I-713/I-55 Killer")

James Willie, 28, was linked to 2 highway murders after he kidnapped and raped a woman who managed to escape and contact police. On Highway 713, police found Willie's 9mm Ruger semi-automatic handgun that matched the weapon used in the Murder of Lori Carswell, 48, found dead near her car on April 2, 2012. On I-55, in Panola County, Tom Schlender, 74, was found dead in his car. Also I-55, in Tate County, a woman was pulled over by what police investigators believed was a fake police officer in an unmarked gold Ford Crown Victoria sedan with flashing lights. When the man approached her car in disheveled plaid shirt, she wisely only lowered the window a bit and asked to see the man's badge and identification, whereupon he became agitated and drove off.

--Source: "Mississippi Highway Shooting Suspect Caught After Rape and Kidnap," ABC News, 5-18-12; "Mississippi Highway Killer May Be Dressed Like Police Officer," Huffington Post, 5-17-12.

# MISSOURI

**KRAJCIR, Timothy Wayne** *("The Highway 3 Rest Stop Killer")*
(see ILLINOIS)

## SELLS, Tommy Lynn
### *("The Cross Country Killer")*

From 1978 to 1999, Tommy Sells hitchhiked and train-hopped across the U.S., leaving a trail of at least 22 murder victims in Missouri, New York, Illinois, Texas, Kentucky, Massachusetts, West Virginia, and he was suspected of up to 70 killings elsewhere. Born June 28, 1964, in Kingsport, Tennessee, his twin sister died from Meningitis at 18 months of age, and that's when he was sent to live with his aunt, Bonnie Woodall, in Holcomb, Missouri around 1966. During his years on the road, he was a carnival worker, drank heavily, did drugs, and was imprisoned several times. His psychiatric diagnoses included "Borderline Personality, Schizoid Personality, Substance Abuse Disorder, Bipolar Disorder, Depressive Disorder and Psychosis." Whatever turned Sells into a multi-state serial killer began in Missouri where Sells committed his first murder in 1980 at age 16 while breaking into a house, where he discovered a man performing fellatio on a young boy; he killed the man in a fit of rage. But his murderous "spree" began with a double murder in 1981, when he raped and killed a woman and also killed a man during a burglary in Forsyth, Missouri. Then in 1985, at age 21, also in Forsyth, he stabbed to death Ena Cordt, 28, and her 4-year old son. According to Sells, he invited Ena to his home where they had sex, he fell asleep, and awoke to find Ena stealing from his backpack. He was convicted in Texas for 6 stabbings inflicted on Kaylene "Katy" Harris, 13, who survived with help from neighbors, and for Murder of Krystal Surles, 10, by slitting her throat. His known victims were:
- Unnamed man - 1980;
- Ena Cordt, 29, Forsyth, Missouri - 7-85;
- Rory Cordt, 4 - 7-85;
- Suzanne Korz in New York - 5-87;
- Russen Keith Dardeen, in Ina, Illinois - 11-87;
- Elaine Dardeen, in Ina, Illinois - 11-87;
- Newborn baby of Elaine Dardeen, in Ina, Illinois - 11-87;
- Pete Dardeen, 3, in Ina, Illinois - 11-87;
- Melissa Tremblay, in Lawrence, Massachusetts - 1988;
- Unnamed co-worker, in Texas - 1989;
- Unnamed woman, picked him up panhandling in Charleston, Virginia - 5-92;
- Stephanie Mahaney, in Springfield, Missouri - 1997;
- Joel Kirkpatrick, 10, in Illinois - 10-13-97;
- Kent Lauten, in Tucson, Arizona - 12-98;
- Debra Harris, 30, Milan, Tennessee - 3-99;

- Ambria Harris, 8, Milan Tennessee - 3-99;
- Haley McHone, 13, in Lexington, Kentucky - 6-13-99;
- Cheryl Harris, Del Rio, Texas - 1999;
- Kaylene Jo"Katy" Harris, 13, Del Rio, Texas (survived; Sells convicted) - 1999;
- Terry Lee Harris, Del Rio, Texas - 1999;
- Krystal Surles, 10, Del Rio, Texas, (Sells was convicted) –1999

In between those murders, he was sentenced in 1993 for the 1992 Malicious Wounding and Rape of a woman he beat with a piano stool, but the charges in West Virginia were dropped. He was then suspected of killing Mary Peres, 9, in San Antonio, Texas. He was also suspected of confessing to murders he may *not* have committed. Sells' Death sentence was carried out by lethal injection at Texas State Penitentiary in Huntsville, on April 3, 2014 when he was 49.

--<u>Source</u>: Jan den Breejen, ITypes.com, 7-4-00; *"Tommy Lynn Sells," Wikipedia*

# MISSOURI UNSOLVED CASES

## *THE I-70 MISSOURI KILLER*

A serial killer is believed to be responsible for 9 murders near I-70 in the Midwest. Six of the murders occurred in different states, and so, at first glance, seemed to be random killings. But each took place at a different shopping mall just off I-70. Nancy Kitzmiller, 24, of St. Charles, Missouri, was shot to death in the Boot Village store off the I-70 where she worked as a manager. Robin Fuldauer, 26, of Indianapolis, was found shot to death at a Payless shoe store off the I-70 where she worked. Patricia Smith, 23, and Patricia Magers, 32 were working at La Bridal Shop off the I-70 in Wichita, Kansas when they were shot to death in the back storeroom. Michael McCown, 40, was shot to death at Sylvia's Ceramics, off the I-70 in Terre Haute, Indiana, on April 27, 1992. Sarah Blessing, 37, was working alone in a gift shop at the Woodson Village Shopping Center in Raytown, Missouri, which is near an access road to I-70. On May 7, 1992, a local auctioneer noticed a stranger walking into his auction house and looking around briefly, then he walking out again. Tim Hickman, who owned a video store, watched the man cross the parking lot and pass by his store. Minutes later, Tim heard a gunshot. He reached his front door just as the man was disappearing around the corner. A grocery clerk saw the stranger as he climbed the embankment to an I-70 access road and vanished. Meanwhile, Tim Hickman went next door to the gift shop and found Sara Blessing laying lifeless in a pool of blood. Police believed the Raytown murder was connected to the earlier shopping mall killings. A multi-state task force was set up. Lab tests confirmed that all 6 victims had been killed by the same gun, most likely a semi-automatic .22 caliber pistol. All were shot where they worked. There were 3 additional murders in Texas in 1993 and 1994 that police believe were the work of the same killer, bringing the number of victims to 9. A composite of the I-70 Serial Killer was made from the Missouri witness' description: Gender: Male; DOB: 1949 to 1959; Height: 5'8" to 6'; Hair: Reddish, sandy; Defining Characteristics: Lazy eyelids and a high forehead. The I-70 murders remain unsolved.

--Source: Sarah J. Clark, *"Police Informed About I-70 Killer 20 Years Later," FOX4kc.com*, 5-3-12; *"The 1-70 Killer,"* Unsolved Mysteries, at unsolved.com

# MONTANA

### BAKER, Stanley Dean Baker; Steven Hurd, Arthur "Moose" Hulse, Harry Stroup
### *"Sons of Satan Killers;"*
### *" The Yellowstone Killers"*

Stanley Baker, 22, a drug addicted hippie hitchhiking on the highway, shot, killed, dismembered, decapitated, stabbed and cannibalized Robert Salem, 40, who gave him a ride. Another hitchhiker, James Schlosser, 22, a social worker from Roundup, Montana, met a similar fate. On June 16, 1970, a hiker stumbled upon a shallow grave off a highway near El Cariso, in southern California. It held the body of Florence Nancy Brown, 29, a schoolteacher from El Toro who worked with handicapped children. Thirteen days earlier, Brown had told her husband she was going to a PTA meeting, got into her car, and vanished. About a month later, July 11, 1970, a man fishing on the Yellowstone River in Montana cast his line into the rushing waters and, instead of a trout, snagged a corpse. It was the remains of James Schlosser, On the previous Friday, the young man had cheerfully set off in his yellow Opel Kadett, after telling his mother that he was looking forward to a weekend hiking in Yellowstone National Park. Schlosser and Brown had been stabbed multiple times, and their bodies mutilated. Brown's right arm had been hacked off and Schlosser's legs, arms and head were missing. And the most chilling detail: Neither corpse had a heart.

Although separated by 1,000 miles, the two killings sparked fears that Schlosser and Brown had fallen prey to a deadly fad - the "devil cult." Working on a tip, California police nabbed Brown's murderers by the end of June. They were part of a loose cult of grubby drug addicts, some teenagers, who called themselves the Sons of Satan. They scraped by, day-to-day, sleeping where they could, stealing and wandering around in search of their next fix. Group leader Steven Hurd, 20, called the devil "father," and boasted that he had eaten Brown's heart to honor Satan. The young mother had been the group's second killing in as many days. The first, on June 2, was Jerry Carlin, a gas-station attendant working the lobster shift. It started as a robbery, but Carlin, 20, a newlywed, wasn't cooperative enough. One of Hurd's acolytes, Arthur "Moose" Hulse, 16, 6 feet tall and 260 pounds, got annoyed. Hulse would later tell a jury, "He kept bugging me." To quiet him down, Hulse whacked Carlin once in the head with the dull edge of a hatchet. When that failed to silence the victim, Hulse turned the hatchet around, and hacked Carlin to death. The take: $73. The next night, Brown, an attractive mother of four stopped at an intersection and was attacked by Hurd's band of killers. They forced their way into her car and drove her to an orange grove, where Hurd stabbed her 20 times. After another short ride, Hurd and his accomplices buried her at the secluded site near the highway. Hurd told investigators that he returned later, alone, dug the body up, mutilated it, then cut out the heart and ate it.

*The Yellowstone Killers* - Stanley Dean Baker, and Harry Stroup, 20, were nabbed after a traffic accident near Salinas, California on July 15, 1970. They had Schlosser's yellow Opel. Upon his arrest, Baker made a startling statement. *"I have a problem,"* he said. *"I am a cannibal."* He then reached into his pocket and pulled out a few small, white objects - finger bones. Baker said they came from Schlosser's hands. He had hacked them off the victim and put them in his pocket, in case, he said, he wanted a snack. Along with the severed digits, Baker had a copy of the "Satanic Bible" in his pocket. Baker freely confessed to what had happened. He told police that he and Stroup had been dropping acid and hitchhiking on July 11 when Schlosser pulled over to offer a ride. They stopped to camp for the night. Sometime after dark, a thunderstorm set Baker's LSD-addled brain into a demonic trance. He could not help himself; Satan told him to stab Schlosser and cut out his heart. *"I ate it, raw,"* he boasted.

Baker pleaded guilty to Schlosser's murder, and was given a Life sentence. Stroup was later convicted of manslaughter and sent to jail for 10 years. Behind bars, Baker apparently forgot about the devil and behaved like a little angel, and by 1985, within 5 years of being jailed, he was paroled. In California, Hulse was quickly tried, and his defense team tried to argue that years of blowing out his brains with booze and drugs rendered him incapable of taking responsibility for his actions. The jury found him guilty and sent him to jail for life. It took five years of psychiatric treatment before Hurd was declared sane enough to stand trial. His attorney portrayed Hurd as a helpless pawn of delusions that Satan was forcing him to kill, and that his addiction to Seconal and LSD had scrambled his brain. After three days of deliberation, the jury decided that Hurd had no one but himself to blame for his actions and that this devil deserved no sympathy. Hurd was sentenced to Life in prison and is still behind bars.
--<u>Source</u>: Mara Bovson, *"Cultists & Cannibals of 1970,"* TheDailyNews.com, 7-18-10

## DRYMAN, Frank
## *("The I-15 Killer")*

Frank Dryer, 19, was a hitchhiking drifter when Clarence Pellett, 59, picked him up during a Spring blizzard in 1951 on the I-15 near Shelby, Montana. Dryman was carrying a loaded gun that he used to kill Pellett by shooting him 7 times in the back as he tried to run way from his attacker. Dryman then took Pellet's car and fled to Canada where he was arrested, then jailed in Montana. Dryman initially received a sentence of Death by Hanging after a quick trial in 1955. But his case became the focus of a battle over the Death Penalty and frontier justice, and he received a new sentence of Life in prison with the help of the Montana Supreme Court. In 1969, after just 15 years in prison, he was paroled. The Montana Department of Corrections said that, today, the soonest a person sentenced to Life in prison could gain parole is 30 years. Dryman skipped out on his parole around 1972 and disappeared. Forty years later, Pellet's grandson hired a PI to track down Dryman, who was then 78 and in Arizona; Dryman was extradited to face a revocation of Parole hearing and again jailed in Montana in 2010. Because Dryer was only 19 in 1951 when he killed Pellet, it was assumed Pellet was his first and only crime, but at age 16 he had been accused of robbing a liquor store; his great aunt testified in his behalf so he was not jailed, and he was also on the loose from 1969 until 2017. Born in 1932, Montana State Prison inmate Frank Dryman died November 6, 2017 at the Lewistown Infirmary in Lewistown.

--<u>Source</u>: Matt Gouras, "*Montana Murderer Captured After 38 Years on the Loose,*" Bozeman Daily Chronicle, 3-24-10.

## KEMPER, Edmund (*"Co-Ed Butcher"*)
## (see CALIFORNIA)

# MONTANA UNSOLVED CASES

## *"THE I-35 PRIEST MURDERS"*

In 1984, Father John Kerrigan was settling into his new role at the Sacred Heart Catholic Church in Ronan, Montana. On the night of July 20, he left a Polish bakery and disappeared. The next day, bloody clothing was found on Highway 35, and a week later his car was found. The car, and a shovel in the trunk, were covered in blood. His body was never found. Experts think his murder may be related to the killing of Father Reynaldo Rivera, who was shot to death in Santa Fe, New Mexico in 1982 at a rest stop after a caller had asked him to come deliver last rites. Kerrigan had spent time in New Mexico not far from Rivera, and both men were members of the Order of Franciscans. But neither mystery has ever been solved, and a connection hasn't been proven.

--<u>Source</u>: Jessica Wick, "*These 6 Famous Homicides in Montana Will Never Be Forgotten,*" OnlyInYourState.com, 9-8-17

## *"THE I-94 BAD ROUTE REST STOP MURDER"*

Sometime in the early morning hours of a bitterly cold Montana morning on November 19, 1985, Dexter W. Stefonek, 67, of Rhinelander, Wisconsin, was brutally murdered at Bad Route Rest Stop on I-94 in Dawson County, Montana. At approximately 10:20 a.m. that morning, Clyde Mitchell, who managed the rest stop for the Montana Department of Transportation, arrived to discover a 1984 Plymouth Horizon with Wisconsin plates engulfed in flames. Mitchell reported the car fire to the Dawson County Sheriff's Office. At first, no one suspected a murder, nor any crime beyond possibly arson. The Plymouth was identified as belonging to Stefonek. It was theorized Stefonek hitched a ride with a trucker, but no trace of him was found for months. Then, on March 8, 1986, William and Cynthia Shaw took some garbage to a private dump site on the land of rancher Bob Reynolds, located approximately 2 miles west of the Whoopup Creek exit. At the dump site, William discovered Stefonek's wallet on the ground. Then the Shaws saw it -- a foot sticking out from under a mattress. Dexter Stefonek's body had been found, and police now knew they had a murder case. The autopsy revealed that Stefonek had been severely beaten and shot twice, execution-style in the back of the head with a large-caliber pistol. The first shot went into strap muscles of his neck. The second shot was fatal. In searching the rest stop building, these words were found penciled into the grout line on the wall in the last stall of the men's restroom: "HOT JOCK SHOT WAD FROM WISCONSIN 11/85 SATURDAY THE 3RD." In 1985, DNA evidence was still relatively unheard of, and video surveillance was uncommon. The one clue upon which the case may hinge was the presence of a blue and white Chevrolet Blazer, with a camper top and Arizona plates, seen parked at the Bad Route rest area that same November morning. The Blazer was never found. The investigation ultimately went nowhere and went cold. Even a profile on *"Unsolved Mysteries"* produced no new clues or tips.

--Source: Jason Stuart, *"Thirty Year Old Bad Route Rest Area Murder Case Remains Unresolved,"* GlendiveRangerReview.com, 11-30-15.

## *"THE I-94 LORA JEAN MURDER"*

Lora Jean was 14 when she ran away from home on April 7, 1972 and never returned. The teenager was last seen in Huntley that morning by a school bus driver as she walked toward I-94. Her body was found 3 weeks later and 250 miles away, near Medora, North Dakota, a short distance off the same highway. She had been sexually assaulted, strangled and stabbed. She had been found by on rangeland adjacent to I-94, evidently caught by her killer at a barbed-wire fence. Her body was found under an old cedar tree a few paces off a worn cattle path. A cross she wore around her neck was found dangling in the tree, and her clothes were strewn on her body. She had been strangled and stabbed in the abdomen Her killer was never identified. The girl's 1972 murder was reopened in late November 2005 when North Dakota Attorney General Wayne Stenehjem announced the creation of a Cold-Case Investigations Squad. Sherrie Kautz and Ella Dugan-Laemmle said they hope to finally put a name to the Lora Jean's killer and 15 unsolved murders and missing-persons cases in North Dakota selected for review by the team. At the time of Lora Jean's murder, the routine use of DNA technology by law enforcement was still about 2 decades away. Lora Jean's mother and one of her sisters have given tissue samples for DNA analysis to help the investigators.. Finding Lora Jean's killer would do more than simply answer a mystery that has tormented her mother. You're frozen in time when there's no solution.

--Source: Greg Tuttle, *"Cold-Case Team Working to Solve 1972 Murder of Huntley Girl"* The Billings Gazette, 1-29-06

## *"THE MONTANA HIGHWAY CHILD KILLER"*

In 1973, the day after she was abducted, the body of 5-year old Siobhan McGuinness was found in a culvert under the I-90, 10 miles east of Missoula Montana. She had been brutalized, raped, beaten about the head and died from multiple stab wounds. In April, 2004, 34 years after her murder, DNA culled from the evidence produced no results, so it has been speculated that her killer has either fled the country, or died.

--Source: *"Her Name Was Siobhan,"* True Crime Report, 12-23-08

# NEBRASKA

### JESPERSON, Keith Hunter
### *("The Happy Face Killer")*

Born April 6, 1955, to Gladys and Lester Jesperson, in Chillawack, British Columbia where he also was raised, Keith Jesperson had an abusive father who beat him and who used electric shocks as punishments. He attempted 2 murders when he was only 10 years old and he was raped at age 14. Strangulation became his preferred killing method, the same method he used as a child to kill animals. Keith Jesperson, an interstate truck driver, claimed that he killed as many as 160 people, just 8 of whom have been confirmed victims, murdered from 1990 to 1995 as he prowled the highways in Nebraska, Oregon, California, Florida, Washington and Wyoming. When a woman falsely confessed to killing Jesperson's lifelong girlfriend, Taunja Bennett, 23, who Jesperson actually brutally beat to death after an argument, Jesperson left a message on a truck stop mirror confessing to Bennett's murder and signed it with a "smiley face." Many of his victims thereafter were transients and prostitutes with no personal connection to him. His confirmed victims were:

- Taunja Bennett, Portland, Oregon - 1-23-92;
- "Claudia," unidentified woman, Blythe, California – 8-30-92;
- Cynthia Lyn Rose, Turlock, California - 9-92;
- Laurie Ann Pentland, Salem, Oregon - 11-92;
- "Carla" or "Cindy," Santa Nella, California - 6-93;
- "Susanne," unidentified woman, Crestview, Florida - 9-94;
- Angela Subrise, Spokane, picked up Washington, to Indiana– 1-95;
- Julie Ann Winningham, Washougal, Washington - 3-10-95

Jesperson was arrested March 30, 1995, claiming 160 to 185 victims, and pled Guilty for the murder of Winningham, pled No Contest for Bennett, was convicted in October 1995, received 3 Life sentences (for murders of Pentland, Winningham, Subrise) and was incarcerated in Oregon.
--Source: Wikipedia

### JOUBERT IV, John Joseph
### *("The I-295 Murders;" "Nebraska Boy Snatcher")*
(see MAINE)

111

## STARKWEATHER, Charles Raymond "Charlie," and Caril Ann FUGATE
### ("Nebraska's Bonnie and Clyde")

"Charlie" Starkweather was an American teenage spree killer who murdered 11 people in Nebraska and Wyoming in a 2-month murder spree between December 1957 and January 1958. During the 1958 murders, Starkweather was accompanied by his 14-year-old girlfriend, Caril Ann Fugate. Born November 24, 1938, in Lincoln, Nebraska, Starkweather was the 3rd of 7 children of working class parents, Guy and Helen Starkweather. He was born with Genu Varum, a mild birth defect that caused his legs to be misshapen and also suffered a speech impediment, which led to constant teasing by classmates. The only subject which Starkweather excelled at was gym, where he found a physical outlet for his rage against those who bullied him. But also began bullying those who had once picked on him, and eventually his rage extended to anyone he happened to dislike. In 1956, Starkweather, 18, was introduced to Caril Ann Fugate, 13. Starkweather had dropped out of high school in his senior year and became employed at a Western Union newspaper warehouse because the warehouse was located near Whittier Junior High School in Lincoln, where Fugate was a student, which enabled him to visit her every day after school. He soon quit that job and became a garbage collector, using the garbage route to plot bank robberies. His personal philosophy by which he lived the remainder of his life was: *"Dead people are all on the same level."* Fugate's family disapproved of Charles, leading the two to run away, after killing Fugate's entire family on November 30, 1957, when they then hit the highway. Their victims were:

- Robert Colvert, 21, gas station attendant;
- Marion Bartlett, 58, Fugate's stepfather;
- Velda Bartlett, 36, Fugate's mother;
- Betty Jean Bartlett, 2, Velda;
- Marion Bartlett's daughter, Fugate's half sister;
- August Meyer, 70, Starkweather's friend;
- Robert Jensen, 17, boyfriend to Carol King;
- Carol King, 16, girlfriend to Robert Jensen;
- C. Lauer Ward, 47, wealthy industrialist;
- Clara Ward, 46, C. Lauer Ward's wife;
- Lillian Fencl, 51, Clara Ward's maid;
- Merle Collison, 34, traveling salesman

On November 21, 1958, Caril Fugate received a Life sentence. She was paroled in June 1976 after 17-1/2 years in prison and settled in Lansing, Michigan, where she married Frederick Clair in 2007. Starkweather was found guilty and received the Death Penalty for the murder of Robert Jensen, the only murder for which he was tried. On June 25, 1959, Starkweather was executed by electric chair in Lincoln, Nebraska

--<u>Source</u>: Wikipedia

# NEVADA

## GALLEGO, Gerald Armond and Charlene Adele GALLEGO
### ("The Sex Slaves Killers")

Gerard and Charlene Gallego were a killer couple who lured young girls and prostitutes from Nevada and California highways and byways into the back of their Dodge van, used them as sex slaves, raped and murdered them. Born July 17, 1946 Gerard Gallego had been married 7 times in 14 years and had been sexually molesting his daughter since she was 6. His wife, Charlene, was born October 10, 1956. Their first known victims, on November 11, 1978, were Rhonda Scheffler, 17, and Kippi Vaught, 16. Charlene picked up the girls on the pretext of offering them marijuana, put them in the back of their van, bound them until Gerard walked the girls to a secluded spot, where he repeatedly raped both girls for hours, then made the girls walk to a ditch where Gerald struck each with a tire iron before shooting them in the head and returned to the van alone. The killer couple then moved on to Reno, Nevada where, on June 24, 1979, Brenda Judd, 14, and Sandra Colley, 13, were lured into their van at the Washtoe County Fair on the promise of making some money delivering leaflets. Charlene drove the van on the I-80 while Gerald repeatedly raped them as Charlene watched in her rear view mirror. Charlene parked at Humboldt Sink, a desolate area, and forced the girls to perform sexual acts on each other. Gerald then swung the shovel at Colley's head, beat Judd to death, and dug a hole in which the naked girls were buried. The girls were listed as runaways for 4 years until their remains were found in November 1999 by a tractor operator. On 4-24-80, the Gallegos kidnapped Stacey Redican and Karen Chipman Twiggs, in Citrus Heights near Sacramento where the Gallegos sexually abused and killed them. Subsequent victims included Linda Aguilar, her unborn child, and Virginia Mochel. On 11-2-80, Gerald spotted Craig Miller, 22, and his fiance, Mary Elizabeth Sowers, 21, standing on the side of the road. Gerald ordered them into the car at gunpoint, and took them to a secluded area where he shot and killed Miller, then took Sowers back to the Gallegos' apartment where he raped her all night and shot and killed her next morning.

In 1984, the Gallegos were tried in both California and Nevada. In exchange for her testimony, Charlene Gallegos was not charged in California; she agreed to plead guilty to Murder and receive a sentence of 16 Years and 8 Months in Nevada. Gerald Gallego was convicted and sentenced to Death in both states. In 1999 Gerard's Death sentence was overturned and he won a new sentencing hearing but the new jury also sentenced him to Death. In Y-2000, nearly 21 years after they disappeared from a Reno fairground, the skeletal remains of Brenda Lynne Judd, 14, and Sandra Kaye Colley, 13, were discovered when a property owner found them in a shallow grave off U.S.

113

Highway 395 north of Reno, just inside neighboring Lassen County, California. They are suspected victims of convicted sex-slave killer Gerald Gallego, who faced execution in both Nevada and California for four other killings. Judd and Colley disappeared in Reno during an evening out at the Washoe County Fair in June 1979. Gallego was implicated in the girls' deaths by his common-law wife, Charlene Williams, who told investigators he sexually assaulted the girls, bludgeoned them to death and buried them in shallow graves. Charlene Gallego was released from prison in July 1997. Gerald Gallego died of rectal cancer July 18, 2002 at Nevada prison medical center.
--Source: Sandra Cherab, "DNA Test Confirms Remains of Sparks Teens," Las Vegas Sun, 2-23-00; Wikipedia; Murderpedia

## KNOWLES, Paul John ("The Casanova Killer")
(see FLORIDA)

## WILDER, Christopher Bernard ("The Beauty Queen Killer")
(see FLORIDA)

# NEVADA UNSOLVED CASES

*"THE I-80 PUMPERNICKEL VALLEY OFF-RAMP DISAPPEARANCES"*

On April 14, 2011, Patrick F. Carnes, 86, disappeared, along with dog, "Lucky," while driving west from Toledo, Ohio to Reno, Nevada, on I-80 in Humboldt County. His Subaru was found abandoned though in perfect working condition, on the wrong side of the highway for the direction that Carnes would have been driving, about 20 miles east of Winnemucca--at the unmarked Pumpernickel Valley Exit 205. The car was devoid of useable fingerprints and all of Carnes' possessions appeared to be intact. Carnes was last seen alive on April 13, 2011 when he was pulled over by a State Trooper, in a dash cam video with Lucky, a 100-pound Akita mix, waving his tail in the back seat. The grainy film caught a tractor trailer with which Carnes seemed to be traveling in tandem. Carnes had been a trucker in Southern California before getting into computers and had an admiration for truckers and trusted them. He mentioned that he had been following the trucker "because he's going to Elko" and that he would "never drive at night again." Five years before Carnes' disappearance, another vehicle was found abandoned on the same spot, in working order, a month after it's driver, Judith Casida of Reno, disappeared. She has never been found. A month before Carnes vanished, Grant Moedl disappeared just after crossing the state line into Idaho. He and his car were later found under water in a reservoir. And in May 2011, Utah authorities were looking for a young man who vanished along the I-80 near Dugway, Nevada and for an elderly hitchhiker vanished in Humboldt County.
--Source: "Elderly Man's Disappearance Linked to Serial Killer?" KTVN-2 2News, KLAS 1 Team Reporter, 6-8-11; "Team of Killers Operating Around I-80," Coast to Coast, "Missing;" "Highway to Hell? Overlapping Disappearances at Pumpernickel Valley Off-Ramp," WordPress, 6-16-14

# NEW HAMPSHIRE

**EVANS, Robert "Bob" (real name Terry Pederson Rasmussen, aka Curtis Kimball, aka Lawrence Vanner)**

Authorities linked at least 6 murders, including 4 or 5 New Hampshire murders, starting from the 1980s, to Terry Pederson Rasmussen, known in New Hampshire as Bob Evans, and Robert T. Evans, a multi-state killer. He used a number of aliases and died in at Susanville, California State Prison in 2010 of natural causes, under the name Lawrence Vanner, while serving a sentence for killing and dismembering his wife, Eunsoon Jun. He was the boyfriend and suspected killer of a New Hampshire woman, Denise Beaudin, who, along with her 6-month old daughter, disappeared in 1981. Evans also killed a mother and 3 girls, one of whom was his daughter, and each of whom were found in steel drums in a New Hampshire's Bear Brook State Park at Allentown, New Hampshire. He had arrests for crimes from bouncing checks in Phoenix, Arizona, to driving a stolen vehicle in San Luis Obispo, California, and evidently racked up thousands of highway miles and many murders along the way
--Source: FOX-61/AP, 1-26-17; WMUR-TV9, 6-10-19

**MAYRAND Jr., Edward H.** (*"The Route 10 Strangler"*)
(see RHODE ISLAND)

**SAMPSON, Gary Lee** (*"The Hitchhiking Carjacker Killer"*)
(see MASSACHUSETTS)

**WILDER, Christopher Bernard** (*"The Beauty Queen Killer"*)
(see FLORIDA)

## NEW HAMPSHIRE UNSOLVED CASES

### *"THE CONNECTICUT RIVER VALLEY KILLER"*

An unidentified serial killer is believed to be responsible for more than 7 knife-murders from 1978 to 1987, in the Connecticut River Valley areas of Claremont, New Hampshire and Vermont. Several of the victims were known to be hitchhiking. The victims are:
- Cathy Millican, 27, New Hampshire - 10-24-78;
- Mary Elizabeth Critchley, 37, New Hampshire - 7-25-81;
- Sylvia Gray, 76, New Hampshire -10-5-82;
- Bernice Courtemanche, 16, hitchhiking on Route 12, New Hampshire - 5-30-84;
- Ellen Fried, 27, New Hampshire - 7-20-84;

- Eva Morse, 27, Route 12, New Hampshire - 7-10-85;

- Lynda Moore, 36, I-91, Vermont - 4-15-86;

- Barbara Agnew, 38, I-91 rest stop at Hartford, Vermont - 1-10-87;

- Jane Boroski, 22 and pregnant, Route 32 (survived) - 8-6-88;

- Carrie Moss, New Hampshire; skeletal remains found in Boston woods - 7-25-89.

Boroski described her attacker for a police sketch and 3 numbers of his license plate; the murders stopped and the cases grew cold after the Boroski attack. One of the suspects was Michael Nicholaou, a Vietnam veteran who served as helicopter pilot and was awarded 2 Purple Hearts, 2 Silver Stars, and 2 Bronze Stars before being charged of strafing civilians in the Mekong Delta in 1970, and for abandoning his camp to seek hand-to-hand individual combat with the enemy armed only with a knife, stating he was "*hunting humans.*" Murder and Attempted Murder charges were ultimately dropped and he received treatment for Post Traumatic Stress Syndrome (PTSD), but then murdered his wife and children before committing suicide. The identity of the Connecticut River Valley Killer is still unknown.

--Source: Dawson Raspuzzi, "*25-Year-Old Vermont Murder Solved by DNA Analysis,*" Brattleboro Reporter, Benington Banner, 7-3-12; "*Connecticut River Valley Killer,*" an Oxygen TV dramatization, 8-26-19

## THE I-89 KILLER

On 12-2-15, unidentified skeletal remains were found by the I-89 just off the southbound Exit 16 in Colchester, New Hampshire.

--Source: "*Human Remains Found by I-89,*" by Cat Viglienzoni

## THE I-95 KILLER

Patricia Webb, 32, had been reported missing July 1, 1989. Her blue pickup was found in the southbound lane of I-95 in Beddeford, Maine, but her skeletal remains were found off Route 3 in Franconia, New Hampshire. July 18, 1989.

--Source: "*Unsolved Crimes in New Hampshire,*" AP, 12-7-09

## "THE ROUTE 112 / VALLEY KILLER"

(see VERMONT)

# NEW JERSEY

## LANE, Adam Leroy  *("The Route 78 Killer")*
(see PENNSYLVANIA)

## ROGERS JR., Richard W.  *("The Last Call Killer")*

Richard Rogers, 55, a former surgical nurse at Mt. Sinai Hospital for 20 years, was convicted of the dismemberment murders of 2 men whose body parts were dumped along New Jersey highways. He was also suspected of murdering at least 5 other gay men, and Thomas Mulcahy, 56, a married bisexual businessman from Sudsbury, Massachusetts, whose body parts were found July 10, 1992, off Route 72 in South Jersey. Anthony Marrero, 44, was a gay prostitute from Manhattan, whose body parts were found May 10, 1993. On July 31, 1993, the head and 2 arms of Michael Sakara of Manhattan, who was linked to Rogers, were discovered off Route 9-W in Havershaw, New York. Rogers' fingerprints were found on the trash bags that contained the victims' body parts.. He was also suspect in the murders of Sakara and Peter Anderson, 54, whose body was found in Pennsylvania, and the 1982 killing of Matthew J. Piero, 25, in Lake Mary, Florida when Rogers was in Florida attending a class reunion. Piero was last seen leaving a gay bar in Orlando on April 10, 1982 and turned up strangled, with multiple stab wounds to his heart and body. On August 19, 1988, Rogers was arrested on Staten Island, accused of drugging, binding and injuring a Manhattan man. Born in 1950, Richard Rogers Jr. was 22 and a graduate student studying French at the University of Maine in 1973 when he became a suspect in the death of Fredric A. Spencer, 22, who lived in his apartment building. Rogers told police he caught Spencer in his apartment and that Spencer came at him with a hammer. Rogers claimed self defense, that he got the hammer away from Spencer and beat Spencer until he died; Rogers was acquitted of Manslaughter. His known victims were:

- Thomas Mulcahy, 56 - found 7-20-92;
- Anthony Marrero, 44 - found 2-10-93;
- Michael Sakara, 55 - found 7-31-93;
- Peter S. Anderson, 54 - found 5-5-91;
- Matthew J. Piero, 25;
- Fredric A, Spencer, 22

On May 28, 2001, Rogers was arrested at Mount Sinai Hospital. When investigators searched his home, they found a bottle of Versed, a sedative that can be used as a date-rape drug, rug fibers consistent with those found with Mulcahy's body, and "several photographs of unknown men on which stab wounds had been drawn," according to court documents. In January 2006, Rogers was sentenced to Life in prison for the murders of Mulcahy and Marrero.

--Source: Damien Cave, *"As Killer Faces Sentencing, His Motive Remains Elusive,"* New York Times, 1-27-06; Murderpedia

**ZARINKSY, Robert** *("Garden State Parkway Killer)*

Robert Zarinsky becasme a suspect when the body of Mary Agnes Klinsky, 18, was found near Telegraph Hill Park inHolmdel, off the Garden State Parkway southbound, now known at Exit 116. She had been raped and beaten to death. In 1976, Zarinsky was sentenced to Life in prison for the 1969 murder of Rosemary Calandriello, 17, of Atlantic Highlands, New Jersey. In 2001 he was acquitted of the 1958 murder of police officer Charles Bernoskie of Rahway, New Jersey. He had also been suspected of the murders of:

- Linda Balabanow, 17, of Union Township, Union County, New Jersey;
- Doreen Carluci, 14, Woodbridge Township, New Jersey;
- Joanne Delardo, 15, Woodbridge Township, New Jersey;
- Ann Logan, 19, of Elizabeth, New Jeresey.

In 2008, he was indicted for the 1968 murder of Jane Durua, 13, of Midletown, New Jersey, but died before the trial could begin.

Source: Wikipedia

# NEW MEXICO

## FRY, Robert
### ("The San Juan Highway Killer")

In the summer of Y-2000, Robert Fry, from Farmington, New Mexico, was 28 when he and a friend offered a ride to Betty Lee, a stranded 36-year-old mother of 5 from Shiprock, New Mexico. Fry stabbed her, stripped her, and bashed in her skull with the swing of a sledgehammer, off a lonely stretch of State Road which intersects with US-160, a 2-lane highway, located in northwestern San Juan County, that passes through desert terrain entirely on the Navajo Nation and is less than a mile long. So Fry had a very short window of opportunity perhaps with the highway's posted speed limit of only 15 miles per hour before reaching its terminus at a toll booth where the highway becomes Four Corners Road and encircles the Four Corners Monument. At Fry's trial 2 years later at Albuquerque he faced the Death Penalty twice more in two separate trials involving gruesome murders of 3 victims. In the 7 years between Fry's trial in 2002 and 2009 when the state repealed the Death Penalty, Fry was also convicted of 3 other murders. He was sentenced to Life in prison for the March 31, 1998, killing of Donald Tsosie, 40, of Ganado, Arizona. Tsosie was beaten with a shovel, his body found nearly a month later at the bottom of a cliff south of Farmington. Fry received 2 Life sentences for the Nov. 29, 1996, killings of Matthew Trecker, 18, and Joseph Fleming, 25. The Farmington men were stabbed and their throats were slashed in the now-defunct "Eclectic," a counterculture store in downtown Farmington.
--Source: Joline Gutierrez Krueger, *"Death Penalty Not Popular With New Mexico Juries,"* The Albuquerque Journal, 10-5-16; Brian Massey, *"Court Upholds Death Sentence Given to Robert Fry,"* 12-8-05.

## NEW MEXICO UNSOLVED CASES

### "CAMINO LA TIERRA STRANGLER"

The decomposed body of James Gossen was found by rabbit hunters on February 6, 1989, in a shallow grave off Camino La Tierra, a highway diamond interchange, in Santa Fe, New Mexico. The cause of death listed on the death certificate was strangulation. Gossen had been reported as a missing person by his wife, Myra Redman (Gossen) in Albuquerque, New Mexico, on or about July 13, 1988. Mr. Gossen's disappearance was suspicious and Ms. Redman suspected foul play. To date, no suspects have been identified for James Gossen's murder.
--Source: New Mexico Department of Public Safety website, *"Cold Case Files,"* http://www.dps.state.php/media/cold-case-files/

## "HIGHWAY 180 KILLER"

On May 27, 1999, electric company workers found a man's mummified corpse chained by the neck to a telephone pole near Highway 180 in Luna County. The victim, presumed to be between 30 to 50 years of age, had been set on fire after being chained to the pole which was half burned. A lighter, presumed to have been used to set the fire, was found near the man's remains.

--Source: The Doe Network, 12-16-14; "*Luna County John Doe*," Unsolved Mysteries," 2015

## "ROUTE 26 KILLER"

On September 4, 1992, hikers discovered several items belonging to Jennifer Pentilla under a tarp in a remote area off State Road 26, between Hatch and Deming, New Mexico. Her body, which has not been not found, was probably dumped somewhere along Route 26. Pentilla had left her home in Missoula, Montana on October 1, 1991, and flew to San Diego where she made frequent contact with family and friends via phone from October 1 to 17, 1991. She was last seen on October 17, 1991 at a Shell service station on Pine Street in Deming, New Mexico, where she called her mother at approximately 9 a.m. A missing persons report was generated on November 1, 1991 by the Missoula, Montana Police Department. She is presumed murdered.

--Source: New Mexico Department of Public Safety website, "*Cold Case Files,*" ."http://www.dps.state.nm.us/index.php/media/cold-case-files/

## "ROUTE 68 KILLER"

On July 29, 2001, at 2:40 a.m., State Police responded to a report of a "man down" in the south bound lanes of State Road 68, north of the town of Espanola. A "John Doe" was taken to University of New Mexico Hospital in Albuquerque with major head trauma and where he died later that day. The State Police Criminal Investigations Section was called upon to investigate. The deceased was identified as 16-year-old Brian Edmonds. Edmonds was last seen at a neighbor's birthday party the night before he was found on the highway. According to several witnesses, he was suffering from a small laceration on his head prior to his death. He left the party to walk to his home, which was a short distance away. He was found on the highway less than a mile from his residence. Although it is presumed she met with foul play, the autopsy of Edmonds could not determine *how* her injuries were received -- whether from a vehicle or from a blow -- therefore the manner of death remains undetermined. No suspects have been identified at this time.

--Source: "*Cold Case Files,*" New Mexico Department of Public Safety website, http://www.dps.state.nm.us/index.php/media/cold-case-files/

# NEW YORK

## BERKOWITZ, David Richard
## ("Son of Sam;" "The 44-Caliber Killer"; "Lovers' Lane Murders")

On April 17, 1977, Valentina Suriani, 18, and Alexander Esau, 20, were shot and killed by the same gun, as they kissed in their parked car near the Hutchinson River Parkway. The significance of the Suriani-Esau murders and their very public Parkway location, is that, this time, the "*.44-Caliber Killer*" left a note in which he referred to himself as "*Son of Sam.*" And while David Berkowitz is known to have killed couples at random in their parked cars - most of them were parked on city roads and "lovers' lanes." But also, what is not generally known, is that the Son of Sam case never actually closed due to Berkowitz's admission that there were *many* murders in which he "*did not act alone*" but allegedly assisted an organized Satanic cult, and that is why there is some disparity between these "*Lovers' Lane Murders*" and murders committed close to highways for which Berkowitz is also credited. Born June 1, 1953, as Richard David Falco, in Brooklyn, his biological mother, Betty Broder, grew up in an impoverished Jewish family and later married Tony Falco, an Italian-American Catholic. The couple ran a fish market together. They separated before Berkowitz's birth when Tony Falco left for another woman, and Broder later had an affair with a married real estate agent named Joseph Kleinman. When she became pregnant Kleinman threatened to abandon her if she kept the baby, so she put David up for adoption but listed Falco as the father so he would appear "legitimate." David Berkowitz was adopted a few days after birth by Nathan and Pearl Berkowitz. Pearl died of breast cancer when David was 14. When his adoptive father remarried the relationship with David was strained but there was no pre-adoption abuse to blame for his outcome. Believing his biological mother died giving birth to him, he grew up feeling intense anger and guilt, also feeling rejected and scorned about being adopted. Berkowitz's killing spree started soon after a reunion with his biological mother, Betty Falco, who he located with the help of an adoption support group. His mother brought to the reunion her other biological child, Roslyn, a sister he never knew about. The discovery that his mother had kept and raised his sibling, while giving him up for adoption, may have resonated with already intense feelings of rejection and abandonment, even though he remained in contact with his half-sister, Roslyn, long after breaking off contact with his mother. The July 29, 1976 to July 31, 1977 confirmed murders not only started shortly after the ill-fated reunion, but also occurred in the same neighborhood as that meeting with his mother. Berkowitz later revealed to another prison inmate that he believed he had been conceived out of wedlock in the back seat of a car, and that his purpose in killing couples in cars was to prevent a repetition of his own conception, birth and abandonment through adoption. He claimed he heard voices in his head and had started over 1,000 fires. Firesetting or fascination with fire is one of 8 "Adopted Child

121

Syndrome" behaviors that adopted killers have in common.

Berkowitz was apprehended August 10, 1988 and has been serving 6 consecutive Life sentences in prison.

--Source: "*Son of Sam Arrested,*" This Day in History (August 10): 1977, History Channel website; David Abrahamson, "*The Mind of the Accused,*" About.com; "*Infamous American Murders,*" Oracle ThinkQuest website, and "*Adopted Killers,*" by Lori Carangelo, 2019

## SELLS, Tommy Lynn *("The Cross Country Killer")*
(see MISSOURI)

### RIFKIN, Joel David, 34
### *("The Long Island Ripper")*

From 1989 to 1993, Joel Rifkin murdered at least 17 women, mostly prostitutes, who he picked up along the Parkway and who he sometimes took to his home to kill, but more often murdered them in his car. Police had been initially searching for Shannan Gilbert, 24, who was working as an escort and was reported missing in May 2010 when she was running away from her driver, Michael Pak, who was waiting for her outside a client's house in Oak Beach. Gilbert was last seen banging on a resident's door and screaming for help before running off into the night. A panicked 911 call from Gilbert that night revealed her saying "*they are going to kill me.*" After bodies and dismembered body parts were piling up in both Suffolk and Nassau counties, it was later learned that some of the murdered prostitutes who knew each other had also "partied with a wealthy man who had plenty of money and drugs." Psychics have talked about "a ring of men who held parties on yachts with prostitutes." A reward of $5,000 was raised to $25,000 for information leading to an arrest. Police received over 1,200 tips via text, email and phone. It was speculated that the killer was former Long Island resident and convicted serial killer, Joel Rifkin. Police finally caught up to Rifkin on June 28, 1993, when state troopers spotted him driving his Mazda pickup truck without license plates on the Southern State Parkway; a high-speed chase ended in Mineola, New York, when he crashed into a utility pole. Troopers detected a foul odor from the back of his truck. It came from the corpse of prostitute and dancer, Tiffany Bresciani, 22, who Rifkin had picked up in his truck on June 24, 1993.

Born January 20, 1959, Rifkin's biological mother was a 20-year-old college student, and his biological father was a 24-year-old college student and army veteran. They were not married and gave him up for adoption when he was 3 weeks old on February 14, 1959 to Benjamin Rifkin who was of Russian Jewish descent, and his wife, Jeanne Granelles, of Spanish descent, who converted to Judaism. Joel considered himself to be an agnostic, having never had a bar mitzvah. The couple adopted another child, a daughter, 3 years later. A shy, awkward child, Rifkin was a target for bullies. He attended religious classes at the Sholem Aleichem Folk School and had an I.Q. assessed at 128, but struggled academically in school due to severe dyslexia.

Rifkin pleaded to "Adopted Child Syndrome" as a mitigating factor in his crimes, as he grew up believing his mother was a prostitute who couldn't afford an abortion. His known victims were:

- Heidi "Susie" Balch, 25, her severed head found on Hopewill golf course - 1989;
- Julie Blackbird (remains never found) - 1990;
- Barbara Jacobs, 31 - 7-14-91;
- Mary Ellen DeLuca, 22 - 1991;
- Yun Lee, 31 - 9-23-91;
- Jane Doe #1 - 1-12-91;
- Jane Doe #2 - mid-winter 1991, body parts found - 5-13-92;
- Jane Doe "Number 6", (never identified, remains never recovered);
- Jane Doe "Number 9", (identity remains anonymous);
- Lorraine Orvieto, 28 - 1992;
- Mary Ann Holloman, 39 - 1-2-92;
- Iris Sanchez, 25 - 5-10-92;
- Anna Lopez, 33 - 5-25-12;
- Violet O'Neill, 21 - 6-92;
- Mary Catherine Williams, 31 - 10-2-92;
- Jenny Soto, 23 - 11-16-92;
- Leah Evans, 28 - 11-16-92;
- Lauren Marquez, 28 - 2-27-93;
- Tiffany Brescianni, 22 (body found in bed of Rifkin's pickup truck) - 4-2-93.

Rifkin was found guilty of 9 counts of Second Degree Murder in 1994 and sentenced to "203 Years to Life" in prison. He denied having anything to do with the New Bedford murders.

--Source: *"Pimp Pleads Guilty to Transporting Hookers Across State Lines--Including one Killed by LI Serial Killer,"* New York Daily News, 4-11-12; *"A Novel Insanity Defense for Joel Rifkin,"* New York Times, 9-25-94; Denise Long, *"Dark Son"*; *"Long Island Serial Killer,"* Wikipedia; *"From Gilgo Beach to Atlantic City, A Serial Killer by the Sea,"* WPIX-11, 3-17-15

# WILDER, Christopher Bernard *("The Beauty Queen Killer")*
(see FLORIDA)

# NEW YORK UNSOLVED CASES

*"THE LONG ISLAND SERIAL KILLER," "THE OCEAN PARKWAY KILLER," "THE GILGO BEACH SERIAL KILLER," "THE SEASHORE SERIAL KILLER,""THE CRAIGSLIST RIPPER"*

An unidentified American serial killer, most often called "The Long Island Serial Killer," is believed to have murdered 10 to 17 people associated with the sex trade over a 20-year period and dumped the bodies along the Ocean Parkway near Long Island beach towns in Suffolk County and Jones Beach State Park in Nassau County.

# NORTH CAROLINA

### WARREN, Lesley Eugene
### ("The Baby Faced Killer")

Lesley Eugene Warren, 22, a former truck driver from the Pisgah Highway area in Candler, North Carolina, was described by police investigators as *"a sexually motivated serial killer."* Warren confessed to murdering 3 women in as many states, and was charged with the August 27, 1993 Kidnapping and Murder of Velma Faye Gray, 42, whose body was found floating in Lake Bowen near the South Carolina Highway 9 bridge, her hands tied behind her back. From 1987 to 1990, Warren, who police also described as *"intelligent, resourceful, but certainly a very dangerous fellow,"* killed female victims who were all attractive, White, and ages 20 to 40. Usually Warren killed his victims close to where he was living. Warren admitted to the murders of Jayme Denise Hurley, 39, and Noel Johnson. Hurley's body was discovered in 1990 in a densely wooded area near Mount Pisgah, North Carolina, near Asheville. He confessed to strangling Johnson and leaving her body in the trunk of her car in a High Point parking garage. Hurley had been Warren's counselor at the Juvenile Evaluation Center in Swannanoa. Johnson had met Warren at a party in High Point. He also confessed to the slayings of Patsy Diane Vineyard of Sackets Harbor, New York in 1987, and Velma Faye Gray of Travelers Rest, South Carolina in 1989. Unaware that Warren was a murder suspect, Asheville police cited him for Failure to Produce a Title to a Motor Vehicle and Misdemeanor Larceny, and released him on a $1,000 bond. Eventually, Warren was sentenced to Death for the murders of Hurley and Johnson.

--<u>Source</u>: Dawn DeCwikiel-Kane, *"Serial Killer Connected to High Point Slaying Subject of Documentary,"* News&Record, Greensboro.com, 8-12-14; *"N.C. Man Held in Serial Killings; Body of One Victim Found in Lake Bowen,"* GoUpstate.com, 7-20-93.

## NORTH CAROLINA UNSOLVED CASES

### *"THE SMALL TOWN STALKER MURDERS"*

Authorities in Lumberton, North Carolina, have no leads in the murders of 7 women, all of whom were found within close proximity of each other. The victims were:
- Abby Patterson, 20;
- Christine Bennet, 32;
- Rhonda Jones;
- Cynthia Jacobs, 41;
- Megan Oxendine, prostitute;
- Lisa Hardin, 36;
- Michelle Driggers, 23, prostitute.

--<u>Source</u>: Jack Newman, *"Is a Serial Killer Stalking the Tiny US Town?"* The Sun, 11-6-17

# NORTH DAKOTA

### BRIDGES, John
### ("The I-94 Killer")

On July 6, 2012, John Bridges, 42, was involved in a car crash on I-94 near the 80th Street overpass, about 3 miles east of Bismarck, North Dakota. His vehicle had gone into the ditch shortly before a North Dakota Highway Patrol trooper came upon it. Lee Clay was dead in the back of the van. But officers said Clay's injuries did not match the severity of the crash. In court, John Bridges admitted he had injected Clay with something that Clay believed to be something to build muscle, but Bridges, annoyed at a perceived slight directed at him by Clay, wrote in the court document that he actually injected Clay with a substance that would cause infection and eventual death. Bridges had also purchased a hatchet and other supplies in Bismarck with which he planned to murder 2 other men and had a plan to dispose of their bodies. Between the I-94 exit and the scene of the crash, Clay saw the hatchet in the van and began to fight with Bridges. Bridges said he left the driver's seat to fight off Clay, eventually taking the hatchet from Clay and killing him with it. He said he also stabbed Clay with a knife. Bridges was sentenced to Life Without Parole for the Murder of Lee Clay, plus an additional 20 years for Class A Felony Kidnapping. Bridges had previously been convicted in Illinois as a juvenile in adult court, of Voluntary Manslaughter. He was also convicted of Aggravated Battery on multiple occasions. His father once told police that his son had said he *"wanted to kill someone just to see what it felt like."*

--Source: Jenny Michael, *"Missoula Man Gets Life in Prison Without Parole for Murder in North Dakota,"* Bismarck Tribune for The Missoulian, 11-27-12

## NORTH DAKOTA UNSOLVED CASES

### *"THE HIGHWAY 2 KILLER"*

Russell Douglas Turcotte, 19, was last heard from July 13, 2002 when he phoned his mother from a truck stop on Highway 2, in Grand Forks, North Dakota. His mother promised to wire him money so he could finish his hitchhiking trip from "a hippie gathering" in Michigan by bus. The money was never picked up and Russell was never heard from again. On November 2, 2002 a rancher found Russell's remains in a tree row near U.S. Highway 2, near Devils Lake, 60 miles west of Grand Forks. His death was ruled a homicide. No arrests have been made in this case. -- Jerome DeCoteau, Robert and Damien Belgarde -- each murdered at Grand Forks in September 2001.

--Source: UNDNews.com

# OHIO

### COLVIN, Dellmus
### ("The Long-Haul Strangler")

In 2006, Dellmus Colvin, an Ohio long-haul trucker, admitted to killing several women along highways across the country, including 6 women in Toledo. Skeletal remains of Dorothea Wetzel, 40, of Toledo were found August 5, 2000, by a man walking his dog near the Maumee River in South Toledo. Colvin categorized her death as *"an intended overdose."* Like Colvin's other victims, Wetzel - who also went by the last name Oviedo and was nicknamed "Angel" - was a known prostitute, according to police and court records. And like several of Colvin's other victims, her body had been wrapped in a blanket and discarded in a desolate area. Colvin, may have carried the bodies of one or two of his victims with him until they were mummified. Calling the 47-year-old Colvin "twisted," assistant prosecutor Tim Braun compared him to Jack the Ripper, the notorious killer of at least 5 prostitutes in the Whitechapel section of London in 1888. *"It's the same motivation. This is having sex with women you hate. He blames them for selling sex for money, but he's paying for them, and then, to feel superior, he kills them,"* Braun said, noting letters that Colvin sent to another prostitute while he was in custody. *"[The letters] are vitriolic and laced with profanity, telling her she is worth nothing,"* Braun said. Investigator Tom Ross, who spent several hours interviewing agreed: *"I think it's a control thing. It's 'I kill because I can.'"* The cases against Colvin abruptly unfolded during the third day of his trial for the murders of Jackie Simpson, 33, whose body was found April 23, 2003, and Melissa Weber, 37, whose body was found May 9, 2005. Colvin admitted, one by one, to killing Simpson and Weber, as well as Lily Summers, 43, whose body was found April 8, 2002; also Jacquelynn Thomas, 42, whose body was found Sept. 2, 2000; and Valerie Jones, 38, whose body was found Jan. 6, 2000. All 5 Toledo area women had been strangled or smothered - their bodies wrapped in sheets and blankets, and dumped. Several were badly decomposed. Braun and another assistant prosecutor, J. Christopher Anderson, yesterday said forensics revealed that at least two of the women were dead long before their bodies were discarded. Police had begun to suspect Colvin of a series of murders more than a year prior, after one prostitute told police critical details following an attack by Colvin. During the assault, she urinated on the sheets in his cab in order to leave her DNA, the assistant prosecutors said. *"She thought he was going to kill her,"* Braun said. *"She was going to do everything she could so that if they came looking for her, they'd find something."* Additionally, she memorized details of the truck Colvin drove at the time. Investigators eventually matched her assailant's DNA with evidence in a string of rapes of local prostitutes and to the murder of Weber, police said. A separate trial against Colvin on 2 rape charges ended in a mistrial. In the meantime, police continued to build their murder cases against him. On the second day of the trial, a man described as "Colvin's best friend" testified

127

that Colvin had asked for cleaning supplies and was in a hotel room where he saw what appeared to be a body covered with a sheet. Ultimately, Colvin gave them the names of the 6 prostitutes he said he killed. Prosecutors did not have enough time to verify Colvin's account of Wetzel's death, but Lucas County Common Pleas Court Judge Thomas Osowik gave Colvin 5 consecutive Life sentences for the other 5 murders, and, under a plea agreement, Colvin's confession allowed him to avoid the Death Penalty.

--Source: Robin Erb and Erica Blake, "*Serial Killers, Victims Invisible to Outsiders*," The Blade,10-24-06; Anya Pham, "*10 Serial-Killing Long-Haul Truckers*," ListVerse, 10-31-15.

## CRUZ Jr., James Robert *("The Truck Stop Killer")*
(see PENNSYLVANIA)

## KNOWLES, Paul John *("The Casanova Killer")*
(see FLORIDA)

## REMBERT Jr., Robert G. "Bobby" *("The I-4 Killer"; "The I-71 Killer")*

Bobby Rembert, a Cleveland truck driver, was suspected of being the "I-4 Killer" and also in the cases of 11 young women missing or murdered along the I-71 from Chillicothe to Cincinnati, Ohio, 4 of whom had been found dumped in creeks or streams flowing from the town. Born March 15, 1970, Rembert, who had previously served time for Voluntary Manslaughter 2 decades prior, was indicted at age 45 on October 14, 2015, on charges of Aggravated Murder, Rape and Robbery, involving 3 victims: Morgan Nietzel, 26, Jerry Rembert, 52 (Robert Rembert's cousin), had each been shot "execution style" to the back of the head, and Kimberly Hall of Cleveland, who had been strangled to death, beaten and raped and her body left in an open field. The last call on her cell phone was to Rembert. On September 21, 2015, Rembert was arrested at a truck stop near Seville, Ohio, in Medina County,

-Source: "*I-4 Highway Serial Killer is a Long-Haul Trucker*," PIBillWarner.wordpress

## SURRATT, Edward
*("The Long-Haul Killer")*

Between 1977 and 1978, over two dozen individuals were murdered along the highways of Ohio and Pennsylvania. Long-haul trucker Edward Surratt would break into homes occupied by couples along the highways and immediately kill the male with a shotgun. He would then kidnap the female, rape her, kill her, and dump her body along the highway. He was arrested in 1978 for raping a mother and daughter in front of their bound husband and father. In 2007, he finally confessed to 6 unsolved slayings that had plagued the Ohio area for 30 years. But police long suspected him of a total of 18 murders.

--Source: Amanda Tullos, "*12 Terrifying Truck Driver Killers Who Committed Murder While on the Road*," Ranker.com/list/truck-driver-crimes/amandatullos

## WICKLINE, William Dean
## ("The Butcher")

Nicknamed "*The Butcher*," William Wickline used his prison time to hone his skill as a meat cutter to later strategically disembowel and dismember his victims, bag the body parts, and dispose of them in trash dumpsters and along highways. Some believed Wickline engaged in human butchery partly for sport. He was convicted, indicted, and/or named as suspect, in 6 homicides in which the victims were dismembered or decapitated or both. In November 1979, Wickline brutally but skillfully murdered Charles "Swampy" Marsh, a known drug dealer in Parkersburg, West Virginia. Marsh was found with his hands handcuffed behind his back, strangled with a phone cord, his head cut off and placed on a night table beside the bed. The killer had taken the time to comb the hair on Marsh's severed head. The medical examiners determined it had been severed with one, or at the most 2 cuts, indicating the killer was a skilled butcher. Tory Gainer, well known to police for illegal gambling operations in Ohio, disappeared in 1978 or 1979. Informants told police Gainer was killed and dismembered, his body parts left in different landfills around Fairfield County. An unidentified man, stabbed to death, decapitated and dismembered in Florida may have been one of Wickline's victims. Some police investigators believe Wickline was also responsible for 2 more killings for which another man was convicted. On August 14, 1982, Wickline argued with drug dealers, Chris and Peggy Lerch, over a $60,000 drug debt. During the argument, Lerch boasted that he had sex with Wickline's girlfriend. Wickline slit Lerch's throat, then decided Mrs. Lerch would also have to be eliminated as a possible witness, so he strangled her while she slept. Wickline's girlfriend testified against him, claiming he threatened to kill her unless she helped him by holding Mrs. Lerch's legs while he strangled her. Both bodies were decapitated and dismembered in the bathtub and their body parts placed in trash bags and deposited around Franklin County. In October 1983, Tony Muncie, 14, of Ohio, disappeared. His body was found 2 days later along a highway in Delaware County. He had been stabbed in the back, his arms severed at the shoulders and elbows, his legs partially severed from his torso. He may have been killed simply because he refused to leave a drugstore that Wickline intended to rob. His known victims were:

- Tory Gainer, Fairfield County, Ohio - 1978 or 1979;
- Charles "Swampy" Marsh, Parkersburg, West Virginia – 11-79;
- Chris and Peggy Lerch, Frankline County, in Ohio – 8-14-82;
- Tony Muncie, 14, in Delaware County, Ohio - 10-83

West Virginia had sought extradition of Wickline from Ohio for the Marsh murder, but reached an agreement saving West Virginia the cost of his trial. Wickline was executed by Lethal Injection in Ohio on March 30, 2004 for the Lerch murders.

--Source: WestVirginiaNewws.blogspot.com, 12-13-10

# OKLAHOMA

### COOK, William Edward Billy "Cockeyed" (*"The Hitchhiker Murders"*)

Billy Cook killed 6 people, including an entire family of 5, during a terrifying 3-week spree across several states in early January 1951. Cook's early life in his native Missouri was an unremitting series of disasters. His mother died when he was 5; his father abandoned him and his 7 siblings. He became a ward of the state before age 10. He had a nasty temper that was exacerbated by the teasing and bullying he endured due to a deformed eye, and eventually ended up in Missouri State Penitentiary. When he was released from prison in 1950 at age 21, he told his father, with whom he briefly reunited after more than a decade of estrangement, that his ambition was now to *"live by the gun and roam."* He drifted from Missouri to California and then eastward again, to Texas. There, in late December 1950, his crimes and killing spree began in Oklahoma, the Mossers — Carl, 33; Thelma, 29; Ronald, 7; Gary, 5; and Pamela Sue, 3 — picked up Cook, who was once again hitchhiking. Cook pulled out the .32 caliber snub-nosed pistol he had bought in El Paso, and told Carl to drive. Over the next 3 days, Cook and the Mossers wove their way back toward Cook's hometown of Joplin, Missouri. On the 3rd day, Cook shot them all -- including the family dog -- and dumped the bodies down a well not far from Joplin. Cook again headed west. Outside Blythe, California, where he had once worked, he took a deputy sheriff hostage. The sheriff's life was spared because the deputy's wife, who had once briefly worked with Cook, *"treated him like a human being and had been nicer than anyone had ever been to him in his life."*

Cook killed once more during his spree, shooting to death a salesman from Seattle named Robert Dewey and dumping his body in a ditch — then kidnapped 2 hunters and forced them to drive him across the border into Mexico. There, in Santa Rosalie, the local police chief, Luis Parra, plucked the .32 from his belt, and arrested him. A short time later, he was handed over to the FBI. William Cook was sentenced to "300 Years in Prison" after being convicted of the Mosser killings in Oklahoma, and was subsequently convicted and sentenced to Death in California for Murder of Robert Dewey. On December 12, 1952, at San Quentin, Cook was executed in the prison's gas chamber. He was 23 years old. Less than a year after he was put to death, a movie based on Cook's spree was filmed by the actress-turned-director, Ida Lupino, as *"The Hitch-Hiker."* The movie is notable not only because it's a better-than-average noir film, but because it's one of the first films ever made in Hollywood that was based on a killer whose crimes were still fresh in the minds of filmgoers.

--<u>Source</u>: Ben Cosgrove, "'*I'm Gonna Live by the Gun and Roam: Portrait of an American Spree Killer*," TIME.com, 4-1-14.

### LAWSON, Carl Wayne

### *("I-35/40 Truck Stop Strangler")*

A woman said she got into Carl Lawson's truck at a Nebraska I-35 truck stop to discuss payment for her to clean the tires and fuel tanks on his truck when he locked the doors and began beating and strangling her until she passed out. She woke up alongside I-35 on the side near the Kansas-Nebraska border where a motorist stopped to help and took her home. Lawson alleged he smoked Crack with the woman at the truck stop, they got into an argument over money she stole from him, and he hit her, opening a cut over her eye. Lawson, 32, was also a "person of interest" in homicide cases in which prostitutes picked up at truck stops were strangled to death and dumped, partially clothed or naked, along I-40 in Oklahoma, Pennsylvania, Indiana, Mississippi, Texas and Arkansas.

--Source: *"Truck Driver is Person of Interest in Serial Killer Investigation,"* Serial Killer News at Crimezzz.net

### WILDER, Christopher Bernard *("The Beauty Queen Killer")*

(see FLORIDA)

# OKLAHOMA UNSOLVED CASES

## *"THE TRUCK STOP KILLER"*

(see ARKANSAS)

# OREGON

**BRAAE, Michael** *("Cowboy Mike," "Barefoot Cowboy." "The I-84 Killer")*
(see WASHINGTON)

**BUNDY, Theodore Robert "Ted"**
*("The Co-Ed Killer;" "The Campus Killer;" "Lady Killer")*
(see WASHINGTON)

### COX, Scott William
*("The Truck Stop Prostitutes Killer")*

In 1993, Scott Cox, 49, a long-haul truck driver, was charged with fatally stabbing Reena Ann Brunson 34, in November 1990, and with strangling Victoria Rhone, 34, in 1991, both truck stop prostitutes. Cox pled "No Contest" to 2 counts of Murder and was sentenced to 25 years in prison. Police examined the deaths of 20 women who frequented truck stops on his route, hoping DNA might link him to additional cases.
--Source: *"Oregon Trucker Who Killed Women Now Free in McMinnville,"* Yamhill Valley News Register, newsregister.com, 2-18-13

**JESPERSON, Keith Hunter** *("The Happy Face Killer")*
(see NEBRASKA)

**KONDRO, Joseph** *("The 'Uncle Joe' Killer," "The Longview Serial Killer")*
(see WASHINGTON)

**WOODFIELD, Randall "Randy" Brent** *("The I-5 Killer")*
(see CALIFORNIA)

## OREGON UNSOLVED CASES

### "THE HIGHWAY 101 KILLER"; "THE OREGON COASTAL KILLER"

The 5 known victims were walking along coastal Highway 101 when they vanished. In 1992, Jennifer Esson, 15, and Kara Leas, 16, were found strangled to death and covered with brush at an old logging road near Highway 101. Melissa Sanders, 17, and Sheila Swanson, 19, were found off Highway 20. Kelly Disney, 13, disappeared in 1984, her skull found near a reservoir north of Newport. Joan Hall, who disappeared in 1983. S has never been found.
--Source: *"Is There a Serial Killer on the Oregon Coast?"* KATU News, 3-16-09

132

# PENNSYLVANIA

**CHRISTOPHER, Leonard** (*"The Frankford Slasher"*)
(see PENNSYLVANIA UNSOLVED CASES)

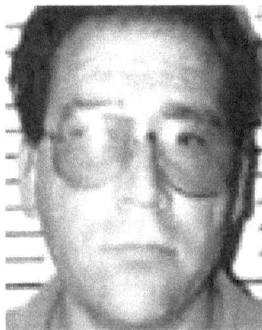

### CRUZ Jr., James Robert
### (*"The Truck Stop Killer"*)

James Cruz seemed like a typical family man, working hard as an Ohio truck driver to support his wife and daughter. Little did his family know, Cruz had a dark secret: he was a truck stop killer. In 1997, Cruz, picked up 17-year-old runaway, Dawn Marie Birnbaum. The Indiana teen's body was found dumped in a snow bank at a truck stop near I-80 in March 1993, 3 days after she ran away from a reform school in Maine. She died from strangulation, a yellow cord still wrapped around her neck when she was found. Police were able to connect Cruz to the murder by his DNA and by looking at his truck route. He was in the area at the time Birnbaum went missing, and her DNA was discovered in his car. A special Task Force was coordinated in an effort to try to prove Cruz's involvement in a string of unsolved similar strangulation murders of mostly prostitutes along Routes 26 and 550 in Pennsylvania and 8 other women discovered near Ohio interstate highways who had been strangled and sexually assaulted. When Cruz, 36, was sentenced to Life in prison for Birnbaum's murder, the Task Force disbanded and the Pennsylvania and Ohio prostitutes' murders remained unsolved.
--<u>Source</u>: Amanda Tullos, *"12 Terrifying Truck Driver Killers Who Committed Murder While on the Road,"* Murderpedia and Ranker.com/list/truck-driver-crimes/

**KRAJCIR, Timothy Wayne** (*"The Highway 3 Rest Stop Killer"*)
(see ILLINOIS)

### LANE, Adam Leroy
### (*"Route 78 Killer"*)

Adam Lane, a truck driver, used the highways to randomly hunt and kill his victims, then calmly walked back to his big rig parked at a nearby truck stop and drove away. He snuck up on Darlene Ewalt in the dark as she sat on her patio at her Harrisburg, Pennsylvania home at 2 AM, chatting on her cell phone with a friend about an upcoming cruise. Her husband was sleeping upstairs as Lane slit her throat and stabbed her so violently she died in minutes. And 11 days later, on

133

July 19, 2007, at midnight, Lane pulled into a truck stop near the home of Monica Massaro, 38, who he attacked with his knife, fatally cutting her throat, and continued to stab her multiple times after her death. He then walked back to his truck and drove away. Less than 24 hours later, on July 20, 2007, in Chelmsford, Massachusetts, a woman spotted a man hiding in the bushes and called police. But the man disappeared before police arrived. A few hours later, police received a frantic 911 call from Kathy Crowley about a man, dressed all in black and wearing a black mask, staring in, banging on her door trying to get in. Police arrived within minutes but the suspect was gone; 90 minutes later, the same man showed up at Kevin and Jeanie McDonough's home a mile or two away. While they slept, their daughter Shea, 16, was awakened by a man in black standing over her with one hand over her mouth and a knife in the other. He told her not to scream or he'd kill her, but she cried out, waking her parents in the next bedroom. Her father was able to overpower the intruder and Shea called 911. When police arrived, they found Adam Lane being held down by the parents. Evidence found at the scene included 2 large hunting knives hanging from his belt with knife sheaths, choking wire, a Chinese "throwing star," a leather mask with the eyes and mouth cut out, "trophies" from Lane's previous victims, and a DVD titled "*Hunting Humans*." Lane pled guilty to the murder of Massaro, since his knife, which still had her blood on it, provided the DNA evidence.

--<u>Source</u>: "*Hunting Humans: Serial Killer Stalks Homes Along Highways*," ABC News, 5-14-09.

# PENNSYLVANIA UNSOLVED CASES

## "THE FRANKFORD SLASHER"

From 1985 to 1990, the Frankford neighborhood of Philadelphia was shaken by a series of unsolved murders. Dubbed "*The Frankford Slasher*," the killer was believed responsible for the deaths of 9 or more women over 4 years. The first victim was discovered on August 8, 1985 when the body of Helen Patent, 52, was found, nude from the waist down, her blouse pulled u to expose her chest, in a railway maintenance yard. She had been stabbed 19 times and sexually assaulted. Five months later, Anna Carroll, 68, was found stabbed to death in her apartment. Like the first victim, she was nude from the waist down and had her blouse pushed up. When Carol Dowd, 46, was found murdered behind a fish market in 1990, authorities looked at one of the employees, Leonard Christopher, as a suspect. He was eventually given a Life sentence for Dowd's murder and was also accused of being the Frankford Slasher. However, since Christopher was Black, he did not match the description of the White male seen with the other victims. Also, the Slasher murdered Michelle Dehner — believed to be his last victim — *after Christopher was already in jail*. Many think Christopher did not kill Dowd, was not the Frankford Slasher, and the real killer continues to get away with murder.

--<u>Source</u>: Wikipedia

## "THE REDHEAD MURDERS"
(see ARKANSAS)

# RHODE ISLAND

**MAYRAND JR., Edward H.** *("The Route 10 Strangler")*
(see MASSACHUSETTS)

**VELEZ, Jovani; Raul OTERO; and Ramon ESCOTTA**
*("I-95 Providence Shooters")*

Three men charged in connection with a shooting on I-95 in Providence mistook the victim's car for another vehicle. Authorities charged Jovani Velez, 20, Raul Otero, 22, and Ramon Escotta, 23 with Assault and battery, Drive-by Shooting, and other crimes. The victim was identified as Giovanni Camacho. He told troopers that bullets came flying through his driver's side window as he was driving to work, but he wasn't hit. The suspects crashed their car near the I-46 overpass. Witnesses who saw the crash reported seeing 3 men flee from the car. Evidence was gathered from the crash scene and they were taken into custody. About 30 minutes later, police received a call about 3 suspicious men at the Marriott Hotel. Police would not comment on the 3 new suspects, nor whether the men are suspected of any other unsolved highway shootings or murders in Rhode Island.
--Source: "*3 Men Charged in RI Highway Shooting*," Turnto10.com, 9-16-15.

# RHODE ISLAND UNSOLVED CASES

## *"THE I-95 KILLER"*
(see also CONNECTICUT)

On September 30, 2002, Christopher Schmeller, 31, was reported missing by friends. On October 10, 2002 the Westerly Rhode Island Fisherman was found about 10 feet down an embankment in a wooded area near the weigh station just off I-95 in Waterford, Connecticut, where dead bodies had been left there before. There was no indication that Schmeller's case, labeled a homicide, is linked to the other bodies found in the same area, but police from both Connecticut and Rhode Island and have worked on the case. A friend of Schmeller's had reported that he was last seen at the Superior Court House in Wakefield, Rhode Island, and was nervous about finding a ride home.
--Source: "*Questions Surround Rhode Island Man's Death*," Rhode Island Cold Cases, ctcoldcases.com/RhodeIsland.html.

## *"THE ROUTE 3 KILLER"*

Benjamin Bailey, 17, had last been seen on Route 3, about a quarter mile from his home. On November 28, 1964, Bailey's body was found, fully clothed, his face submerged in Lake Tigoue, in Coventry, Rhode Island.
--<u>Source</u>: *Connecticut Cold Cases,* Ctcoldcases.com

# SOUTH CAROLINA

### GASKINS, Donald Henry "Pee Wee"
### *("The Redneck Charles Manson")*

"Peewee" Gaskins' first murder victim was a hitchhiker who he tortured before sinking her body in a swamp in September 1969. She was the first of many hitchhikers, male and female, who he randomly picked up and killed for pleasure while driving around the coastal highways. Born March 13, 1933 in South Carolina, he and his siblings were neglected by his single mother in childhood. When a year old, he drank a bottle of kerosene which caused him to have convulsions until age 3; he also suffered from "Night Terrors." He was small for his age, hence he was called "Peewee," and never knew his first name was "Donald" until his first court appearance for gang raping the sister of a fellow school drop-outs and for a string of robberies. In reform school, he was repeatedly raped by other inmates. After escaping from the school, getting married, and voluntarily returning to complete his sentence, he was released at age 18 in 1951 and briefly worked on a tobacco plantation. In Gaskins' autobiography, *"Final Truth,"* he claimed he had *"a special mind"* that gave him *"permission to kill."* In 1953, he was charged with Attempted Murder after using a hammer to attack a teenage girl who he claimed insulted him, and was sentenced to 6 years in prison where he was again raped, but this time fought back and cut the throat of his attacker, which added another 3 years to his sentence b u t he escaped from prison by hiding in the back of a garbage truck and fled to Florida where he took a job with a traveling carnival, was re-arrested, and paroled in 1961. He reverted to committing robberies and fencing stolen property. Two years after his parole, he was arrested for Rape of a 12-year old girl, fled while awaiting sentencing, but arrested in Georgia and sentenced to 8 years. His known victims were:

- Female hitchhiker - 1969;
- Hazel Brazell (claim of self defense);
- Girl, 12, in Florida (fled before sentencing);
- Janice Kirby, 15, Sumter, South Carolina - 11-70;
- Patricia Ann Alsbrook, 17, Sumter, South Carolina - 11-70;
- Doreen Dempsey, 23, her daughter, age 1; her unborn baby - 1973;
- Silas Barnell Yates, (contract hit) - 1975;
- Margaret "Peg" Cuttino, 13

While on Death Row for killing another man on Death Row with an explosive device, he confessed to journalist Wilton Earle to having committed 100 to 110 murders -- by stabbing, suffocating, mutilating his victims, and even cannibalizing some of them.
--Source: Wikipedia

### JONES Jr., Timothy Ray *("The Highway 10 Shooter")*
(see ALABAMA)

# SOUTH DAKOTA

### ANDERSON, Robert Leroy and GLENN WALKER
### ("The Tire Popper Killers")

Robert Leroy Anderson and Glenn Walker, friends since childhood, together kidnapped and killed 2 women on the County Road by suffocation and strangulation, Larisa Dumansky, in 1994, and Piper Streyle in 1996. A third victim in 1994, Amy Anderson (not a relative), escaped. To facilitate the abduction of Dumansky, and the attempted abduction of Anderson, they used a device called a "tire popper" to "pop" or flatten the victim's tire and compel her to stop and get out to look, with the killers approaching as if to offer help. Anderson grabbed Amy and tried to drag her over to a ditch. She wrestled her way out of his grasp and ran down the road, terrified, flagging down a passing motorist and got away. That year, 4 more women were murdered at Sioux Falls. On April 8, 1998, Anderson was sentenced to Death, but on March 3, 2003, he committed suicide by hanging himself in his cell. In Y-2000, Glenn Walker was sentenced to 30 Years in Prison for his role in the kidnappings and Attempted Murder of Amy Anderson but was released in 2015.
--Source: "Escaping a Serial Killer," KSFY-ABC,11-6-14; John Hult,Argus Leader,12-22-15

## SOUTH DAKOTA UNSOLVED CASES

### "THE HIGHWAY 314 KILLER"

On December 12, 1992, a car stopped at a remote intersection on the highway at Yankton Sioux Indian Reservation in Lake Andes, South Dakota. It was cold and the road was icy. The driver, Arnold Archambeau, 20, his girlfriend, Ruby Bruguier, 19, and Ruby's cousin, Tracy Dion, 17, had been drinking when the car crashed in a frozen ditch. Tracy recalled, "We ended up upside down in the ditch and Ruby and I were in the car. Arnold wasn't in the car." It was not until after Spring thaw, in early March 1993, that a passing motorist saw a body in the ditch, just 75 feet from the accident site. It was Ruby Bruguier, her glasses and shoes missing, clothes in tact; but the body was very decomposed. The next day they found the body of Arnold submerged in the water about 15 feet away from where we found Ruby. Arnold's body was very well kept, his skin color was fine and he was not frozen to the ground. A witness claimed to have seen Arnold, accompanied by 3 other people on New Year's Eve, almost 3 weeks after he was reported missing. Ruby's father, Quentin Bruguier, had his own theory: "They had to die someplace else. Somebody had to come and put them back in there again, to make it look like that's where they died." An opportunistic highway killer is suspected.
    --Source: Unsolved Mysteries, unsolved.com

138

# TENNESSEE

### BOYER, John Wayne
### ("The Long-Haul Killer")

John Wayne Boyer, a long-haul trucker, confessed to murdering at least 4 of the many women he is believed to have murdered and dumped along state highways. In 2005, the body of Jennifer Smith, 25, was found alongside a highway in Tennessee. It took about 2 years for Smith's identity to be established. Boyer was extradited to Tennessee in 2015 to face charges in her death. He further admitted to two other murders, which solved two missing persons cases, each over a decade old. At the time, Boyer was already serving time for Second Degree Murder of North Carolina resident, Scarlett Wood, 31, in 2003. They had both attended a party at a motel in Wilmington, North Carolina. Because he'd been seen with Wood at the party, police questioned truck driver John Wayne Boyer, who stated that she'd left while he'd been sleeping. Over a year later, a battered body with stab wounds was discovered, and it was almost another 2 years before the body was confirmed to be that of the missing woman. Boyer was arrested in 2006, convicted of Second-Degree Murder, and sentenced to 12 years in prison. In 2007, with the discovery of new murder victims, law enforcement officials found a match to the DNA samples taken from Jennifer's body. After his arrest, Boyer was compelled to give a DNA sample, which linked him to Smith. In 2009, Boyer confessed to the slaying of Jennifer Smith, granting justice to both her and her family. In Boyer's confession he admitted to picking up Smith at a truck stop. From there, the two were engaged in a physical altercation, resulting in the death of Smith. Boyer was sentenced to 30 Years in prison for the murder of Jennifer Smith.
--Source: Rachel Townsend, "*Justice for Jennifer: Woman's Murderer Sentenced to 30 Years in Prison,*" State Gazette, 3-13-16.

### GOBLE, Sean Patrick
### ("The Asheboro Highway Killer")

Sean Goble admitted that, while he was a long-haul truck driver, he picked up his victims at gas stations and truck stops along the Interstates, later dumping their bodies further down the road. He is kept under lock and key in a Tennessee prison, convicted in 1995 of killing 2 women in Tennessee, and was convicted of killing a 3rd woman in Orange County, North Carolina. Authorities suspect he is responsible for many more deaths.

139

Goble, a high school dropout who had a criminal record that included cocaine possession and passing bad checks, was a big man, weighing 310 pounds and standing 6 feet 3 inches, but acted like a teddy bear, according to family and friends. Goble often phoned them while on the road, at times crying, and brought friends jewelry and clothes when returning from trips -- items belonged to his victims, police reports say. Goble considered himself a lady's man, often bragging to investigators about his romantic exploits. Nicknamed "The Wild One," which Goble had emblazoned across the cab of his black Peterbilt truck, Goble slipped up when he left a thumbprint on a plastic bag found wrapped around the neck of one of his victims. His known victims were:

- Brenda Kay Hagy, 45, of Bloomington, Indiana, dumped in Tennessee - 1995;
- Sherry Tew Mansur, 34, of Clearwater, Florida, dumped along the I-40 - 1995;
- Alice Rebecca Hanes, 36, of Ohio, dumped in Kingsport, Tennessee - 1995.

Goble killed Hagy of Bloomington, Indiana, at a service station in Tennessee and dumped her body along I-81 in Virginia. He killed Hanes, a prostitute from Ohio whose body was found in Kingsport, Tennessee. The body Mansur of Clearwater, Florida, was found along the I-40. Authorities from at least 7 other states questioned Goble about dozens of similar unsolved deaths that occurred along his known truck routes. All those victims were prostitutes who were smothered or strangled. Several unsolved cases involving women's bodies being dumped along U.S. highways share similar characteristics to Goble's known crimes: Victims with missing shoes or panties, and witnesses who saw a black Peterbilt in the area where the bodies were discarded. Authorities believed the killer used the CB handle "Stargazer," according to archived news reports. Authorities in Asheboro found an assortment of women's shoes and panties in Goble's home. Unsolved murders, matching Goble's modus operandi and whereabouts at the time, number in the dozens -- including in New York, Pennsylvania, Ohio and Indiana. Several women were murdered or vanished in circumstances similar to those involving Goble while he drove trucks in the md-1990s. In North Carolina, those cases include:

- A woman's skull found in Asheboro - late 1990s;
- An unidentified woman last seen at a Burlington truck stop – 1990;
- Cheryl Mason, a prostitute whose body was found in Guilford County - 1991;
- Nona Cobb, whose body was found along I-77 near Elkin;
- Unidentified woman, body found in western Guilford County - 2-19-95.

Goble received 2 "Life" sentences for the Tennessee murders and 14 years in the North Carolina case. It will be 100 years before he's eligible for parole

--<u>Source</u>: *"Asheboro Serial Killer May Have More Victims,"* The Courier-Tribune, 2-23-15

# MENDENHALL, Bruce D.
## ("The Truck Stop Serial Killer"; "The Rest Stop Killer"; "The Prosti Killer")

Bruce Mendenhall, a long-haul truck driver, is a serial killer whose victims were prostitutes. He confessed to 6 murders in Kentucky, Tennessee, Indiana, Georgia, and Alabama and was suspected of 9 more at truck stops in 4 different states. Born April 14, 1951, Bruce Mendenhall, had run for mayor in 1997 when he lived in the small farming town of Albion, Illinois, where he was married with 2 daughters in their 20s and when he confessed to at least 6 homicides. He was arrested June 26, 2007, at a TA truck stop along I-24 in Nashville, Tennessee, where the body of Sara Nicole Hulbert, 25, a prostitute, was found dead with gunshot wounds. The detective noticed a tractor-trailer rig that matched the description of one spotted shortly before Hulbert's body was found. When he searched the semi, he saw blood in several places -- the inside of the driver's door, and inside a trash bag behind the driver's seat. A search warrant recovered over 300 items from the truck, including a .22 caliber handgun, a rifle, weapons cartridges, a razor blade, black tape, latex gloves, a night stick, condoms, and sex toys. Also on June 26, 2007, Latisha Yvonne Miller, 28, a prostitute, was reported missing. Indianapolis police searched truck stops where he claimed they would find 2 bodies, and found nothing. But blood found in Mendenhall's truck matched the DNA of Miller. Mendenhall implicated himself and was charged with the murder of Symantha Winters, 48, whose body was also found June 26, also shot with a .22 caliber handgun and stuffed in a trash can at a Lebanon, Illinois truck stop. Alabama police in Birmingham charged Mendenhall with the murder of Lucille Gretna Carter, 44, who, in July 2007, was found nude in a trash bin with a plastic bag taped around her head. Samples from bloody clothing and 200 items found in his truck, including weapons and sex toys, turned up DNA from 5 different women. On October 24, 2016, Kentucky State Police say Carma Purpura, 35, of Indianapolis, Indiana. who was found off Louie B. Nunn Parkway in Barren County, Kentucky. On August 15, 2011, there was yet another victim of The Truck Stop Killer, Mendenhall. She was initially reported missing on July 11, 2007. Mendenhall was charged with Purpura's death -- and multiple others when blood from at least 10 people was found in the cab of his truck. Mendenhall also claimed he killed Belinda Cartwright, a Georgia prostitute, and Robin Bishop, a Tennessee prostitute, at truck stops. He was also suspected of the stabbing death of Tammy Zywicki, 21, in Missouri.

His known victims were:

- Tammy Zywicki, 21, Lawrence County, Missouri - 8-3-92;
- Andrea Hebdrix-Steinert, Evansville, IN - 10-29-97;
- Dusty Shuck, Mount Airy, Maryland - 5-06;
- Belinda Cartwright, Georgia – 2001;
- Latisha Yvonne Milliken, 28, Millersville, Tennessee – 2-07;
- Carma Purpura, Indianapolis, IN, found Barren County, Kentucky - 10-24-16;
- Sherry Drinkard, Lake Station, Indiana - 12-22-07;
- Nicole Hulbert, 25, Nashville, Tennessee - 6-26-07;

- Symantha Winters, 48, Lebanon, Illinois - 6-26-07;
- Lucille Gretna Carter, 44, Birmingham, Alabama - 7-07;
- Deborah Ann Glover, Suwanee, Georgia - 11-29-07;
- Jennifer Annette Smith, Bucksnort, Tennessee - 4-05;
- Michelle Carter - 2007;
- Robin Bishop (possible victim), Tennessee - 7-1-07

Mendenhall was arrested July 26, 2007, and found guilty for the murder of Sara Hulbert. While in prison awaiting trial, he was sentenced to 30 years in prison for Soliciting Murder for Hire of a police detective stemming from 4 slayings in 3 states. ----Source: Criminal Minds, wikia.com/Bruce_Mendenhall; WTHR-13 Eyewitness News, Nashville, TN; *"A Body Found in Kentucky Identified As Victim of Truck Stop Killer,"* WKRN, Glasgow, Kentucky, 10-24-16; and *Wikipedia.*

## TENNESSEE UNSOLVED CASES

*"THE REDHEAD MURDERS"*
(see ARKANSAS)

# TEXAS

## BARROW, Clyde Chestnut and Bonnie Elizabeth PARKER
### ("Bonnie and Clyde")

Bonnie and Clyde drove existing highways from Texas to Minnesota, Colorado to Mississippi, and through the central United States during the 1930s Great Depression. Their 2-year spree of robbing people and killing when cornered or confronted, finally ended with their demise in a hail of bullets on Highway 154 in Louisiana, before the 1950s interstates were constructed, and warrants their inclusion as highway serial killers. The 12 victims were:

- John N. Bucher of Hillsboro, Texas - 4-30-32;
- Eugene Moore of Atoka, Oklahoma - 8-5-32;
- Howard Hall of Sherman, Texas - 10-11-32;
- Doyle Johnson of Temple, Texas - 12-26-32;
- Malcolm Davis of Dallas, Texas - 1-6-33;
- Harry McGinnis of Joplin, Missouri - 4-13-33;
- Wes Harryman of Joplin, Missouri - 4-13-33;
- Henry D. Humphrey of Alma, Arkansas - 6-26-33;
- Major Crowson of Huntsville, Texas - 1-16-34;
- E.B. Wheeler of Grapevine, Texas - 4-1-34;
- H.D. Murphy of Grapevine, Texas - 4-1-34;
- Cal Campbell of Commerce, Oklahoma - 4-6-34

While Bonnie Parker was present at 100 or more felonies during the 2 years she was with Clyde Barrow, she was not the cigar-smoking, machine gun-wielding killer depicted in newspapers of the day. But photos found at one of their hideouts in Joplin, Missouri, introduced the public to new criminal "superstars" with the most titillating trademark of all—illicit sex. Bonnie and Clyde were wild, young, and undoubtedly slept together. Bonnie Parker, born October 1, 1910 in Rowena, Texas (southwest of Dallas) was the 2nd of 3 children. Her father, Charles Robert Parker, was a bricklayer who died when Bonnie was 4. Her mother, Emma Krause Parker, then moved her family to her parents' home in Cement City, now known as West Dallas, where she worked as a seamstress. On September 25, 1926, at age 15, in her second year in high school, Bonnie married Roy Thornton. Their marriage, marked by his frequent absences and brushes with the law was short-lived. In 1929, Bonnie lived with her mother and worked as a waitress in Dallas. Clyde Barrow, born March 24, 1909 in Ellis County, Texas, (southeast of Dallas) was the 5th of 7 children of Henry Basil Barrow and Cumie Talitha Walker, a poor farming family. The family migrated to Dallas in the early 1920s as part of a wave of resettlement from impoverished nearby farms to the urban slum known as West Dallas, where they spent their first months living underneath their wagon until Henry had put together enough money to buy a tent for

the family. Clyde was first arrested in late 1926, after running away when police confronted him over a rental car he had failed to return on time. His second arrest, with brother Buck, was for possession of stolen turkeys. Despite having legitimate jobs during 1927 through 1929, he also cracked safes, robbed stores, and stole cars.  In 1930, he was sent to Eastham Prison Farm. While in prison, Barrow, who was 5 foot 6 inches, killed an inmate who had repeatedly sexually assaulted him. That was Clyde Barrow's first killing, although another inmate already serving a Life sentence took the blame. Barrow's mother successfully petitioned his release. He paroled February 2, 1932 from Eastham Prison a hardened and bitter criminal. The Barrow Gang, assembled by Clyde Barrow and Ralph Fults, included Raymond Hamilton, W.D. Jones, Buck Barrow and Henry Methvin who did not hesitate to shoot anyone, lawman or civilian, who got in their way. Clyde and Fults began a series of small robberies of stores and gas stations to collect enough money and firepower to launch a liberation raid against Eastham Prison and seek revenge against the Texas prison system for the abuses Clyde suffered while serving time. Clyde's favored weapon was the M1918 Browning Automatic Rifle (called a "BAR"). Clyde met Bonnie on January 5, 1930 at the home of Clyde's friend, Clarence Clay, in West Dallas.  Most historians believe Parker joined Barrow because she was in love with him. She remained his loyal companion as they carried out their crime spree. On April 19, Bonnie and Fults were captured in a failed hardware store burglary in Kaufman, Texas, and were jailed. Bonnie was released after the grand jury failed to indict her. On April 30, Clyde was the driver in a robbery in Hillsboro, Texas, during which the store's owner, J.N. Bucher, was shot and killed. Although Clyde had stayed in the car, he was accused of murder. On August 5, when Sheriff C.G. Maxwell and his deputy, Eugene C. Moore, approached them in a parking lot, Clyde and Hamilton opened fire, killing the deputy and gravely wounding the sheriff. This was the first time Clyde Barrow and his gang killed a lawman; eventually, they reached a total of 9. On January 16, 1934, Clyde orchestrated the escape of Raymond Hamilton, Henry Methvin, and other prisoners in the infamous "Eastham Prison Breakout of 1934." The brazen raid achieved Clyde's overriding goal -- revenge on the Texas Department of Corrections -- but also attracted the full power of the Texas and federal government to the manhunt for Bonnie and Clyde.  Highway Patrol boss L.G. Phares offered a $1,000 reward for "the *dead bodies* of the Grapevine slayers."  Texas Governor "Ma" Ferguson added $500.  A posse was led by former Texas Ranger Frank A. Hamer of the Texas Department of Corrections, who began tracking the pair on February 12, 1934. The posse, concealed in the bushes, heard Barrow's stolen Ford V8 approaching at a high speed.  Bonnie and Clyde were ambushed and killed in their stolen car as the lawmen opened fire, shooting a combined total of about 130 rounds on a dusty stretch of Louisiana State Highway 154 near Sailes, Bieville Parish, Louisiana, May 23, 1934.
--<u>Source</u>: Wikipedia; "*A Memorial: 12 Victims*," Texashideout.trpod.com/victims.html

## CORLL, Dean Arnold
### *("The Candy Man," "The Houston Mass Murders")*

Born Christmas Eve, December 24, 1939, Dean Corll, from an early age, lured young boys with free candy from his parents' Corll Candy Company. From 1970 at age 31, until 1973, in Houston, Texas, he would offer rides to teenage boys and young men who he picked up along the highway and city streets, and abducted, raped, tortured and murdered at least 28 of them. On August 8, 1973, Corll was shot to death by Elmer Wayne Henley, one of his accomplices who claimed self defense.
Source: Wikipedia

## KNOWLES, John Paul *("The Casanova Killer")*
(see FLORIDA)

## LUCAS, Henry Lee *("The Orange Socks Killer"; "The Highway Stalker; "The Confession Killer")* and OTIS ELWOOD TOOLE

Henry Lee Lucas was a one-eyed, snaggle toothed multi-state serial killer. His Death sentence was for the confessed murder of an unidentified woman in her 20s who was found strangled on Halloween eve in 1979, off I-35 in Williams County, Texas. Known in media as "Orange Socks," she was nude, except for the pair of orange socks that were pulled over her feet. Lucas claimed that he and his lover, Otis Toole, who may have killed as many as 600 people, went on 30-year killing spree together, from 1960 to 1983. Lucas confessed to murdering more than 200 people in Texas, Michigan and possibly Florida. Born August 23, 1936 in Blacksburg, Virginia, Lucas was one of 9 siblings born to Viola and Anderson Lucas, abusive, alcoholic parents. His mother was a sex worker who would force him to watch her have sex with clients and cross dress in public. His father lost both legs in a railroad accident. Lucas lost one eye at age 10 after his mother ignored that the eye was infected as result of a fight. Lucas had a low IQ and his sexual deviancy formed in his teen years. It included having sex with his sister and with dead animals. On January 11, 1960, Lucas stabbed his mother to death in Tecumseh, Michigan, during an argument, and was sentenced to 20 to 40 years in prison at Jackson State Penitentiary in southern Michigan, for Second Degree Murder. But after 2 suicide attempts, he was admitted to Iona State Mental Hospital and paroled in 1970, after serving 10 years. Lucas confessed to 28 unsolved murders and later recanted his confessions. His known victims were:
- Laura Burnsey, 17 - 1951;
- Tammy Alexander, "The Caledonia Jane Doe," 20s, Williams County Texas - 1979;
- Unidentified "Orange Socks," found Williamson County, Texas - Halloween 1979;
- Carol Cole, Louisiana (believed to be a false confession) - 1980;

- Carolyn Cervenka, 19, Taylor, Texas - 6-6-82;

- Viola Lucas, Tecumseh, Michigan - 1-11-60;
- Frieda "Becky" Powell, 15 - 1982;
- Kate Rich, 82 - 1982;
- Maria Rae Sharp, 25, Millard County, Utah - 1983;
- Woman in Provo, Utah - 1983

His Death sentence was changed to Life by then Texas Governor George W. Bush. Lucas died in prison of a heart attack on March 12, 2001. Otis Toole was born March 5,1949, in Jacksonville, Florida His mother was a Christian extremist; his sister sexually abused him and they dressed him in women's clothes. His alcoholic father abandoned him. Toole confirmed Lucas' statements that, together and separately, they picked up and killed *hundreds of hitchhikers on the Interstate*. Toole, a serial arsonist, was sexually excited by firesetting and engaged in necrophilia and cannibalism. He was convicted of 6 counts of Murder. Both Lucas and Toole had boasted they killed many more. Toole confessed to the 1981 murder of Adam Walsh, 6-year old son of John Walsh who hosts the TV series, *"America's Most Wanted."* He wsn't convicted due to loss of evidence and that he then recanted. The boy was abducted from a Sears department store at the Hollywood Mall in Hollywood, Florida, July 27, 1981. The boy's severed head was found 2 weeks later in a drainage canal alongside Florida's Turnpike in St. Lucie County, Florida. Toole died in prison from liver failure, September 15, 1996.
--Source: Biography.com; *"Utah Officers Still Convinced Texas Inmate Killed 2 in Utah,"* DesertNews.com 12-3-90; Wikipedia.

### McDUFF, Kenneth Allen
*("The Broomstick Killer")*

Kenneth McDuff murdered 9 to 14 victims from August 6, 1966 when he was 20, to March 1, 1992. On October 14, 1989, the body of Sarafia Parker was discovered along the I-35 corridor, 48 miles south of Waco, but his return to prison was for a parole violation for making death threats to a youth in Rosebud, Texas. Born on March 21, 1946, in Rosebud, Texas, he had 3 siblings. McDuff's mother, Addie McDuff, was wellknown around her town as "the pistol packin' momma" because of her habit of carrying a firearm and her violent tendencies. McDuff was known to shoot his .22 rifle at living creatures and was often getting into fights with boys older than he was. With these tendencies, he was well known by the sheriff of his hometown. McDuff and his newfound friend, Roy Dale Green, were driving around central Texas when they came across Robert Brand, 18, his girlfriend Edna Louise Sullivan, 16, and his cousin Marcus Dunman, 16, who were standing beside their car parked near the highway in Everman, Texas. McDuff and Green approached the vehicle and ordered the 3 people into the trunks of both cars. McDuff drove his victims down the highway, stopping at a field where he shot to death Brand and Dunman. The woman was raped by both McDuff and Green and then strangled by

McDuff with a 3-foot long piece of broomstick from his car which earned him the nickname, *"Broomstick Killer."* They then dumped her body in the bushes at the side of the highway. The following day when the murder was announced on the radio, Green felt guilty and turned himself in to police. In exchange for his testimony against McDuff, he was given a lesser sentence. McDuff went to trial and was sentenced to Death for Murder of Robert Brand. As result of the suspension of the Death Penalty in 1972, and the overcrowding in Texas prisons, many prisoners were not serving out their full sentences. As a result, McDuff was given parole in October 1989. In 1991, while working at a Quik-Pak market, McDuff developed a fascination with his senior manager's wife, Melissa Northrup. On many occasions, he mentioned wanting to rob the store and "take" Melissa. Her husband grew worried when she didn't return home one night following her shift and an investigation was launched. Eyewitnesses were able to identify McDuff in the area of Melissa Northrup's abduction, as well as at the site where Colleen Reed was kidnapped. A month later, the body of Melissa Northrup was discovered. Around the same time, the body of Valencia Kay Joshua, a prostitute, who was last seen searching for McDuff's dorm room, was found in the woods. On October 10, 1991, in Waco, McDuff picked up Brenda Thompson, a drug addicted prostitute. Despite that, at a Waco Police Department highway checkpoint, Thompson repeatedly kicked the windshield of McDuff's truck, cracking it, in an effort to alert police nearby, McDuff sped away as police gave chase, and eluded police under cover of night. Her body was not found until 1998, in a wooded area near US-84 where McDuff had inflicted a torturous death on her. Five days after Thompson, on October 15, 1991, McDuff picked up Reginia DeAnne Moore, 17, a prostitute, and drove her in his pickup truck to a remote area beside Highway 6 where her body was discovered, her arms and legs tied with her stockings. McDuff is also believed to have killed Cynthia Rose Gonzalez, 23, who found dead on September 21, 1991 in a creek bed one mile west of I-35. On December 21, 1991, he kidnapped Colleen Reed at an Austin carwash, in plain sight of witnesses, together with an accomplice, Alva Hank Worley. Worley admitted to raping Reed but denied participating in her murder. McDuff moved to Kansas City where he worked at a refuse collection company and lived under the assumed name Richard Fowler. On May 1, 1992, Gary Smithee, a co-worker, was watching *"America's Most Wanted"* on TV, recognized McDuff who was featured on the program, and phoned Kansas City Police who searched Fowler's name and found he had been arrested for soliciting prostitutes -- which led to the discovery that his fingerprints were the same as McDuff's. McDuff's known victims were:

- Robert Brand, 18, Everman, Texas;
- Edna Louise Sullivan, 16, Everman, Texas;
- Marcus Dunnam, 16, Everman, Texas;
- Serafia Parker - 9-14-89;
- Melissa Northrup - 1991;
- Valencia Kay Joshua – 1991;
- Cynthia Rose Gonzalez, 23, Arlington, Texas - 9-21-91;
- Brenda Thompson, Waco, Texas - 10-10-91;
- Regina DeAnne Moore, 17, Texas - 10-15-91;
- Colleen Reed, Austin, Texas - 12-21-91;
- Brenda Thompson – 1991

On February 18, 1993, a jury opted to sentence McDuff to Death. He was executed by lethal injection in Huntsville, Texas, November 17, 1998 at age 52.
--<u>Source</u>: *"The Broomstick Killer,"* CrimeMuseum.org; Murderpedia

### RHOADES, Robert Ben
### *("The Long-Haul Trucker Killer")*

Robert Rhoades, a long-haul truck driver, is believed to have tortured, raped and killed more than 50 women and young girls before his arrest in 1990, although only 3 were confirmed victims in 1989 to 1990. Born November 22, 1945, in Council Bluffs, Iowa, Rhoads was raised by his mother alone, although his father returned from overseas when Robert was still in school. His first arrest at 16 while in high school was for Tampering with a Motor Vehicle. After graduation, he joined the Marine Corps. That same year, his father was arrested for molesting a 12-year old girl and subsequently committed suicide. In 1967, Robert was arrested again for Theft; in 1968 he was dishonorably discharged from the military, married 3 times, had a son with his first wife. He is best known for taking a photo of his last known victim, Regina Kay Walters, 14, who he picked up with her boyfriend, Ricky Lee Jones, both runaways from Pasadena, Texas, moments before strangling her with bailing wire in an abandoned barn in Illinois in April 1990. It is believed Jones was killed immediately, though his body wasn't found until March 3, 1991 in Laramar County, Mississippi, and was not identified until July 2008, while Walters was kept for a long time, based on the photo and the degree of hair growth and bruising she sustained. Rhoades' first confirmed victims were Candace Walsh and her husband, Douglas Zyskowski, in January 1990. The couple was hitchhiking when Rhoades picked them up in his truck while on a long-haul journey. As with Jones and Walters, he immediately killed Zyskowski and dumped his body along the I-10 in Ozona, Texas, where it was not found until 1992, and kept Walsh for over a week, torturing and raping her multiple times before dumping her body in Millard County, Utah. In the early morning of April 1, 1990, Arizona State Trooper, Mike Miller, found a truck at the side of the I-10 freeway with its hazard light on, about 50 miles north of Phoenix. Miller discovered a nude woman inside the truck, alive, but handcuffed to the door and screaming. She had welts on her body, cuts on her mouth, and a horse bridle secured around her neck. In Rhoades' briefcase, investigators found alligator clips, leashes, handcuffs, whips and dildos. He had told the woman in his cab that he had been torturing women for 15 years as he crisscrossed America by highway. After failing to talk his way out of the situation, Rhoades was arrested and later charged with Aggravated Sexual Assault, Sexual Assault, and Unlawful Imprisonment. After further investigation, the arresting detective was able to make a connection to the Houston case and noticed a pattern stretching over the course of at least 5 months. In executing the warrant for Rhoades' home, police found photos of a nude teenager, later identified as Regina Walters, whose body was found in September 1990, and also photos of Candace Walsh, whose body was found that October. His known victims were:
- Candace Walsh, Milford County, Utah - 1-90;

148

- Douglas Zyskowsky, Ozona, Texas - 1-90;
- Regina Kay Walters, 14, Illinois - 4-90;
- Ricky Lee Jones, Illinois - 4-90;
- Woman, (survived) - 4-4-90

In Illinois, Rhoades was sentenced to Life Without Parole, but in March 2012, he was transferred to Ozona, Texas, where he was charged with the murders of Zyskowski and Walsh. Although prosecutors wanted to seek the Death Penalty, Rhoades accepted 2 Life sentences in a plea deal so that if he ever got out of prison in Illinois, he would be behind bars in Texas for the rest of his life. Prosecutors told media that Rhoades is suspected of additional murders as trucking records show that Rhoades regularly traversed 22 states. The FBI declined to comment on its ongoing investigation.
--Source: Texas Observer, 11-7-12; and Wikipedia

## SELLS, Tommy Lynn *("The Cross Country Killer")*
(see MISSOURI)

### SMITH, Kevin Edison
*("The I-45 Killer")*

In April, 2012, Kevin Edison Smith, a refinery worker from Port Arthur, Texas, was convicted of murdering a 13-year-old girl in Texas City, along the I-45 corridor, and dumping her body under an interstate bridge. He was sentenced to Life without parole, and some investigators believe he may have been involved in other I-45 murders.
--Source: Alex Hannaford, *"Highway Injustice,"* Texas Observer, 11-7-12.

## SUFF, William Lester *("Riverside Prostitute Killer")*
(see CALIFORNIA)

### STALLINGS, Mark Roland, and WILLIAM LEWIS REECE
*("The I-45 Killers")*

For over 3 decades, the FBI chronicled at least 32 dead women on either side of the I-45, along the 50-mile stretch of Gulf Freeway between Houston and Galveston, Texas, dating back to 1971 when 3 Galveston girls disappeared; 2 were found in Turner's Bayou in Texas City, the 3rd in Galveston Bay; 6 more who lived close to the Gulf Freeway in Alvin, Dickinson, Sagewood and Houston, were

149

found in watery graves over the next few months. Mark Roland Stallings, 34, had been working close to the I-45 on the Calder property when the bodies were found. In April 1997, Laura Smither, 12, disappeared while jogging near her home. Her decapitated body was found in a Pasadena retention pond 3 weeks after her disappearance. In August, 1997, Jessica Cain, 17, of Tiki Island, went missing after having theater dinner party with friends at Benningan's in Webster. Cain was found 19 years later, buried in a field off East Orem Drive. Her truck was found parked in an emergency lane off I-45, not far from her home. Stark similarities in several earlier cases suggested that a single serial killer was active in the Calder Road area that had been called *"The Killing Fields"* and *"Highway to Hell"* since the 1970s. In September 2016, grand jury in Galveston County, Texas, decided there was enough evidence to charge William Reece with the murders of Jessica Cain and Laura Smither. He had already been charged in Oklahoma with the kidnapping death of Tiffany Johnston, 19, who disappeared from an Oklahoma carwash in 1997, and Reece has also been linked to the 1997 death of Kelli Ann Cox, 20, a North Texas University student, whose bones were dug up in Brazoria County, Texas, in March 2016. He was serving a 489-year sentence in the Texas Department of Corrections for Aggravated Assault and an Escape Attempt and became a Murder suspect after writing a letter to the Fort Bend County Sheriff confessing to the murders of 2 Houston women 10 years before; then clues surfaced in the I-45 Murders in the Calder Road area. The victims were:

- Tiffany Johnston, 19 - 1997;
- Laura Smither, 12 - 1997;
- Jessica Cain, 17 - 1997;
- Kelli Ann Cox, 20 – 1997

Police now worry that the same stretch of Calder Road has served as a hunting ground for multiple killers who found or dumped bodies of people killed elsewhere.

--<u>Source</u>: Courtney Fischer, *"William Reece Indicted in Murders of Cain, Smith,"* ABC-13 News online, 9-1-16; Mary Alys Cherry, *"Man Confesses to I-45 Murders,"* Chron.com (a Hearst Publication), 11-7-01; Crimesider Staff/AP, *"Serial Killer Charged in 1997 Murders of 2 Texas Girls,"* CBS News online, 9-2-16

## WILDER, Christopher Bernard (*"The Beauty Queen Killer"*)
(see FLORIDA)

## WOOD, David Leonard
(*"The Desert Killer"*; *"Highway 54 Killer"*)

David Wood was convicted of 6 serial murders of young women who disappeared from El Paso, Texas, between May 13, 1987 and August 27, 1987; remains of all 6 were found buried in the desert close to U.S. Highway 54. The 6 victims were:

- Ivy Susanna Williams, 23;
- Desiree Wheatley,15;
- Karen Baker, 20;
- Angelica Frausto, 17;

- Rosa Maria Casio, 24;
- Dawn Marie Smith, 14

He was also indicted for 5 other victims:

- Marjorie Knox, 14, Chapparal, New Mexico - 2-14-87;
- Melissa Alaniz, El Paso, Texas - 3-7-87;
- Cheryl Vasquez - 6-28-87;
- Unidentified woman, El Paso, Texas (survived rape) – 9-19-87;
- Unidentified woman, El Paso, Texas (survived rape) – 9-19-87

On January 14, 1993, Wood was sentenced to Death for the first 6 murders. One of his earlier victims, a 12-year old girl who survived, testified that, in 1977, Wood had grabbed her as she was walking home and raped her underneath a freeway bridge. Another woman testified that when she was 23, Wood gave her a ride home from work when he raped her. Marjorie Knox, 14, disappeared from Chapparal, New Mexico, on February 14, 1987, and 3 weeks later on March 7, Melissa Alaniz vanished from El Paso. On June 28, Cheryl Vasquez-Dismukes disappeared. On September 19, 1987, an El Paso prostitute complained to police that one of her "tricks" had driven her into the desert near grave sites where he pulled a knife and threatened her before she fled on foot. Another prostitute, raped some weeks before, came forward after that report was published; both women commented that their assailant had numerous tattoos. A search of police tattoo files led to the October 22 arrest of David Leonard Wood, an ex-convict with a history of violence against females.

--Source: Murderpedia

# TEXAS UNSOLVED CASES

## "THE TEXAS I-45 KILLING FIELDS"

According to 2010 FBI statistics, Texas was leading the nation with 38 unsolved serial highway homicides -- which is surely a drop in the ocean compared to the actual figure. *"The Texas Killing Fields,"* a 25-acre patch of land situated a mile from I-45, is an area bordering the Calder Oil Field where, in the early 1970s, some 30 bodies of murder victims have been found within the Killing Fields area alone. These were mainly the bodies of girls or young women. Many others have disappeared from this area; their bodies, if they are deceased, are still missing. It is believed that many of the murders were the work of multiple serial killers trolling along the I-45, the logical means for quick access in and out. Many of the victims were aged 10–25 years, and many shared similar physical features. A few of them had similar hairstyles. Very few of these murders have been solved. The known victims are:

- Sharon Shaw, Webster, Texas, 8-4-71; found near Clear Lake – 1-3-72;
- Gloria Gonzales, 19, Houston, Texas - 10-28-71;
- Alison Craven, 12, Houston, Texas, 11-9-71 - found 3-9-72;
- Debbie Ackerman, 15, Galveston, Texas, 11-11-71 - found 11-13-71; Last seen outside ice cream store with Maria Johnson;
- Maria Johnson, 15, Galveston, Texas, 11-11-71 - found 11-13-71; Last seen outside ice cream store with Debbie Ackerman;
- Kimberly Pitchford, 16, Houston, Texas, Last seen at school – 1-3-73;

- Suzanne Bowers, 12, Galveston, TX; 5-21-77; found Alta Loma, Texas - 3-25-79;
- Brooks Bracewell, 12, Dickinson, Texas - 4-3-81; Last seen with Georgia Geer at a convenience store;
- Georgia Geer, 14, Dickinson, Texas - 4-3-81; Last seen with Brooks Bracewell at a convenience store;
- Sandra Ramber, 14, Santa Fe, Texas, still missing – 0-26-83;
- Heide Villareal-Faye, 23, League City, Texas, 10-10-83 - found 4/84; Last seen at a convenience store;
- Laura Miller, 16, League City, Texas, 9-10-84 - found 2-3-86; Last seen at a convenience store;
- Shelley Sikes, 19, Texas City, Texas - 5-24-86; Car found abandoned on I-45; Still missing;
- Suzanne Rene Richardson, 22, Galveston, Texas, still missing – 10-7-88;
- Lynette Bibbs, 14, Houston, Texas, last seen with Tamara Fisher – 2-1-96;
- Tamara Fisher, 15, Houston, Texas, last seen with Lynette Bobbs – 2-1-96;
- Tot Harriman, 57, League City, Texas, Last seen driving. Still missing - 7-12-01;
- Sarah Trusty, 23, Algoa, Texas, 7-12-02, last seen biking - found 7-26-02;
- Teressa Vanegas, 16, Dickinson, Texas, 10-31-06 - found 11-3-06; Last seen leaving the Green Caye subdivision;
- Krystal Baker, 13, Texas City, Texas, last seen at a convenience store - 3-5-96;
- Jane Doe - 2-3-86;
- Janet Doe - 3-8-91

The fields have been described as *"a perfect place for killing somebody and getting away with it."* After visiting some of the sites of recovered bodies in League City, Ami Canaan Mann, director of the film, *"Texas Killing Fields,"* commented, *"You could actually see the refineries that are in the south end of League City. You could see the I-45. But if you yelled, no one would necessarily hear you. And if you ran, there wouldn't necessarily be anywhere to go"*.
--<u>Source</u>: Alex Hannaford, *"Highway Injustice,"* Texas Observer, 11-7-12

## THE CANYON LAKE HIGHWAY KILLER

In February 1993, Emily Jeanette Garcia, 15, simply boarded a city bus in San Antonio for a health services appointment to find out when her baby was due. But she never made her appointment. Instead, she was kidnapped and raped, beaten and strangled over a 12-day period before a road crew found her battered body dumped on an old stretch of Texas highway off US 281 in Canyon Lake, Texas.
--<u>Source</u>: Christian McPhate, *"10 Notorious Unsolved Texas Murders,"* Texas Observer, 5-17-16

## THE I-30 DALLAS-FT WORTH KILLER

A U.S. Postal Service employee was found fatally shot inside a truck on I-30, Dallas police said. The employee was found in a USPS box truck on the Dallas-Fort Worth Turnpike Freeway. Homicide detectives and US postal inspectors responded, but police did not indicate what might have happened. The victim has not been named yet. A photo from the scene shows the truck resting beside a guard rail. On February 8, a marked Dallas police squad car was shot at about one mile from the fatal shooting of the Postal Service driver. The police officer was not injured, CNN affiliate KTVT reported.

--Source:   Amir Vera, *"A US Postal Service Employee Was Found Fatally Shot Inside A Truck on Interstate 30, Dallas Police Said,"*  CNN, 2-19-18

# UTAH

## BUNDY, Theodore Robert "Ted"
*("The Co-Ed Killer;" "The Campus Killer;" "Lady Killer")*
(see WASHINGTON)

## BOUTAIN, Austin and Kathleen BOUTAIN
*("1-70 Carjacking Killer Couple")*

On October 27, 2017, after Austin Boutain, 24, accompanied by his wife, Kathleen, Boudain, randomly killed Mitchell Bradford Ingle, 63, in Golden, Colorado, slitting the victim's throat. Now a drifter couple on a violent run, having stolen Ingle's truck and guns, they fled on the I-70, arriving in Salt Lake City, next day. There, the Boutains set up a camp in Red Butte Canyon area of Salt Lake City, eventually coming up with their plan to kidnap an unsuspecting Utah motorist and either kill the driver in the Utah Canyon or take him along and kill him in Tennessee. On October 30, 2017, the Boutains eyed the cars from higher vantage point, waiting for the "right" one. But as the afternoon beat on, Kathleen's patience frayed. Every time she pointed out a vehicle to her husband, Austin hesitated. Another vehicle would come up. *"Don't want witnesses,"* he'd say. Or it was *"too light out still."* He was taking too long to find a victim. Finally she told Austin he was a coward. He responded by pulling out a handgun and pistol whipped his wife for questioning his resolve to kill. Kathleen ran off down the dirt road out of the canyon. When his wife did not return, Austin walked down the hill and knocked on the black car's window to ask whether the driver knew which way Kathleen had gone. No answer. He knocked again, his temper flaring as the car was driving away, and repeatedly fired into the driver's side window until the gun clicked empty, killing the Chinese student, Guo ChenWei, 23. That was the last act that authorities attribute to the Boutains, including a murder attempt with a crossbow, an actual murder with a knife, and bizarre plans for cross-country kidnap plot. In Colorado, the couple intended to steal Ingle's RV but it was too bloody, so they ransacked the RV, taking money, prescription drugs, a rifle, handguns, ammo, knives, blankets, clothes, and Ingle's green F350 Ford truck. While Ingle's body lay undiscovered in the trailer, the couple traveled the I-70 in the stolen truck to

153

Salt Lake City, picking up a couple at a truck stop, and gave the truck to the couple so they would not have to dispose of it. Both faced Murder charges in Utah and and Colorado.

--Source: Paighten Hawkins, "*At least 64 People Were Killed in Homicides in Utah This Year,*" The Salt Lake Tribune, 12-31-17; "*Gunman Who Killed Chinese Student in US Car Jacking Surrenders After Manhunt,*" South China Morning Post, AP and Reuters,11-1-17; Kyle Swenson, "*University of Utah Shooting Details Released in Court Documents,*" The Washington Post, and The Standard Examiner, 11-17-17.

**LUCAS, Henry Lee** *("The Orange Socks Killer; ""Confession Killler")*

(see TEXAS)


**VALFEADES, Timothy Jay** *("The Vampire Trucker")*

(see MINNESOTA)


**WILDER, Christopher** *("The Beauty Queen Killer")*

(see FLORIDA)


# UTAH UNSOLVED CASES

## *"THE I-80 UTAH SUITCASE KILLER"*


In May of 2015, Utah Highway Patrol was called to the scene where a body was found inside a suitcase dumped just north of the westbound lanes of I-80 near Saltair, Utah. An autopsy was performed and police say the victim, who died as result of a shooting, is believed to have been there for several weeks to several months. She is a middle-aged female, unknown ethnicity, long dark hair, tattoo on her left wrist of a pink breast cancer ribbon, mastectomy of right breast, wearing a red and white tank top, red button-up shirt and jeans. Police were working on a lead about a missing Las Vegas woman with a similar description.

--Source: Good4Utah.com, 5-1-15

# VERMONT

**KEYES, Israel** *("The Cross Country Serial Killer")*
(See ALASKA)

### MORRISON, David Allan
### *("The Highway Strangler")*

Sarah Hunter, 36, a golf pro at the Manchester Country Club at the time, was reported missing the morning of Sept. 19, 1986, and her vehicle was found later that day at a gas station in Manchester Center on Vermont Historic Route 7-A. a north-south state highway in Bennington County, Vermont. Over 2 months later, Hunter's body was found in a wooded area near a cornfield in Pawlet, Vermont. She had been sexually assaulted and was strangled to death a short time after being abducted. David Allan Morrison, 52, one of the first suspects in the case and who was interviewed twice following Hunter's disappearance, moved to California in January 1988, leaving his 1968 Chevrolet Impala at a friend's house in Arlington, Vermont. While in California,

Morrison held-up an adult bookstore, then led police on a brief chase. He was driving the same gray Hyundai that he stole from a female newspaper carrier in an attack the week before in Chula Vista, California. The 20-year-old woman had been delivering papers in a Chula Vista trailer park when Morrison came behind her with a gun, forced her into her car and made sexual advances toward her, police said. She jumped out of the moving car, resulting in stitches to her face. He was arrested in Oceanside, California for Kidnapping, Attempted Murder, and Sexual Assault of the newspaper carrier, and given a "20 Years to Life" sentence in that case. Following the arrest, Vermont State Police seized Morrison's vehicle and vacuumed it for trace evidence but there was not enough evidence at the time to charge him with Sarah Hunter's murder. More than 20 years later, after significant advancements in DNA testing, hair strands collected from the vehicle positively connected Sarah Hunter to Morrison's vehicle and detectives were granted an arrest warrant for Morrison for First Degree Murder. Morrison denied killing Hunter but did not deny strangling her. According to the affidavit, Morrison has been identified and/or convicted in 4 other cases with a modus operandi similar to Hunter's case, in which he approached lone females, abducted them using a firearm or physical force, and transported the victims to remote areas before sexually assaulting them. There remain a number of unsolved homicides from the mid-1980s in Vermont and New Hampshire, including at least 7 murders believed to be linked to an unidentified person dubbed *the "Connecticut River Valley Killer,"* but authorities have no reason to believe Morrison may be that killer.
--Source: Dawson Raspuzzi, *"25-Year-Old Vermont Murder Solved by DNA Analysis,"* Brattleboro Reporter, Benington Banner, 7-3-12; Kristina Davis and Lisa Rathke, *"DNA Links San Diego Man to Golf Pro's Slaying,"* The San Diego Tribune, 7-19-14.

## SCHAEFER, Gary Lee
### ("The Kidnap Rapist-Killer"; "The Valley Killer")

In the late 1970's and early 1980's, 2 killers roamed the scenic region in search of victims. Gary Schaefer, a Vermont native, born in 1951, was captured but the other remains uncaught. His first victim was likely Cathy Millican, 26, her body found on September 25, 1978, in a wetlands preserve near New London, New Hampshire. She had been stabbed to death. He kidnapped, raped and murdered Sherry Nastasia, 13, and in 1981 he did the same to Theresa Fenton. But in 1982, Deanna Buxton, 17, survived his attack in Brattleboro. On April 9, 1982, Shaefer abducted Catherine Richards in Springfield and drove her to a remote location where he forced her to felate him before he crushed her skull with a rock. It was not until Schaefer had claimed his 3 victims that the Valley Killer struck again on May 30, 1984. Eva Morse was last seen hitchhiking in Charlestown, New Hampshire, after leaving work on July 10, 1985. Her corpse was found by a logger on April 25, 1986, with knife wounds. In a plea deal, Schaefer pled guilty to Kidnapping, Sexual Assault, and Second Degree Murder, charges dismissed regarding Fenton, and was sentenced to "30 Years to Life" at the federal penitentiary in Leavenworth, Kansas.
--Source: Murderpedia

# VERMONT UNSOLVED CASES

## "THE ROUTE 112 / VALLEY KILLER"

From 1970 to 2004, 30 women vanished in the tiny states of Vermont and New Hampshire. Of the 30, 10 were found, brutally murdered, while 19 were never found. Throughout the 1990s, Vermont and New Hampshire were at the top of the list of states that were nearly free of violent crimes and murder. But there are also 60 *unsolved* homicides in Vermont and New Hampshire that occurred during that period, and media dubbed the unknown serial killer as "*The Valley Killer*" and "*The Route 112 Killer.*" February 9, 2004, Maura Murray, 19, was driving on Vermont Route 112 which begins in Vermont, when she swerved into a snow bank on a sharp icy curve hitting a guard rail. There were several witnesses. Murray said she was fine and had called AAA on her cell phone. About 10 minutes later, both a Haverhill Police Officer and a New Hampshire State Police Officer arrived on the scene. Maura Murray had vanished. Gone with Murray were her credit and bank cards. On March 19, 2004, Brianna Maitland, 17, of Sheldon, Vermont, also vanished. Her abandoned car was found next day at Montgomery, Vermont, off Vermont 118. The car had plowed backward into the side of a vacant farmhouse, its headlights still on. It was speculated that the "Route 112 Killer" had abducted both girls who have not been found to date.
--Source: "*Missing Girl Case: Reward to Expire*," Rutland Herald, 6-24-17; Natalie Finn, "*The Disappearance of Maura Murray: Everything You Need to Know About the Baffling Unsolved Case,*" ENews, eonline.com, 9-30-17.

156

# VIRGINIA

## MATTHEW JR, Jesse Leroy
### ("The US 29 Hitchhiker Killer")

Jesse Leroy Matthew Jr, 33, was linked by forensic evidence to the murder of Morgan Harrington, a 20-year old Virginia Tech Student last seen hitchhiking along US-29 outside Charlottesville in 2009. He was also indicted for the Murder of Hannah Graham, an 18-year old Virginia Tech student who was last seen on surveillance footage from the Tempo Bar at the Downtown Mall, that showed Matthew with his arm around Graham and that Graham appeared drunk or sedated. Over the previous decade, Matthew left 2 colleges where he was a student, after being of a sexual assault at each college. On June 10, 2015, after his trial began, Matthew entered an Alford Plea, (in which a defendant does not admit guilt but concedes that the prosecution has enough evidence to win a conviction), and he was convicted in the killing and kidnapping of Hannah Graham.
--Source: *CNN*, 10-29-14; NBC News, 6-10-15; and *Wikipedia*

## KNOWLES, Paul John ("The Casanova Killer")
(see FLORIDA)

# VIRGINIA UNSOLVED CASES

## "THE COLONIAL PARKWAY MURDERS"
(See also VIRGINIA: ATWELL, Fred)

On October 12, 1986, the first 2 victims, Cathleen Marian Thomas, 27, and Rebecca Ann Dowski, 21, a gay female couple, were found strangled, their throats cut, and their bodies dumped on an embankment of the York River along the Colonial Parkway. On September 23, 1987, in a second double homicide, the bodies of David Lee Knobling, 20, and Robin M. Edwards, 14, turned up, both shot in the back of the head. Knobling's pickup was discovered abandoned in a parking lot with the door open. They had disappeared October 9, 1986 and their bodies found 3 days later in the Ragged Island Wildlife Refuge off the James River. About 6 months later, on April 9, 1987, Richard Keith Call, 20, and his date, Cassandra Lee Hailey, 18, went missing. Call's car was found abandoned on Colonial Parkway but the couple was never found. On September 5, 1989, Daniel Laer, 21, and Anamaria Phelps, 18, disappeared from a rest stop off I-64. Phelps died of a stab wound; it was impossible to tell how Lauer died. Because the cars of the victims in each case were found along the Colonial Parkway with the driver's side window rolled down, authorities suspected the perpetrator was a police officer who got the victims to stop on the Parkway.

Fred Atwell, 62, a former Gloucester, Virginia Deputy Sheriff who had bizarre behaviors, became a suspect in the Colonial Parkway serial murders. Police in Gwinnett County, Georgia, arrested Atwell who was accused of robbing a woman of $100 at gunpoint in Georgia in September of 2011. He reportedly told the woman he had been living in the woods and was hungry. The month before, Atwell was arrested, indicted, and pled guilty in connection with a phony car raffle in which all the proceeds were to go to "The Colonial Parkway Victims Fund." Atwell cashed a check for $270 that was supposed to go for Department of Motor Vehicles fees related to the non-existent cars. Probably the traumatic event culminating in his capture was when he and his wife separated. He was then reportedly "wandering around" and had called a suicide hotline saying he is "a suspect in a serial murder" and wants to commit "suicide by cop." However police managed to take Atwell alive into custody. He was sentenced to 2 years and 8 months in prison for Obtaining Money Under False Pretenses in the fake "Colonial Parkway Victims" fundraiser. However, the Colonial Parkway Murders remain unsolved.

--Source: *Huffington Post*, 9-6-11; *"Killer On The Run,"* Mayhem.net; *"The Colonial Parkway Murders,"* Pilotonline.com, 8-18-10; NBC News, 10-3-14; Wikipedia

# WASHINGTON

### BRAAE, Michael
### ("Cowboy Mike," "The Barefoot Cowboy," "The I-84 Killer")

Michael Braae, had been the focus of a manhunt for a serial killer that extended across Idaho, Washington and Oregon. The search intensified when he was spotted at "garage sales" in those states and at a truck stop on I-84 in Idaho where a high speed chase ensued. After police placed spike strips in his path, which blew out his tires, Braae abandoned his car at the Snake River and jumped into the water in an attempt to elude capture, but a police "bite dog" dragged him to shore. Described as *"not from anywhere -- he's from here and there,"* Braae was a country singer, known as *"Cowboy Mike"* for his cowboy hat, boots and penchant for serenading ladies with his guitar. He was also called *"The Barefoot Cowboy"* in California where he preferred to go shoeless. Braae was the last person seen with Lori Jones, 44, of Washington, who was found naked except for a pillowcase over her head, raped and strangled to death. In June and July of 2001, Jones wasn't the only Washington woman to disappear after being last seen with the man known in bars as "Cowboy Mike." Braae, 48, who lived in a 1970's trailer on what he dubbed a "mini farm" in Pierce County, went on a rampage that left at least one woman dead, 2 women injured (one critically from a gunshot wound to the head), and left one police dog nearly drowned. He's also suspected in the murders of 2 Oregon women in 1997, but the evidence is scant in the other cases and complicated by time, lack of witnesses, and bodies. Susan Ault, a Wahkiakum County woman and girlfriend of Braae's, hasn't been seen since arguing with him in June 2001. Her body was never found. Marchelle Morgan identified Braae as the person who shot her in the head less than a week after Jones was found dead, but her condition had so deteriorated from her brain injury by the time her case went to trial in 2006, that she could no longer testify; the jury deadlocked 11-1 and the judge declared a mistrial.

Braae is serving time for Aggravated Assault and Eluding a Police Officer in a high-speed chase in July 2001. Although he spent much of his time in the Northwest, he also surfaced in Illinois and Florida, had a DUI arrest in Oregon, and was convicted of Assault in California for inflicting corporal injury on a spouse—actually a girlfriend named Teri Conway. According to court documents, Braae met Conway in New Orleans in the summer of 2001 at a cowboy bar, singing karaoke. A month later, he moved to California to live with her and was arrested after twice trying to strangle her. She reported that he would rape her, grab her head and bang it against the headboard, and pin her arms down with his knees. But she didn't know him as *"Cowboy Mike."* Police also wanted to question Braae about the death of Valina Marie Larson, last seen with him September 30, 1997 in Oregon and found in January 1998.

His known victims were:
- Valina Marie Larson, Oregon - 9-30-97;
- 2 Women, Oregon - 1997;
- Lori Jones, 44, Washington - 6-01;
- Susan Ault, Wahkiakum County, never found - 6-01;
- Marchelle Morgan - 6-01;
- Teri Conway, California (survived) - 6-01;

On July 23, 2008, in Washington, he was sentenced to 47 years in prison.

--Source: "Cowboy Mike: The Ladykiller," Seattle News, 7-22-08; ABC News, 7-20-15; and Murderpedia.

## BUNDY, Theodore Robert "Ted"
### ("The Co-Ed Killer;" "The Campus Killer;" "Lady Killer")

Ted Bundy was a prolific multi-state killer and most of his victims were in Washington state. Born November 24, 1946 as Theodore Robert Cowell at the Elizabeth Lund Home for Unwed Mothers (now Lund Family Center), in Burlington, Vermont, to Eleanor "Louise" Cowell, his father's identity was never determined with certainty. Although Ted's birth certificate assigned paternity to Lloyd Marshall, a salesman and Air Force veteran, his mother alleged that his father was "a sailor named Jack Washington" who did not exist in Navy records at the time. But family members suspected it was his mother's violent, abusive father, Samuel Cowell, who beat his wife and the family dog, once threw his wife's younger sister, Julia, down the stairs, sometimes spoke of unseen presences, and would fly into a violent rage when the subject of Ted's paternity was raised. For the first 3 years of his life, he was raised by his mother's parents, Samuel and Eleanor Cowell, "as their own," to avoid the stigma of his out-of-wedlock birth, and his mother had to pretend to be his "older sister." Julia recalls awakening from nap to find knives on her bed and 3-year old Ted standing by her bed, smiling. In 1950, his mother fled from the violence, changing her name from Cowell to Nelson, and left Ted with cousins, Alan and Jane Scott, in Tacoma, Washington. His grandmother, Eleanor, a timid and obedient woman, periodically underwent electro-convulsive treatment for Depression. In 1951, his mother met and married Johnny Culpepper Bundy, a hospital cook, and Bundy formally adopted Ted. Subsequently, his mother conceived children with Johnny Bundy. Although Johnny tried to include Ted in family outings and activities, Ted remained distant. Ted later complained to his girlfriend that Johnny wasn't his "real father," wasn't very bright, and didn't make much money. Ted expressed a lifelong resentment toward his mother for lying about his parentage. Biographer, Ann Rule, believed he obtained his birth certificate in 1969 when he began college at University of Washington where he studied Psychology. Ted said he had been obsessed with crime magazine stories involving sexual violence, particularly those accompanied by photos or illustrations of dead or maimed bodies, and in adolescence began peeping into windows to observe women undressing. Although he was liked in high school, he did not know or understand how to have social interactions or relationships. In high school years, he was arrested twice on suspicion of Burglary and Auto Theft but his record was expunged when he reached 18. He told psychologist, Art Norman, that he killed 2 women in Atlantic City in 1969 while visiting family in Philadelphia. To homicide detective, Robert D. Keppel, he hinted at a murder in Seattle in 1972 when he graduated UW, and another in 1973 involving a hitchhiker near Tacoma, Washington, the same year he was accepted University of Puget Sound (UPS) Law School at Tacoma. In 1974, he abruptly ended his relationship with his girlfriend, Stephanie Brooks, without explanation, and began skipping classes. He later stated *"I just wanted to prove to myself I could have married her."* There is no consensus on exactly when Ted Bundy began killing women, but his earliest *documented* homicide occurred at the time he broke off with Brooks -- Shortly after midnight on January 4, 1974, he entered the basement apartment of Karen Sparks (aka Joni Lenz or Terri Caldwell) a dancer and student at UW. He bludgeoned the sleeping woman with a metal rod from her bed frame, sexually assaulted her with a speculum (a medical tool for examining body orifices), causing extensive internal injuries. She remained unconscious for 10 days but survived with permanent brain damage. In the early morning hours of February 1, 1974, Bundy broke into the basement room of Lynda Ann Healy, a UW undergraduate, who he beat unconscious, dressed her in blue jeans, a white blouse and boots, and carried her away. Female college students continued disappearing in the Tacoma-Seattle area at the rate of about one per month.

Witnesses reported seeing a man with his arm in a sling, carrying books and a light brown or tan VW Beetle. Bundy wore an arm sling or leg cast to convince women to help him carry or load his books or briefcase to his car, including in broad daylight, once alleging he needed to carry items to a sailboat from his VW. Another time he murdered two women in a restroom near a picnic area. In June 1974, Bundy was working at the Washington State Department of Emergency Services (DES) in Olympia -- the government agency involved in the search for the missing women. In August 1974, Bundy received a second acceptance -- from University of Utah Law School -- and moved to Salt Lake City. He said that on his way, on September 2, he raped and strangled a still unidentified hitchhiker in Idaho, then photographed and dismembered her -- the first in a string of his new victims. Next, on October 2, 1974, he abducted 16-year old Nancy Wilcox in Holladay, a suburb of Salt Lake City, and dragged her into a wooded area, intending to "de-escalate" his pathological urges, he said, by raping and releasing her. However, while trying to silence her, he strangled her by accident, he claimed, and buried her in Capitol Reef National Park; her remains were never found. In November 1974, several women disappeared from towns surrounding Salt Lake City. In mid-May 1975, three of Bundy's former co-workers at DES-Washington, Carole Boone, who he had dated while at DES, and Elizabeth Kloepher, who suspected Bundy of the killings, visited him in Salt Lake City and stayed at his apartment for a week. Bundy would not disclose details about his alleged romances in Utah with Boone, Kim Andrews, or Sharon Auer. Bundy was arrested in August 1975, when a Utah Highway Patrol Officer pulled him over for a routine traffic stop. The officer, noting the front passenger seat of the VW was missing, searched the car and found a ski mask, a second mask fashioned from pantyhose, a crowbar, handcuffs, trash bags, a coil of rope, an ice pick, and other items initially assumed to be burglary tools.

There were multiple trials and imprisonments and Bundy made multiple escapes, eventually being captured and charged with more murders. He chose to represent himself, and while questioning his witness, Carole Ann Boone, in court, he asked her to marry him and she said yes -- constituting a legal marriage. He turned down a plea deal that would have saved him from a Death sentence and on February 10, 1980, Bundy was sentenced to Death by electrocution for a third time.  In October 1982, Carole Ann Boone gave birth to a daughter and named Bundy as the father -- While conjugal visits were not allowed at Raiford Prison, inmates were known to pool their money to bribe guards to allow them intimate time alone with their female visitors. Bundy ultimately confessed to 30 homicides but the true total is unknown. Published estimates have run as high was 100 victims or more.  On the evening before his execution, Bundy reviewed his victim tally with Detective Bill Hagmaier on a state-by-state basis:

- 11 in Washington
- 8 in Utah;
- 3 in Colorado o 3 in Florida;
- 2 in Oregon (both unidentified);
- 2 in Idaho (one unidentified);
- 1 in California (unidentified)

Following is a chronological summary of the 20 identified victims and 5 survivors:

1974

Washington, Oregon

- January 4 - Karen Sparks, 16 (often identified as Joni Lenz in Bundy literature): Bludgeoned and sexually assaulted in her bed as she slept; survived;
- February 1 - Lynda Ann Healy, 21: Bludgeoned while asleep and abducted; skull and mandible recovered at Taylor Mountain site;
- March 12 - Donna Gail Manson, 19: Abducted while walking to a concert at Evergreen State College; body left (according to Bundy) at Taylor Mountain site, but never found;
- April 17 - Susan Elaine Rancourt, 18: Disappeared after attending an evening advisors' meeting at Central Washington State College; skull and mandible recovered at Taylor Mountain site;
- May 6 - Roberta Kathleen Parks, 22: Vanished from Oregon State University in Corvallis; skull and mandible recovered at Taylor Mountain site;
- June 1 - Brenda Carol Ball, 22: Disappeared after leaving the Flame Tavern in Burien; skull and mandible recovered at Taylor Mountain site;
- June 11 - Georgann (often misspelled "Georgeann") Hawkins, 18: Abducted from an alley behind her sorority house, UW; skeletal remains recovered at Issaquah site;
- July 14 - Janice Ann Ott, 23: Abducted from Lake Sammamish State Park in broad daylight; skeletal remains recovered at Issaquah site;
- July 14 - Denise Marie Naslund, 19: Abducted four hours after Ott from the same park; skeletal remains recovered at Issaquah site; Utah, Colorado, Idaho;
- October 2 - Nancy Wilcox, 16: Ambushed, assaulted, and strangled in Holladay, Utah; body buried (according to Bundy) near Capitol Reef National Park, 200 miles (320 km) south of Salt Lake City, but never found;

- October 18 - Melissa Anne Smith, 17: Vanished from Midvale, Utah; body found in nearby mountainous area;
- October 31 - Laura Ann Aime, 17: Disappeared from Lehi, Utah; body discovered by hikers in American Fork Canyon;
- November 8 - Carol DaRonch, 17: Attempted abduction in Murray, Utah; escaped from Bundy's car and survived;
- November 8 - Debra Kent, 17: Vanished after leaving a school play in Bountiful, Utah; body left (according to Bundy) near Fairview, Utah, 100 miles (160 km) south of Bountiful; minimal skeletal remains (one patella) found, but never positively identified as Kent's;

1975
- January 12 - Caryn Campbell, 23: Disappeared from hotel hallway in Snowmass, Colorado; body discovered on a dirt road near the hotel;
- March 15 - Julie Cunningham, 26: Disappeared on the way to a tavern in Vail, Colorado; body buried (according to Bundy) near Rifle, 90 miles (140 km) west of Vail, but never found;
- April 6 - Denise Oliverson, 25: Abducted while bicycling to her parents' house in Grand Junction, Colorado; body thrown (according to Bundy) into the Colorado River 5 miles (8.0 km) west of Grand Junction, but never found;
- May 6 - Lynette Culver, 12: Abducted from Alameda Junior High School in Pocatello, Idaho; body thrown (according to Bundy) into what authorities believe to be the Snake River, but never found;
- June 28 - Susan Curtis, 15: Disappeared during a youth conference at Brigham Young University; body buried (according to Bundy) near Price, Utah, 75 miles (121 km) southeast of Provo, but never found;

1978
Florida
- January 15 - Margaret Bowman, 21: Bludgeoned and then strangled as she slept, Chi Omega sorority, FSU (no secondary crime scene);
- January 15 - Lisa Levy, 20: Bludgeoned, strangled and sexually assaulted as she slept, Chi Omega sorority, FSU (no secondary crime scene);
- January 15 - Karen Chandler, 21: Bludgeoned as she slept, Chi Omega sorority, FSU; survived;
- January 15 - Kathy Kleiner, 21: Bludgeoned as she slept, Chi Omega sorority, FSU; survived;
- January 15 - Cheryl Thomas, 21: Bludgeoned as she slept, eight blocks from ChiOmega; survived;
- February 9 - Kimberly Diane Leach, 12: Abducted from her junior high
- school in Lake City, Florida; skeletal remains found near Suwannee River State Park

On January 24, 1989, minutes before Bundy's execution, Detective Hagmaier queried Bundy about unsolved cases in Illinois, Vermont (Curran case), Texas, and Miami. He denied involvement in any of them. Bundy's third Death sentence was the one carried out at Florida's Raiford Prison. Bundy was 42.

--<u>Source</u>: Wikipedia; Ann Rule, *"The Stranger Beside Me,"* 1989, 2000, 2009.

**JESPERSON, Keith Hunter** (*"The Happy Face Killer"*)
(see NEBRASKA)

**KONDRO, Joseph**
(*"The 'Uncle Joe' Killer"*;
*"The "Longview Serial Killer"*)

Joseph Kondro disposed of at least 3 young girls' bodies in heavily wooded areas along the I-5 that runs down the Washington and Oregon coasts and is suspected of murders of up to 70 missing girls. Born May 19, 1959, as Don Lee Durant, he was one of 7 children born to his Native American parents, Elizabeth Marie and Curtis Durant. When he was born, he was taken from the hospital to Michigan Children's Aid Society of Detroit because his parents had fallen on hard times and could not care for him. The Durants were grief stricken by the loss of their son and had refused to sign relinquishment, but he was adopted anyhow by a White couple, John and Eleanor Kondratovich. This was during "the Sixties Sweep" also termed "The Baby Scoop Years," when adoptable infants were taken from unwed mothers and Naive American children in particular were systematically removed from their parents on reservations in order to be "Christianized." His adopters named him "Joe" and also called him "Joey." They later changed their own and his last names to Kondro. Around age 7, Joey's school classmates bullied him about his skin color being darker than his parents, even calling him "nigger." And that's when Eleanor told him he was adopted. He never felt he belonged and had a lot of anger that he took out on other kids. In 4th grade, he poured gasoline on a boy who had a painful bad sunburn and killed some newborn kittens by bashing them with his baseball bat - the first of many animal killings. As early as age 5 or 6, while still in kindergarten, he learned that if he had something a girl wanted, he had the power to make her do anything he wanted -- including take off their clothes. Although he, himself, was never molested, by age 7, he was sexually deviant, preferring to experiment with innocent young blonde girls. Kondro explained *"I got away with it because they never told anyone... Even as a kid, before I actually murdered anyone, I did wonder how far I could take my sexual desires and increasing fantasies that included killing."* In adulthood, he resided in Longview, Washington, preying mostly on 7-year olds while married with children of his own who he never molested, perhaps because his children provided a sense of biological connectedness that he didn't have with his adoptive family. Then one day, Emily, 7, and Jessica, 14, told their mothers what he had done to them and he did jail time. Still, the mothers of the girls he molested seemed to not want to believe that the charismatic "Uncle Joe" could do such a thing, so he was able to continue his secret life. But from then on, when a little girl would get into his car, it was a done deal -- *"I knew I was going to kill her."* Rima Danette Traxler, a pretty, blonde 8-year old, disappeared May 15, 1985. By then, Kondro was drinking and drug addicted, as were some of his neighbors. Rima's parents had warned her not to accept rides from strangers, but he was "Uncle Joe" to her and to his other neighbors, and he knew what password Rima's mother had given her -- *"Unicorn"* -- which he used to convince her that her mother wanted him to pick her up.

164

The many unoccupied cabins in wooded areas along the I-5 near his home provided a place where he could take his time with his victims. After I sexually assaulted her, to reinforce the kill, I put my weight on her as I strangled her with both my hands. And as she exhaled her last breath, *I put my mouth over hers to take in her last breath for myself.* Why I did that, I don't know... If you could put a meter on my emotions, it would flat line -- I don't know where my emotions are." On November 21, 1996, 12-year old Kara Patricia Rudd was missing. By being a "local" who everyone knew and liked, Kondro could take the time he needed to "groom" his neighbors' young daughters while becoming a trusted friend and drinking buddy of their parents to the extent they considered him to be like a family member. One of a search team found Kara's body at an abandoned house, beneath a rotting VW. When charged and convicted of Kara Rudd's murder, Kondro had already been in jail for Child Rape and Molestation of 3 girls, ages 7, 9 and 10. In a plea deal, he avoided the Death Penalty by confessing to the Murder of Rima Traxler and disclosing where her remains could be found. He was sentenced to 55 years in prison with no chance of parole, to be served at Walla Walla Penitentiary in Washington state. But it had been more than 10 years between the 2 murders and authorities were unable to find Rima Traxler's remains which animals may have long ago carried away.

Investigator Scott McDaniel interviewed Kondro about more than 70 other killings and disappearances, in some of which Kondro remains a suspect, most notably the disappearance of 8-year old Chila Silversmith from Kalama, Washington, where Kondro had been working at the time. His known victims were:
- Emily, 7 (unreported molestation);
- Jessica, 14 (unreported molestation);
- 3 Unnamed Girls, 7, 9. 10, (for Child Rape and Molestation);
- Rima Danette Traxler, 8, Longview, Washington - 5-15-85;
- Kara Patricia Rudd, 12, Longview, Washington - 11-21-96;
- Chila Silvernails, Kalama, Washington, 8.

On May 3, 2012, at age 52, Joseph Kondro died in prison, from End Stage Liver Disease due to Hepatitis C.

--Source: Lori Carangelo, "*KONDRO: The 'Uncle Joe' Killer,*" Access Press, 12-19-15.

## RIDGWAY, Gary Leon
## (*"The Green River Killer"; "Route 99 Killer"*)

Gary Ridgway's slayings began in 1982 when young runaways and prostitutes began disappearing along Route 99. Ridgway murdered at least 49 women in Washington state from 1982 until he was caught in 2001 and told investigators that he killed 75-80 women along Route 99 in King County, Washington. Born February 18, 1949 in Salt Lake City, Utah, but raised along Seattle, Washington's Pacific Coast Highway, Gary Leon Ridgway was the second of Mary and Thomas Ridgway's three sons. His home life was somewhat troubled; relatives have described his mother as domineering and have said that young Ridgway witnessed more than one violent argument between his parents. His father was a bus driver who would often complain about the presence of sex workers. Ridgway had a bed wetting problem until he was 13, and his mother would wash his genitals after every episode. He would later tell defense psychologists that, as an adolescent, he had conflicting feelings of anger and sexual attraction toward his mother, and fantasized about killing her. Ridgway is dyslexic and was held back a year in high school. Ridgway's IQ was recorded as being in the "low eighties" When he was 16, he stabbed a 6-year old boy, who survived the attack. Ridgway had led the boy into the woods and then stabbed him through the ribs into his liver. After serving in Vietnam, Ridgway worked painting trucks for 30 years. He was married 3 times, was fanatical about religion, but was also a frequent customer of prostitutes. He brought many of them to his home and strangled them, then left their bodies in remote, wooded areas. The first few bodies turned up along Green River. After DNA evidence from victims matched Ridgway's DNA, he was charged in December 2001 with 4 counts of Aggravated Murder and eventually pled guilty to 48 counts of Aggravated First Degree Murder. In a plea deal to avoid execution, Ridgway agreed to reveal where he had hidden the bodies of several young women who had never been found. He was then sentenced to Life in prison in December 2003, having committed more confirmed murders than any serial killer in history.

--Source: Biography.com and Wikipedia

# WASHINGTON, D.C.

## MUHAMMAD, John Allen, and Lee Boyd MALVO
### *("The Beltway Snipers")*

The Beltway Sniper attacks were a series of coordinated shootings that took place over 3 weeks in October 2002 in several locations throughout the Washington, D.C., metropolitan area and along I-95, in Washington, D.C., Maryland and Virginia; 10 people were killed and 3 other victims were critically injured in Virginia. The rampage was perpetrated by John Allen Muhammad (then aged 42), and Lee Boyd Malvo (then 17), driving a blue 1990 Chevrolet Caprice sedan. Their crime spree began in February 2002 with murders and robberies in the states of Alabama, Arizona, Florida, Georgia, Louisiana, Texas, and Washington, which resulted in 7 deaths and 7 injuries, bringing the total victim count to 17 deaths and 10 injuries. In September 2003, Muhammad was sentenced to Death. One month later, Malvo was sentenced to 6 consecutive Life sentences without the possibility of parole. On November 10, 2009, Muhammad was executed by lethal injection at the Greensville Correctional Center near Jarratt, Virginia.
--Source: Wikipedia; CrimeMuseum.org

## WASHINGTON, D.C. UNSOLVED CASES

### *"THE FREEWAY PHANTOM"*

"The Freeway Phantom" is the name given to an unidentified serial killer known to have abducted, raped and strangled 6 young female victims in Washington, DC, from April 1971 to September 1972, their bodies dumped on several Interstate highways. On 4-25-71, Carol Spinks, 13, was sent by her older sister to buy groceries about 1/2 mile from her home, just across the border into Maryland. Her body was found 6 days later on an embankment next to the northbound lanes of I-295, about 1500 feet from Suitland Parkway. On 7-8-71, Darlene Johnson, 16, was abducted on her way to work. Eleven days later, her body was found just 15 feet from where Spinks was found on I-295. A witness reported having seen Johnson in a black car driven by an African-American male, shortly after her abduction. On 7-27-71, Brenda Crockett, 10, was sent to the store by her mother. Three hours later, Brenda called home, crying, "A White man picked me up and I'm heading home in a cab," adding that she believed she was in Virginia, then abruptly said "bye" and hung up. A short time later, Brenda phoned again, repeating what she said previously but indicating she was "alone in a house with a White man." Brenda's mother's boyfriend asked Brenda to have the man come to the phone. Heavy footsteps were heard in the background and Brenda said "I'll see you," and hung up.

a few hours later, a hitchhiker discovered Brenda's body in a conspicuous location on Route 50, near Baltimore, Washington Parkway, in Prince George's County, Maryland. Authorities concluded that the kidnapper had the child call home to throw off the investigation and buy time until he could perpetrate her killing and disposal. On 10-1-71, Nenomoshia Yates, 10, was walking home from a Safeway store in Northeast Washington, DC, when she was kidnapped, raped and strangled. Her body was found within a few hours of her abduction just off the shoulder of Pennsylvania Avenue in Prince George's County, Maryland, when *"Freeway Phantom"* was first used in media. On 11-15-7, Brenda Woodward, 18, boarded a city bus to return to her Maryland Avenue home; 6 hours later, a police officer discovered her body, stabbed and strangled, near an access ramp to Route 202 at the Baltimore-Washington Parkway. A coat had been placed over her chest and one of its pockets contained a note from the killer: *"This is tantamount to my insensitivity to people, especially women. I will admit the others when you catch me... if you can! Freeway Phantom."* The Phantom's final victim, a year later on September 5, 1972, was Diane Williams, 17, who was last seen alive boarding a bus. A short time later, her strangled body was found dumped alongside I-295 just south of the D.C. line. Despite several county, state and FBI investigations of potential suspects, including a member of a gang known as "The Green Vega Rapists," who was serving time and who was not a perpetrator in these cases but who identified one of the perpetrators and crime details not known to the public "on condition that he not be identified." A political candidate at the time leaked the information about the break in the case and the whistleblower then denied he had provided any information and declined any further interviews. The Freeway Phantom files maintained by the lead detective at the time were lost, and detectives involved either retired or died, so the cases went cold. In 1977, Robert Elwood Askins was charged with abducting and raping a 24-year old woman inside her Washington, DC home and had served cyanide-laced whiskey to 5 prostitutes at a brothel, resulting in one death; 2 days later, he stabbed to death another prostitute. He referred to himself as a "woman hater," had collected newsclips in which a Judge used the word *"tantamount"* -- a unusual word choice also in the note written by "The Freeway Phantom." He was determined to be criminally insane, but his crimes didn't fit the profile of "The Freeway Phantom" and he denied having anything to do with *those* murders, stating he *"didn't have the depravity of mind required to commit any of the crimes."* --<u>Source</u>: Wikipedia

168

# WEST VIRGINIA

### FALLS, Neal  *("The Escort Killer")*

Neal Falls, lived in Henderson, Nevada, from 2000 to 2007. During that time, the bodies of 3 prostitutes were found dismembered along highways. A 4th sex worker was reported missing but was never found. Falls was being investigated in connection with unsolved sex worker cases in at least 9 states, including West Virginia, including deaths and dismemberment of many of the women. A female escort identified only as "Heather" met Falls, then 45, through Backpage.com, an online classified ad portal often used by men seeking prostitutes. When Falls arrived at Heather's home, he pointed a 9mm handgun at her chest, asked her, "Live or die?" and tried to strangle her. She grabbed Falls'

gun when he set it down to overpower her, and shot him one time in the head, killing him instantaneously. In the back of Neal Falls' car, police found several sets of handcuffs, several long knives, a box cutter, two axes, a machete, a sledgehammer, a bulletproof vest, another gun, shovels, a rubber tub large enough to hold an adult, bleach and other cleaning supplies that could be used to help dispose of a body, and a list containing the names of escorts.

–Source:  *"Sex Worker in West Virginia Shoots Dead 'Serial Killer',"* BBC-News - U.S. and Canada, 7-27-15; HuffPost Crime, 7-24-15; KPTV, 7-28-15; *"Textbook Case: W.VA. Sex Worker Stopped a Serial Killer, Authorities Say,"* NBC News, 7-29-15

### WICKLINE, William Dean *("The Butcher")*

(see OHIO)

# WISCONSIN

**EYLER, Larry** (*"The Interstate Killer"*)
(see ILLINOIS)

**ZAMASTIL, William Floyd** (*"The I-15 Freeway Killer"*)
(see CALIFORNIA)

**ZELICH, Steven**
(*"The Wisconsin Suitcase Murders"*)

When highway workers found the bodies of 2 women stuffed in suitcases along a rural highway at Geneva, Wisconsin, William Zelich, 52, had been a police officer with the Allis, Wisconsin Police Department from February 1989 until his resignation in August 2001. That was a few months after a prostitute told police they had struggled when she tried to flee Zelich's home. Zelich was charged with 2 counts of hiding a corpse after dental records were used to positively identify Jenny Gamez, 19, who had lived with several foster families since age 5 and who went missing from her foster father's Cottage Grove home in 2012. Another victim had been identified as Laura Simonson, 37, reported missing from Farmington, Minnesota, in November 2013. Simonson's father, Richard Wierson, said she struggled with mental illness and that he has cared for her 7 children. She was found naked except for a collar, with a rope around her neck and a gag in her mouth. Homicide charges were filed. Zelich confessed that he killed one in late 2012 or early 2013 in Kenosha County, and the other in November in Rochester, Minnesota. He bound and killed them, then kept their bodies for months, either in his vehicle or home
--Source: KARE11.com/story/news, 6-25-14; *"Second Victim Identified in Wisconsin 'Suitcase Murders',"* CBS News, 6-30-14; and NY DailyNews.com, 7-1-14

## WISCONSIN UNSOLVED CASES

### *"THE HIGHWAY 78 JANE DOE"*

The skeletal remains of a woman, age 45 to 65, were found in Caledonia, Columbia County, Wisconsin on May 8, 1982. The body was found in a wooded area near Highway 78. It is believed that she had died elsewhere and was disposed of at that location. In 2014, the remains were transported to Virginia for additional testing including DNA profiling.
--Source: *"List of Unidentified Victims in the United States,"* Wikipedia

# WYOMING

## ALCALA, Rodney James
### *("The Dating Game Killer")*

Rodney Alcala is worthy of mention as a multi-state serial rapist-killer who traversed the nation's interstates, leaving known victims in California, Washington, New York, and Wyoming. He was dubbed *"The Dating Game Killer"* for appearing on the popular television program in the middle of his murder spree, when, as "Bachelor Number 2," he won a date with Cheryl Bradshaw who refused to go out with him, as she found him to be "creepy. Bradshaw was lucky. Alcala was known to approach his female victims by pretending to be a photographer and asking them to pose for him before physically assaulting and strangling them until they lost consciousness, then waiting until they revived, and repeating this process several times before finally killing them and leaving the bodies posed. Born Rodrigo Jacques Alcala Buquor, August 23, 1943, in San Antonio, Texas, to Raoul Alcala Buquor and Anna Maria Gutierrez, Rodney Alcala. In 1951, his father moved the family to Mexico, abandoning them 3 years later. His mother moved Rodney and his siblings to suburban Los Angeles when he was about 11. He joined the U.S. Army as a Clerk at 17, had a nervous breakdown while AWOL, was diagnosed with Anti-social Personality Disorder by a military psychiatrist and discharged on medical grounds. Later, various psychiatric experts at is trials diagnosed him with Narcissistic Personality Disorder, Personality Disorder, and (by expert Vernon Geberth) with Malignant Narcissistic Personality Disorder with Psychopathy and Sexual Sadism. Alcala graduated from UCLA School of Fine Arts, later studied film under Roman Polanski at New York University.

His first known crime was in 1968 when a motorist observed him luring Tali Shairo, age 8, into his Hollywood apartment. The girl was found alive but raped and beaten with a steel bar. Her parents refused to allow her to testify against Alcala who fled and enrolled in the NYU film school using the name John Berger. In 1971, he obtained a counseling job at a New Hampshire arts camp for children, as John Burger. In 1971, Cornelia Michel Crilley, 23, a TWA flight attendant, was found raped and strangled in her New York apartment; her murder went unsolved until connected to Alcala in 2011. When charged with the murder of Christine Thornton, 28, Alcala was already on Death Row at Corcoran State Penitentiary in California, convicted of murder in California in 1980 in the killing of Robin Samsoe, 12, and in 2010 for the killings of Jill Barcomb, Georgia Wixted, and Charlotte Lamb. In January 2013, Sweetwater County Wyoming authorities charged an imprisoned serial killer with the 1977 murder of 28-year old Christine Ruth Thornton, whose unburied remains were found by a rancher in 1982 on public lands near the intersection of US-30 and I-80 in southwest Wyoming. But the remains could not be identified for decades, although it was determined to be a homicide victim who was about 6 months pregnant when she died. Alcala had taken a photo of Thornton on his motorcycle when she disappeared but claimed *"She was alive when I left her."* DNA samples taken from Thornton's sisters were a familial match to the victim. His victims were:

1968
- Tali Sairo, age 8 (Hollywood, California; survived);

1971
- Cornelia Michel Crilley, age 23 (New York;);

1974
- "Julie J," age 13 (Huntington Beach, California; survived);

1977
- Jill Barcomb, age 18 (Los Angeles, California;
- Ellen Jane Hover, age 23 (New York);
- Georgia Wixted, age 27 (Los Angeles, California;
- Antoinette Wittaker (suspected; Washington);
- Pamela Jean Lambson age 19 (San Francisco. California);
- Christine Ruth Thornton, age 28 (near US Hwy 80, Wyoming)

1978
- Charlotte Lamb, 31 (El Segundo, California);
- Joyce Gaunt; (suspected, Washington)

1979
- Monique Hoyt, age 15 (California);
- Jill Parenteau, age 21 (Burbank, California);
- Robin Samsoe, age 12 (Huntington Beach, California)

In 2019, Huntington Beach and New York City Police Department released 120 of Alcala's photographs and sought the public's help in identifying them to determine if any were Alcala's additional victims; 900 additional photos could not be made public because they were sexually explicit. In the first few weeks after photos were released, 21 women had come forward to identify themselves and at least 6 families believed they recognized loved ones who had disappeared years ago and were never found, but none could be positively connected to a missing person case or unsolved murder until 2013 when a family member recognized the photo of Christine Thornton, age 28.

--Source: Elise Schmelzer, *Star Tribune*, (Caspar, Wyoming). " *Serial Killer charged in Connection to 1977 Wyoming Cold Case,"* 9-20-16; Wikipedia.

## EATON, Dale Wayne
## ("The Li'l Miss Murder;" "The I-20/25 Killer")

"The Li'l Miss Murder" is the name given to the case of Lisa Marie Kimmell (July 18, 1969 - April 2, 1988), who disappeared somewhere along on the I-25 to I-20 while driving home from Colorado to Billings, Montana. She had left her job at Arby's in Denver on March 25, 1988. Highway Patrol records showed that she was stopped for speeding in Douglas, Wyoming, just before she disappeared. Eight days later, her body was found floating in the North Platte River near Casper, Wyoming, by a local fisherman. She had been hit on the head with a blunt object, stabbed 6 times in the chest and abdomen, then taken to the Old Government Bridge and thrown into the river. The autopsy showed the head wound would have killed her in a matter of minutes even if she had not been stabbed. The autopsy also determined that she had been bound, beaten and raped, for at least 6 days. In 2002, investigators a DNA profile was developed and the CODIS database matched the DNA to Dale Wayne Eaton, 57, of Moneta, Wyoming, who was then serving time in Englewood federal prison at Littleton, Colorado on an unrelated weapons charge. July 2002, Lisa Kimmel and her car, with the license plate "LIL MISS" which gave the case it's name, were found buried on Eaton's property with DNA evidence from semen linking him to her rape-murder.

Dale Eaton was born February 10, 1956. At 16, he tried to set his parents' house on fire which resulted in his mother's hospitalization. His father was abusive to him; his mother, the one person in his life who was supportive, was mentally ill, so at 16, at the time of his first psychiatric evaluation which determined that he had serious emotional problems, he ran away. At 17, Eaton got caught committing an Assault with a Deadly Weapon and Theft, and was turned over to the Juvenile Authority at Lookout Mountain School for Boys. From 17 to 19, he did well in reform school, learned to weld with proficiency. At 19, he became involved with a 16-year old girl. She left him for another man and he was devastated, resumed stealing and had multiple incarcerations. At 25, he seemed to be a more productive member of society, helping to build a church he attended, and was a member of the Operating Engineer's Union. At 26, he married but on their wedding night she wanted a divorce, although they remained married, constantly arguing, with her hitting him, though he never hit her back. They had 2 children when they divorced in 1979, got back together, and broke up several times. He threatened to commit suicide, and was diagnosed with Depression and "Thought Disorder." His suspected and confirmed victims were:

- Unidentified Female, 25-30 - 4-26-82;
- Belinda Grantham, 20-35 - 8-7-82;
- Naomi Kidder - 9-10-82;
- Lisa Marie Kimmel, 18 ("Li'l Miss") who he kept longer - 4-2-88;
- Patricia Candace Walsh, whose body was found in Utah - 1990;

- Scott Zykowski, found near El Paso, Texas - 1990;
- Amy Wroe Bechtel, 24 - 7-24-97;
- Kathleen Pehringer - 9-12-97;
- Shannon and Scott Breeden attacks - failed attempts to murder when Scott stabbed Eaton and Eaton was arrested, took a plea agreement, served 2-5 years suspended sentence in a halfway house.

On April 17, 2003, Eaton was charged with First Degree Murder (of Lisa Kimmel), Premeditated Murder, Aggravated Robbery, First Degree Sexual Assault, Second Degree Sexual Assault, and Aggravated Kidnapping. On March 2, 2004, Eaton was sentenced to Death. His Appeal was rejected and he remains the only prisoner in Wyoming on Death Row.

--Source: Bancroft, Eyers and Bennett, Radford University Department of Psychology, Radford, Virginia; and Wikipedia

## JESPERSON, Keith Hunter *("The Happy Face Killer")*
(see NEBRASKA)

# ADDENDUM

## 55 FACTS ABOUT SERIAL KILLERS

- A serial killer is someone who has murdered three or more people over a period of more than a month, with a cooling-off period between murders. The motive is usually based on psychological (often sexual) gratification, though the motives may also include anger, thrill, money, and attention seeking.[1]

- According to the FBI, more than 70% of serial killers experienced problems related to substance abuse. While only a few serial killers were actually addicted to alcohol and substances, many of them encountered them in their youth.[6]

- Many serial killers had sexually stressful childhood experiences[3]
- 

- Dr. Harold Shipman (1946–2004) a most prolific serial killer in modern history with over 250 murders ascribed to him, was a British doctor who murdered his patients. He hung himself in his cell in 2004, a day before his 58th birthday.[2]

- The blockbuster movie "*Se7en*" is a creepy thriller about a serial murderer who kills his victims in accordance with the seven deadly sins (lust, greed, gluttony, sloth, pride, anger, envy). Another blockbuster about a serial killer is the Oscar-winning *Silence of the Lambs*.[2]

- America's first serial killer was Dr. H. H. Holmes who confessed to 27 murders in the late 1890s. He said he "could not help the fact he was a murderer, no more than a poet can help the inspiration to sing."[3]

- Almost all serial killers admit that they started by acting out their fantasies on small animals before they moved to humans and that animal torture brought them a great source of pleasure. Given that most serial killers are from dysfunctional families, such pathological and abnormal behavior may be ignored. Jeffrey Dahmer's father, for example, had no qualms that his son performed animal dissections.[4]

- Former FBI Special Agent Robert K. Ressler (1937–2013) is the man credited with coining the term "serial killer" in 1971.[2]

- Steven Egger, in his book *Murder Among Us*, notes that serial murderers are frequently found to have an unusual or unnatural relationship with their mothers (Hitchcock's Norman Bates is an archetype).[2]

- While many serial killers were abused or beaten as children, there are exceptions. Jeffrey Dahmer had an apparently normal upbringing, yet became a horrific sex murderer. However newsstories mentioned his feeling rejected. His father wrote a book, "*A Father's Story*," which searches for explanations for his son's deviance.[2]

- A study that focused on a group of sociopaths who had been adopted as infants showed biological relatives of sociopaths were 4–5 times more likely to be sociopathic. [But no similar study focused on adoptees raised by sociopathic adoptive parents]; researchers note it's easier for "bad seeds to blossom in bad environments."[2]

- Many serial killers report having an abnormally strong sex drive and many fantasized about dead women rather than living ones.[4]

- *Crime Times* reports that psychopaths have a greater fear threshold and are less likely to respond to fear-inducing stimuli or even be immune to fear. Their startle reaction was significantly less than the average person, meaning they need a higher level of thrill or stimulation in order to have an intense experience.[2]

- Most serial killers suffered child abuse. Neglect and child abuse not only impair a child's self esteem, but also interfere with the ability to function in society, succeed academically, and form healthy relationships with people.[4]

- There are six phases of the serial killer's cycle: 1) the Aura Phase, where the serial killer begins losing a grip on reality; 2) the Trolling Phase, when the killer searches for a victim; 3) the Wooing Phase, where the killer lures his victim in; 4) the Capture Phase, where the victim is entrapped; 5) the Murder or Totem phase, which is the emotional high for the killer and, finally, 6) the Depression phase, which occurs after the killing.[2]

- Many serial killers will keep "souvenirs" of their crimes. When Ted Bundy was asked why he took Polaroids of his victims, he said, *"When you work hard to do something, you don't want to forget it."*[4]

- Very few serial killers turn themselves in. Only Ed Kemper called the police to confess. He waited at a telephone booth to be picked up.[2]

- Between 30%–38% of psychopaths show abnormal brainwave patterns, or EEGs.[4]

- Most psychiatrists note that psychopaths cannot be successfully treated.[2]

- Criminologists estimate that at least 86% of male serial killers are heterosexual. While numerically less, homosexual serial killers include some horrific monsters, such as John Wayne Gacy (1942-1994), Jeffrey Dahmer (1960-1994), William George Bonin (1968-1980)].[3]

- John E. Robinson is dubbed the *"first Internet serial killer."* After being released from prison in 1993 for running a prostitution ring, using the name "Slavemaster" he started to lure women in chat rooms to his home, where he murdered them.[6]

- The FBI's "Crime Classification Manual" places serial killers into three categories: organized, disorganized, and mixed (those who exhibit both organized and disorganized traits). Organized serial killers are often socially adequate, may have a wife or children, and plan their crimes methodically. Disorganized serial killers

176

are far more impulsive and have fewer friends.[6]

- Some historical notorious serial killers include the 15th-century nobleman Gilles de Rais who fought alongside Joan of Arc during the Hundred Years War. After she was executed, he lured young boys to his castle where he would torture, sexually assault, and kill them.[6]

- Nearly 70% of serial killers received extensive head injuries as children or adolescents. Some researchers believe that the prefrontal cortex (the area involved in planning and judgment) does not function properly in psychopaths.[4]

- In 20th-century America, the serial killer has come to embody a host of gnawing anxieties—anxieties about runaway crime, sexual violence, and breakdown of civil conduct.[3]

- Although it is impossible to predict if a child will grow up to be a serial killer, the three warning signs of future psychopathic behavior are 1) animal torture, 2) prolonged bed-wetting, and 3) juvenile pyromania. Criminologists call these symptoms "The Triad" [Kirschner and many other psychologists have recognized Adopted Child Syndrome][4]

- While many children wet the bed, this behavior may be a sign of a deeper pathology when it persists beyond the age of 12. Over 60% of serial killers were still wetting their beds as adolescents.[4]

- California has the highest number of serial homicide cases in the U.S. in the 20th century, at 16% of the national total.  This compilation attests to existence of highway serial killers, specifically, in very state

- The United States has the highest number of serial killers, with 76% of the world's total. And the majority are adopted[7] .Europe comes in a distant second with 17%.[2]

- England has produced 28% of Europe's serial killers, Germany 27%, and France 13%.[2]

- Most serial killers in the U.S. are Caucasian (84%); approximately 16% are African American. [2] Men constitute the overwhelming preponderance of serial killers, at over 90%.[2]

- While women make up just a very small percentage of serial killers, they constitute the majority of victims: 65%.[2]

- The first serial sex killer of the modern era was Jack the Ripper, who slaughtered five London streetwalkers.[2]

- It is rare for serial killers to prey on people from another race. Consequently, because most serial killers are white, so are most of their victims (89%).[4]

- In the United States, a great majority of serial killers are single, white males from

- lower to middle class backgrounds. However, there are also Hispanic, Asian, and African serial killers. But, according to the FBI, whites are not more likely than any other race to be serial killers based on percentages.[6]

- The motives of serial killers generally fall into four categories: 1) visionary (someone who feels compelled by entities such as God or the Devil to murder); 2) mission-oriented (to rid the world of homosexuals or prostitutes or to cure a societal ill); 3) hedonistic (someone who derives pleasure from killing); and 4) power- or control-hungry. The categories overlap considerably.[6]

- A historical survey of serial killers would have to begin at least as far back as the Roman emperor Caligula, who derived great pleasure in torture and murder.[2]

- The majority of serial killer arrests are by patrol officers doing their everyday duties and unrelated to the ongoing serial murder investigation. Larry Yeler was arrested during a traffic stop for a parking violation; Ted Bundy during a traffic stop for a stolen car.[4]

- Most serial killers are young: 44% started when they were in their 20s, 26% in their teens, and 24% in their 30s.[4]

- In almost 15% of serial murder cases, the victims are chosen entirely at random.[2]

- From an early age, many serial killers are intensely interested in voyeurism and fetishism and other paraphilia. Many start as peeping toms before moving onto the house breaking, rape, and murder.[4]

- In an effort to establish precise criminal classifications, the FBI distinguishes between serial killing and spree killing. A serial killer always experiences an emotional "cooling-off" period between his crimes, a hiatus that lasts anywhere from days to years. A "spree killer" in contrast, is someone who murders a string of people in several locations with no cooling off period.[3]

- Serial killers usually come from families that are dysfunctional and debilitating. They are rarely remembered by classmates because they did not have close friends. Often, they grow up lonely and isolated.[4]

- Without any social structure in his life, a serial killer is unable to have normal sexual relationships and is thus forced into solo sexual activities. In some cases, they turn to obsessive masturbation, as in the case of Soviet serial killer Andrei Chikatilo (1936–1994), who had scars on his genitals due to aggressive masturbation.[4]

- Unlike some people with significant mental disorders such as schizophrenia, psychopaths can seem normal and often charming, in a state of adaptation psychiatrists call "the mask of sanity."[4]

- Studies suggest that serial killers have an average or low-average IQ, but are

-  perceived as having above-average intelligence. Only serial bombers had an average IQ above the population mean.[5]

- While many serial killers have an average IQ, there are exceptions. Harold Shipman, a successful general practitioner working for the NHS was one of the world's most prolific serial killers with up to 250 murders being ascribed to him.[5]

- A board game called "Serial Killer" created controversy when it was put on the market. The winner of the game was the person who had the highest body count at the end of the game. The game came packaged in a plastic body bag.[6]

- The most prolific female serial killer in history is Elizabeth Bathory (1560–1614). After her husband's death, she and 4 accomplices were accused of torturing and killing as many as 600 girls and young women although convicted of 80.[2]

- Historians note that legends such as werewolves and vampires were inspired by medieval serial killers.[6]

- There are several subcultures that revolve around the hundreds of serial killers. This subculture includes the sale, collection, and display of serial killer memorabilia, which has been dubbed "murderabilia."[6]

- A Chicago band named Macabre has an entire catalogue of songs devoted to serial killers. The band calls their music "murder metal."[2]

- Many serial killers are fascinated by authority. They've attempted to become police officers or security guards or served in the military. Ted Bundy, the Hillside Stranglers, and John Gacy posed as police officers to gain access to their victims.[4]

- Because of their psychopathic nature, serial killers do not feel sympathy for others. They learn to *simulate* normal behavior by observing others, but it is a manipulative act. Henry Lee Lucas described being a serial killer as being "like a movie-star; you're playing a part." They covet being in the role of authority.[4]

-

Excerpted compilation by Karin Lehnardt for Factretrieve.com,12-30-16

**REFERENCES**
[1] Bryant, Clifton D. and Dennis L. Peck. *Encyclopedia of Death and the Human Experience*. Thousand Oaks, CA: Sage Publications, 2009. [2] Schechter, Harold and David Everitt. *The A to Z Encyclopedia of Serial Killers*. New York, NY: Pocket Books, 2006. [3] Schlesinger, Louis B. *Serial Offenders: Current Thought, Recent Findings*. Boca Raton, FL: CRC Press, 2000. [4] Scott, Shirley Lynn. "What Makes Serial Killers Tick?" *Crime Library*. 2014. Accessed: June 26, 2014. [5] "Serial Killer Information Center: Serial Killer I.Q." *Radford University*. Updated September 16, 2012. Accessed: June 26, 2014. [6] Stone, Michael H., M.D. *The Anatomy of Evil*. Amherst, NY: Prometheus Books, 2009. [7]"*Adopted Killers,*" Access Press.

# SERIAL KILLER MURDERABILIA

Buying and selling "murderabilia" is legal but It sensationalizes the horrific for purely selfish reasons. So is it moral? For some, that's a difficult question. Eight states have passed laws that prevent inmates from profiting from the sale of their mementos or "murderabilia" - Alabama, California, Florida, Michigan, Montana, New Jersey, Texas and Utah. Most of the inmates whose wares end up online sit on the nation's Death Rows, or are serving long sentences or Life Without Parole, so adding to their sentence for breaking the law on selling murderabilia is not a deterrent.

A Christmas card from Ted Bundy signed "God bless you, Peace, Ted," was listed on a Murderabilia website for $4,999.99 and a similar card for sale on another site was offered for $3,000. Charles Manson's locks of hair are often up for bid; one lock sold for $800. Manson's ID Card went for $850.

Although murderabilia is now discouraged by eBay, copies of the book, "*Helter Skelter,*" about the Manson Family murders, signed by the author, Vincent Bugliosi, are currently offered at $200 to $300, but as one such auction was about to end, the highest bid for one book was $20.

The Arts Factory, an art gallery in Las Vegas, displayed several paintings by John Wayne Gacy, a professional clown turned serial killer – paintings that he painted while on Death Row, which also included portraits of Elvis, Hitler and Charles Manson – offered for between $2,000 and $12,000 intending a percentage of the proceeds to be donated to the National Center for Victims of Crime; however the Center refused to accept the money. A competing Murderabilia website, "*Serial Killers Ink,*" offered Gacy's "Pogo the Clown" for $2,750 and his "Skull Clown" painting which sold for $1,100.

In 2011, in an online auction, Ted Kaczinski's, *Unibomber "Manifesto"* alone sold for $17,000, with the auction proceeds going to the Unibomber's victims. And within 5 years of the sentencing of Dennis Rader, the "*BTK Killer,*" who murdered 10 people in Kansas between 1974 and 1991, several of Rader's possessions were selling on several murderabilia sales and auction websites – including Rader's drawing, "*Factor X,*" the entity he believed "made him kill," and was listed for $3,000; or for $40, Rader fans could buy "a sample of dirt from one of his houses."

On January 1, 2014, Keith Jesperson *("The Happy Face Killer")* who produced over 1,500 drawings during his 16-year incarceration, told The Oregonian reporter, Bryan Denson, that some of the items on murderabilia sites are "knockoffs" with forged signatures, including lots of art that corrections officers and police investigators sometimes walk off with, to either market it or keep it until it's worth more.

"*MurderAuction.com*" is a website run central California man, William Harder, who has visited and occasionally established friendships with more than 70 incarcerated murderers and serial killers. Texas banned Harder from its prisons, while California found it disturbing that anyone should profit from someone else's murder and suspected he might be the outside contact alluded to by James Munro, convicted as an alleged accomplice to the *"Freeway Killer,"* William Bonin, when Munro, who is of low IQ, in an effort to elicit media attention told a prison psychologist that he planned to "continue what serial killer Bonin started." But California's CDC ultimately decided it had no grounds to ban Harder from visiting prisoners as Texas did. Harder stated *"This is a capitalist society. To tell me I can't sell something I collected is about as un-American as it gets."*

And the ACLU agreed that it is a "free speech" issue.

The Christmas card on the next page, received from serial killer Joseph Kondro, one of many cards and letters I received from killers whose stories I compiled, is an example of Murderabilia. Kondro wanted to disclose how and where he had disposed of his other, still-missing young female victims, but the plea deal he was offered in Washington state only applied to one disclosure in exchange for avoiding the Death Penalty in that case only; further admissions (of up to 70 victims he is suspected of making disappear) would each separately result in Death sentence. On his Christmas card, Kondro commented on a legislative bill I proposed to a Washington state legislator that could enable prosecutors to structure a plea deal that could avoid a Death sentence permanently if a serial killers' disclosures result in finding multiple named victims' remains as agreed, so the families could have closure. The proposed bill was never considered, and Kondro died in prison at age 52, taking those secrets to his grave.

–The Author

The perfect gift for everyone on your list...

I'm glad to here that your doing better. Thank you for your christmas greetings. I'm a little baffled about "Rima's Law". Are you or your Organization spear heading this endeavor? And if so, would you like some help from me to help get this passed? How can I help?

My brother has asked me several times about recieving pictures of our family members from me, but I only have my originals. I know you have copies in your files and would appreciate it if you would consider sending him those copies. The ones I would like for him to recieve are these: Pictures of: Grandmother Bertha, Mother Marie, Leo & pat Bowden. AND any of me as an adult.

Please stay in contact with ME about any issue's concerning "Rima's Law" and please send me any future updates on "Rima's Law" and my book for my Review. Question. Don't you think that KATA Rudd should be apart of a Legislative Bill also?

Brothers Address':
Clifford Durant
#08053-040
FCI- Fort Dix
POBOX 2000
Fort Dix, NJ.
08640

For God so loved the world that He gave His one and only Son, that whoever believes in Him shall not perish but have eternal life.
JOHN 3:16 NIV

Jesus.

May God's perfect gift
fulfill the desires of your heart—

on Christmas and always.

Forever gratefull
Joseph Kehn

---

## Christmas card from Highway Serial Killer, Joseph Kondro

Note: I choose NOT to sell any serial killer murderabilia out of respect for the victims and their families.
-The Author

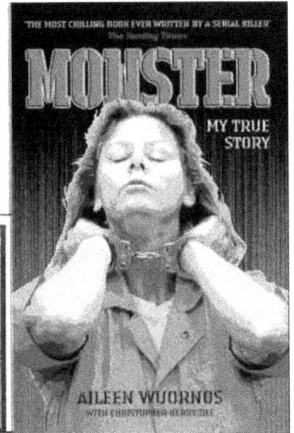

# Highway Serial Killers' Auctioned Murderabilia

Row 1: Lawrence Bittaker *("Toolbox Killer")* with William Bonin
*("Freeway Killer")*; Randy Kraft ("*The Scorecard Killer*"
posing at jail with paper gun); Zodiac Killer Wanted Poster;

Row 2: Ted Bundy ("*Co-Ed Killer*")Wanted Poster & Christmas card;
Aileen Wournos ("*Damsel of Death*") signed Biography

# BIBLIOGRAPHY

Addison, Brian, *"1970-1983: Randy Kraft, The Freeway Killer,"* Long Beach Post, 2-21-13

Bancroft, Stephanie, and Joshua Ayers, Emma Bennett, *"Dayle Wayne Eaton, The Lil Miss Killer,"* Department of Psychology, Radford University, 11-14-11

Blanco, Juan Ignacio, *"Patrick Kearney: The Trashbag Killer – The Freeway Killer,"* Murderpedia, Murderpedia.org

Borson, Mara, *"Two Killers Leave a Trail of Bodies Along Interstate 5 in the 1980s,"* New York Daily News, 3-23-14

Bott, Michael, *"Murderabilia Collector Defends Hobby, Website, in Spite of Criticism by Victims' Families,"* KXTV, 4-3-15

Bovsun, Mara, *"Murder Down the Freeway;"* *"The Justice Story,"* NY Daily News, 3-25-08; and *"Hitchhiker Kept as Sex Slave for Seven Years as 'Girl in Box Under Captors' Bed,"* NY Daily News, 3-9-14

California Department of Corrections and Rehabilitation, Research on William George Bonin and James Michael Munro

Carangelo, Lori, *"Kondro: The Untold Story of the Longview Serial Killer,"* Access Press, 2014

Clark County Prosecutor, *"Aileen Carol Wuornos,"* clarkprosecutor.org

Dalmas, Robin, *"What Killed Hitchhiking?"* NBCNews.com, 2013

Darby, Tom, *"The Mystery of Pumpernickel Valley Exit,"* TomDarby.Net, 3-5-13

Denson, Bryan, *"'Happy Face Killer' Keith Jesperson Shares Thoughts on Halting Online Trade of Murder Momentos,"* OregonLive, 1-29-14

Dolan, Lynn, and Jonathan Abrams, *"The Highway That Crime Cruises,"* Los Angeles Times, 2-27-06

Dubois, Steven, *"Oregon Trucker Who Killed Women Now Free in McMinnville,"* Yambill Valley NewsRegister.com, 2-8-13

Farmer, Frances, *"Frances Farmer's Revenge: Munro"*

Farrell, Paul, *"Ali Syed Named As California Freeway Shooter,"* Heavy.com, 2-19-13

Glover, Scott, *"FBI Makes a Connection Between Long-Haul Truckers, Serial Killings,"* Los Angeles Times, 4-5-09

Graysmith, Robert, *"Zodiac"*

Grollmus, Denise, *"'Happy Face Killer' Keith Hunter Jesperson Racks Up More Victims,"* True Crime Report, truecrimereport.com, 12-22-09

Hannaford, Alex, *"Highway Injustice,"* Texas Observor, 11-7-12

Hicks, Jerry, *"Bonin Accomplice Wants Freedom or Death, Not the Truth,"* Los Angeles Times, 6-18-98

Hunter, Michelle, *"No Ties Surface Between 2 Female Victims Found Dead on I-10 Overpasses,"* The Times-Picayune, 6-10-15

Jensen, Thom, *"Is There a Serial Killer on the Oregon Coast?"* KATU News, Katu.com, 3-16-09, updated 10-29-13

Johnson, Sheila, *"Blood Highway,"* Pinnacle, 2008

Keller, Robert, *"Bundy: Portrait of a Serial Killer"*

Kirschner, David, Phd, *"Son of Sam and the Adopted Child Syndrome,"* Adelphi Society for Psychonalysis and Psychotherapy Newsletter, June 1978;

Lang, Louise, *"Dark Son,"* Avon, 1995

Lohr, David, *"Mississippi Highway Killer May Be Dressed Like Police Officer,"* Huffington Post, 5-17-12

Mejdrich, Kellie, *"Aliso Viejo Man Worries About Possible Parole of 'Freeway Killer,'"* Orange County Register, 1-23-14

Morrison, Blake, *"Along Highway, Signs of Serial Killings,"* USA Today, 10-5-10

Munro, James Michael *("Freeway Killer"),* Letters from Prison (5-13-09 to 12-19-09), and online interviews and writings)

Murphy, Mary, *"From Gilgo Beach to Atlantic City: A Serial Killer by the Sea,"* New York PIX11, 3-17-13

Nelson, Joe, and Wes Woods, *"High Desert Known for Body Dumping,"* The Sun, and Inland Valley Daily Bulletin, 11-13-13

Newsweek Staff, *"Killers on the Road: The FBI's Highway Map,"* Newsweek, 4-17-11

O'Brien, Darcy, *"The Hillside Stranglers"*

Ramsey, Nancy, *"Portraits of a Social Outcast Turned Serial Killer..."* New York Times, 12-30-03

Reston, Maeve, *"Jury Convicts Man of 4 Serial Killings,"* Los Angeles Times, 6-28-06

Rocha, Veronica, *"Death of Two Men Found... on Area Freeways Investigated,"* Los Angeles Times, 10-23-14

Rosewood, Jack, *"The Toolbox Killers"*

Rule, Ann, *"Green River Running Red: The Real Story of the Green River Killer,"* 2005

Strand, Ginger, *"Killer on thr Road: Volence and the American Interstate,"* Uiversity of Texas Press, 2014

Wilson-Buterbaugh, Karen, *"The Baby Scoop Era,"* 2017

Welborn, Larry, *"The Killer Kept His Victims' Bodies in Refrigerator,"* The Orange County Register, 7-8-11

Wuornos, Aileem, *"Monster: My True Story,"* John Blake, 2004

# HIGHWAY KILLERS INDEX

*44-Caliber Killer, The,* 121

*Alaska Highway Killer, The,* 19-20

Alcala, Rodney James, 171-172

Anderson, Robert Leroy, 6,138-139

*Asheboro Highway Killer,* 140-141

Baker Stanley Dean, 43,107-108

*Baby Faced Killer, The,* 125

*Barefoot Cowboy,* 132,159

Barrow, Clyde Chestnut, 143-145

*Baseline Killer, The,* 23

*Baton Rouge Killer, The,* 89

*Bayou Killer, The,* 89

Beaumeister, Herbert Richard, 6,83

*Beauty Queen Killer,* 44,70,114,131

*Beltway Snipers, The,* 167

Berkowitz, David, 6,121-122

Bianchi, Kenneth Alessio, 6,29-30

Bierbodt, Lonnie, 79

Biggs, Benjamin "Ben," 85

Bissell, Hayward, 6,13

Bittaker, Lawrence Sigmund, 6,30-31

*Black Canyon Freeway Killer,* 24

Boutain, Austin, 153

Boutain, Kathleen, 153

*Blue Gremlin Killer, The,* 98

*Bluegrass Parkway Disappearances,* 88

Bolin, Oscar Ray, 65

Bonin Jr., William George, 6,31-33

*Bonnie and Clyde,* 11,143-145

Boyer, John Wayne, 139

Boyette Jr., William "Billy," 6,13

*Bra Murders, The,* 57-58

Braae, Michael, 77,132,159

Bridges, John, 126

*Broomstick Killer, The,* 146-147

Brown Debra, 87

Bunday, Thomas Richard, 19

Bundy, Theodore "Ted," 2,6,33,51,65,77,
132,153,160-163,176,178-179,
181,184-184

Buono, Angelo, 6,29-30,33

*Butcher, The,* 129,169

*Butcher Baker, The,* 19

*Butcher, The Co-Ed,* 37,109

Butts, Vernon Robert, 31-33

*California's "Bonnie and Clyde
Spree Killers,"* 41-44,87

*Camino La Tierra Strangler* 119

*Campus Killer, The,* 132,160-163

*Candy Man, The,* 145

*Canyon Lake Highway Killer,* 152

Carignan, Harvey Louis, 99-100

Carr III, Robert Frederick, 55,65,89,103

*Casanova Killer, The,* 15,67,75,114,128,145,
157

Christopher, Leonard, 133

Clark, Michael Andrew, 33

*Co-Ed Butcher, The,* 37,109

*Co-ed Killer, The,* 2,33,51,97,132,160-163

Coffman, Cynthia, 41

Coleman, Alton, 87

Collins, John Norman, 97

*Colonial Parkway Murders,* 157

Colvin, Dellmus, 127-128

Conde, Rory Enrique, 65

*Confession Killer,* 145,153

*Connecticut River Valley Killer, The,*
115-116

Cook, William Edward "Bill," 115-116

Corll, Dean Arnold, 6,145

*Cowboy Mike,* 132,159

Cox, Scott William, 132

*Craigslist Ripper, The,* 122

*Cross County Killer,* 21,82,88,92,96,105,
122,149,159

Cumberland, Rachel, 103-104

Cruz, Akeem, 92,128,133

Cruz Jr, James Robert, 128,133

*Damsel of Death, The,* 72

Daughtrey Jr., Earl, 14,74-75

*Dating Game Killer, The,* 171-172

*Daytona Beach Trucker Killer,* 73

Delage, Richard Tobias, 55

*Desert Killer, The,* 150

Dieteman, Samuel John, 24

Dominique, Ronald, 87

*Dora Doe Killer,* 28

*Double Knot Strangler* 74-75
Dryman, Frank, 108-109
Duncan III, Joseph Edward, 6,33,77-78
Eaton, Dale Wayne, 173-173
Edwards, Mack Ray, 9,33-34
*Escort Killer, The,* 169
Escotta, Ramon, 135
Evans, Donald Leroy, 66,89,103
Evans, Robert "Bob," 115
Eyler, Larry, 79-81,84,87,170
Falls, Neal, 169
Famalaro, John Joseph, 34-35
*Federal Highway Killer, The,* 73
*Flat Tire Killer, The,* 34-35
Ford, Wayne Adam, 6,35
Fort Lauderdale Kiiler, 73
Frankford Slaser, The, 134
Free, Lewis Lamar, 14
*Freeway Killer, The,* 33-34,38
*Freeway Killers, The,* 31-33
*Freeway Phantom, 167*
Fry, Robert, 119
Fugate, Caril Ann, 112
Gallego, Charlene Adele, 6,113
Gallego, Gerald Armond, 6,113
Garden State Parkway Killer, 116
Gaskins, Donald "Peewee," 6,137
*Geneva County Massacre,* 17
*Gilgo Beach Serial Killer, 122*
Goble, Sean Patrick, 139-140
Gore, David Allen, 66-67
Goudeau, Mark, 23
*Green River Killer, The,* 165-166
Greenawalt, Gary, 23-24,26
Groves, Vincent Darrell, 51
Hansen, Robert Christian, 19-20
*Happy Face Killer, The,* 36,67,111.132,164,
        174
*Harv The Hammer,* 99
*Haunted Highway 365 Killer, 28*
Hausner, Dale Shaun, 6,,24
Hernandez, Alexander, 35
*Highway 2 Killer, The,* 126
*Highway 3 Rest Stop Killer,* 81, 105-106,122
*Highway 10 Killer, The,* 15
*Highway 18 Killer, The,* 28
*Highway 21 Murders The,* 15

*Highway 21 Sniper, The,* 14
*Highway 34 Killer, The,* 85
*Highway 41 Strangler,* 65
*Highway 52 Shooter, The,* 17
*Highway 54 Killer, The,* 150
*Highway 78 Jane Doe, The,* 170
*Highway 80 Killer, The,* 15,75
*Highway 84 Shooter, The,* 17
*Highway 101 Killer, The,* 132
*Highway 101 Murders,* 47-48
*Highway 101 Sniper,* 33
*Highway 18 Killer, The,* 120
*Highway 231 Killer, The,* 18
*Highway 285 Killer, The,* 52
*Highway 314 Killer,The,* 138
*Highway Killer, The* 65
*Highway Stalker, The,* 145
*Highway Strangler, The,* 41,155
*Hillside Stranglers,The,* 29-33,179,186
*Hitchhiker Killer, The,* 41-43,55,89,103
*Hitchhiker Murders,* 68-69,130
*Hitchhiking Carjack Killer,* 95
*Honolulu Strangler,* 76,155
*Hoosier Highway Killer, The,* 79
*Houtson Mass Murders, The,* 145
Howell, William David, 56-57
Hulse, Arthur "Moose," 43
Hurd, Steven, 43,107-108
*I-2 Killer, The,* 46
*I-4 Killer, The,* 128
*I-5 Stranglers, The,* 36-37,45
*I-10 Spree Killers,* 13
*I-10 Killer, The,* 33,37
*I-10 Louisiana Killer, The,* 91
*I-10 Phoenix Sniper,* 24
*I-15 Freeway Killer, The,* 45,170
*1-17 Black Canyon Killer,* 24
*I-20/25 Killer, The,* 173-174
*I-25 Serial Shooter, The,* 52
*I-30 Dallas-Ft Worth Killer,* 152
*I-35 Priest Murders, The,* 109
*I-35/40 Truck Stop Strangler,* 131
*I-40 Rest Stop Killer,* 26
*I-40 Trucker Killer, The,* 23-24
*I-40 Valentine Sally Truck Stop Murder,* 25
*I-45 Killer, The,* 149
*I-45 Killers, The,* 149

I-65 Serial Killer, The, 88
I-70 Carjacking Killer Couple, 153
I-70 Kansas Killer, The, 86
I-70 Missouri Killer, 106
I-70 Multi-State Killer, The, 86
I-70/US-6 Colorado Serial Killer, The, 52-54
1-71 Killer, The, 128
I-75 Child Killer, The, 98
I-80 Killer, The, 79,85
I-80 Pumpernickel Valley Offramp
        Disappearances, The, 114
I-80 Utah Suitcase Killer, 154
I-84 Killer, The, 159
I-84 Vernon Murders, The, 59
I-89 Killer, The, 116
I-91 Connecticut Killer, 60
I-94 Bad Route Rest Stop Murder, The,
        109-110
I-94 Killer, The, 126
I-94 Lora Jean Murder, The, 110
I-95 Connecticut Killer, The, 60
I-95 Georgia Killer, The, 75
I-95 Killer, The (New Hampshire), 116
I-95 Providence Shooters, 135
I-117 Murders, The, 13
I-210 Spree Shooter, The, 35
I-295 Murders, The, 92,111
I-713/I-55 Killer, The, 104
I-182 Killer, The, 89
Interstate Killer, The, 79,84,87,170
Interstate Strangler, The, 83
Jesperson, Keith Hunter, 6,36,67,111,132,
        164,174
Jones Jr, Timothy Ray, 15,137
Joubert IV, John Joseph, 6,92,111
Kane, Lawrence, 48
Kearney, Patrick Wayne, 6,36-37
Kemper III, Edmund Emil, 8,37,109,176
Keyes, Israel, 6,21,92,155
Kibbe, Roger Reece, 36,45
Kidnap-Rapist Killer, The, 156
Killing Cousins, The, 66
Knowles, Paul John, 6,15,67-68,75,114,
        128,145,157,182-183,185
Kondro, Joseph, 132,164-165
Kraft, Randy Steven, 6,38-40,98
Krajcir, Timothy Wayne, 81-82,105,133

Lady Killer, The, 132,160-163
Lane, Adam Leroy, 117,133
Lake Elsinore Killer, The, 43
Last Call Killer, The, 117
Lawson, Carl Wayne, 131
Lee, Deandra Marquis, 15
Lee, Derrick Todd, 89-90
Lewis, Gerald Patrick, 15-16,75
Li'l Miss Murder, The, 173-174
Long-Haul Killer,The, 35,128,139
 Long-Haul Strangler, 127-128
Long-Haul Trucker Killer, 148
Long Island Ripper, 122-123
Long Island Serial Killer, 92
Longview Serial Killer, 123,132,164-165
Los Angeles 101 Freeway Killer, 47
Lovers' Lane Murders, The, 121
Lucas, Henry Lee, 6,8,51,145-146,154,
        179,
Lupinacci, Robert, 57-58
Luther, Thomas Edward, 51-52
Malvo, Lee Boyd, 167
Marlow, James Gregory, 41,87
Maryland Truck Stop Unknown
        Child Killer, The, 94
Matthew Jr, Jesse Leroy, 6,157
Mayrand Jr., Edward H., 95,115,135
McDuff, Kenneth Allen, 146-147
McLendon, Michael Kenneth, 6,17
Mendenhall, Bruce, 6,75,87,141-142
Merritt, Leslie Allen, 24
Merritt Parkway Killer, 57-58
Michigan Murders, The, 97
Miley, Gregory Matthew, 32
Miller, Brian Patrick, 24,57-58
Montana Highway Child Killer, 110
Morrison, David Allen, 41,155
Mothers and Daughters Killer, 94
Muhammad, John Allen, 167
Mullin, Herbert William, 41-43
Murder-Mobile Killer, The, 56
Nebraska Boy Snatcher, 92
Nebraska's Bonnie and Clyde, 112
Nemechek, Francis Donald, 86
New Bedford Murders, 96
Norris, Ray Lewis, 6,30-31
Oakland County Child Killer, 98
Ocean Parkway Killer, The, 122

Orange Socks Killer, The, 51,145,153
Oregon Coastal Killer, The, 132
Ortega Highway Killer, 38
Otero, Raul, 135
Parker, Bonnie Elizabeth, 143-145
Pennell, Steve Brian, 63-64
Prosti Killer, The, 142
Prostitute Murders, The, 51
Pugh, William "Billy" Ray, 32
Rasmussen, Terry Pederson, 115
Redhead Murders, The, 26-27,88,134,142
Redneck Charles Manson, 137
Reece, William Lewis, 145
Rees, Melvin Davis, 6,93
Rembert Jr., Robert "Bobby," 128
Rest Stop Killer, The, 66,89,103,142
Rhoades, Robert Ben, 148-149
Rice, Mary Craig, 6,13-14
Richardson Highway Killer, 19
Ridgway, Gary Leon, 6,165-166
Rifkin, Joel, 6,122-123
Riverside Prostitute Killer, 43,149
Roadside Strangler, The, 58
Rogers Jr., Richard W., 117
Ross, Michael Bruce, 6,58-59 44
Route 2 Killer, The, 61
Route 2 Tanana Spree Killer, 21-22
Route 3 Killer, The, 136
Route 8 & New Bedford Murders, 61
Route 10 Strangler, The, 95,115,135
Route 16 Killer, The, 61
Route 26 Killer, 120
Route 40 Corridor Murders, 63
Route 55 Shooter, The, 44
Route 68 Killer, The, 120
Route 78 Killer, The, 117,133
Route 99 Killer, The, 165-166
Route 112/Valley Killer, The 116,156
Route 244 Shooter, The, 62
Sampson, Gary Lee, 95
San Juan Highway Killer, 119
Santa Rosa Hitchhiker Murders, 47-48
Sasser, Christopher Bruce, 17
Schaefer, Gary Lee, 68-69,156
Schaefer, Gerard John, 6,68-69
Scorecard Killer, The, 38
Scott, Jason Thomas, 94

Seashore Serial Killer, The, 122
Sells, Tommy Lynn, 6,82,88,95,105-106, 122,149
Serial Confessor, The, 69
Serial Shooters, The, 24
Seward Highway Killer, The, 22
Sex Beast, The, 93
Sex Slaves Killers, The, 113
Sick Ripper, The, 56
Silka, Michael Allen, 21-22
Small Town Stalker Murders, The, 125
Smith, Kevin Edison, 149
Son of Sam, 121-122
Sons of Satan Killers, 43
Stallings, Mark Roland, 149-150
Stano, Gerald Eugene, 60
Starkweather, Charles Raymond, 112
Stephani, Paul Michael, 101
Stroup, Harry, 43
Suff, William Lester, 6, 43,149
Sullivan, Ross, 48
Surratt, Edward, 128
Sweetheart Murders, 50
Syed, Ali, 44
Taconic Parkway Killer, The, 56
Tamiani Trail Strangler, 65
Texas I-45 Killing Fields, 151-152
Tire Popper Killers, The, 138
Tison, Gary Gene, 23-24,26
Toolbox Killers, The, 30-31,186
Toole, Otis Elwood, 51,145-146
Trash Bag Murders, The, 36
Truck Stop Killer, The, 27,75,84,87,128,131
Truck Stop Prostitutes Killer, 132
Truck Stop Serial Killer, The, 142
Twilite Killer, The, 15-16,75
"Uncle Joe" Killer, The, 164-165
US-13/Route 40 Corridor Killer, The, 63-64
US 29 Hitchhiker Killer, The, 157
Valfeades, Timothy Jay, 101-102,154
Valley Killer, The, 156
Vampire Trucker, The, 101-102,154
Vanner, Lawrence, 115
Velez, Jovani, 135
Walker, Glenn, 138-139
Want Ad Killer, The, 99
Ward, Ronald James, 126

Warren, Lesley Eugene, 25
Waterfield, Fred, 66
*Weepy Voice Killer, The*, 101
*West Side Serial Killer, The*, 76
Wickline, William Dean, 129,169
Wilder, Christopher, 44,70-71,115,131,150
Williams, John Robert, 84,103-104
Willie, James D., 84,103-104
Wilson, Waldorf "Wally," 104
*Wisconsin Suitcase Murders*, 170
Wood, David Leonard, 150-151

Woodfield, Randall Brent, 6,36,44-45,132
Wuornos, Aileen Carol Pitman, 6,8,72,
    184-186
*Yellowstone Killers, The*, 43
*Ypsilanti Ripper, The*, 97
Zamastil, William Floyd, 25,45,170
Zarinsky, Robert, 118
Zelich, Steven, 170
*Zodiac Killer, The*, 48-50

abandon(ed), abandonment,
    -by father, 81,121,130,146
    -by mother, 58,72,80
    -by parents, 121
addiction, 30,108,202
    (see also substance abuse)
accepted police practice, 54
adopt, adopted, adoptee, adoption,
    29-31,33,69,72,81-82,96,121-123,
    160,164,176-177,179,185,200-201
    -informally adopted, 29,32
    -"unadoptable," 69
Adopted Child Syndrome, 121,123,177,
    185 (see also "triad of
    behavior")
*"Adopted kids like me seek out rejection..."*
    69
Aggravated Assault (see Assault)
Agravated Battery (see Assault)
Aggravated Kidnapping, 174
Aggravated Robbery, 174
Aggravated Sexual Assault,
    (see Assault)
Aggravated Murder (see Murder)
Alford Plea, 157
"America's Most Wanted," 8,146-147
animalistic level (of functioning, 69
arson (see fire, fire-setting)
Assault,
    -Aggravated Assault, 13,24,68,
       74,150,159
    -Aggravated Assault with
       Intent to Kill, 74
    -Aggravated Battery, 80,126
    -Aggravated Sexual Assault,
       148
    -Malicious Wounding, 106
    -Simple Assault, 74
Baby Scoop era
    (see Sixties Sweep)
Banks, Tyria, 72
beating, beaten, (victim), 22,26,42,60,
    80,89-91,97,109,110,118,128,152,
    173
    -by mother, 37,44
    -by parents, 175

    -by stepfather(s), 80
    -bludgeoned, 34,60,63,85,99,
       114,161-163
    -pistol whipped, 153

    -with blunt object, 64,85,173
    -with hammer, 57,63-64,99-100,
       117,137
    -claw hammer, 99
    -pick hammer, 38
    -sledgehammer, 3,119,169
    -with hatchet, 107,126
    -with shovel, 119
    -with steel bar, 171
bite marks, 38,92
body(-ies),
    -buried, 24,55,57,68,96,113,
       161-163
       -along highway, 33,
          107,169
       -on killer's property,
          in backyard,
          83,173
    -burned, 17,39,91,97,120
    -cannibalize(d), 38,68,92,107-
       108,137,146
    -car/vehicle, 98
    -dismembered, 13,35,38,40,66,
       79,80,95,107,122,129,
       161,169
    -in desert, 150
    -in dumpster, 73,79,88,129
    -in field, 149,151-152
    -in freezer, 35
    -in refrigerator, 27,186
    -in shallow grave, 15,23,114
    -in suitcase, 154,170
    -in trunk of car, 18,58,87,125,
       146
    -in water or drowned, 35,90-91,
       101,159
    -severed body; cut in half,
    -severed breast, nipples, 46,
       135,64

-severed finger(s), 97,108
  -severed head, decapitated, 37,
    39,123,129,146
  -unburied, 171
  -under freeway, 10
bully, bullied, bullying, tease(d),
  teasing, 19,37,64,92,112,130,164
Calder  Road Killing Fields, -Oil
  Field, -property, 149-151
cannibal(-ism,-ized,-izing), 38,6,92,107-
  108,137,146
CALTRANS,  10,33,38
Carjack (-ed,-er,-ing), 13-14,44,94-95,
  115,153
CARMEL (see code breaker)
castrate(d), castration, 38-39
child molester (see sex crimes:
  molestation)
code breaker, 50
  -CARMEL, 50
  -super computer, 50
crime statistics, 198
Death Penalty, 20,35-36,38,41,64,80-
81,92,96,108,112,119,128,147,149,165,182
  (see also executed, execution)
decapitated (see body,-ies: severed
  head, decapitated)
Depression, 143,160,173,176
  - Depressive Disorder, 105
  -Thought Disorder, 173
dismembered (see body,-ies:
  dismembered)
DNA, 28,37,46,50,53-54,64,66,76,79,88-89,
  95,110,114,116,127,132-34,139,
  141,155,166,170,172-173
  -Touch DNA," 50
drugs (see substance abuse)
dump(-ed,-ing), dump site,
  (see bodies)
Eastham Prison Breakout of 1934, 144
Edwards, Edward Wayne, (see
  Zodiac Killer suspects)
electroshock therapy, 70
execute(d), execution, 23-24,33,59,64-65
  67,69,72-73,87,90,92,109,112,114
  129-130,147-148,162-163,166-

167,177
  -brain blister, 92
  -by electric chair, 92,112
  -by gas chamber, 130
  -by hanging, 108
  -by lethal injection, 29,35,59,65,
    67,72,87,106,129,147,
    167
"execution style," 73,128
exposed, flashing, Public Indecency
  (see sex crimes)
expunged, 161
FBI, 1-=11,21,41,46,49,52,73-74,79,87,
  96,130,149,151,175-176,178,185-
  186,199
  -Behavioral Unit, 10
  -Crime Classification Manual,
    176
  -Highway Murders Map, 10-11
  -Highway Serial Killings
    Initiative, 10
fingerprint(s), 25,53,114,117,147
  -handprint(s), 50
  -palm print, 49
fire-setting, 16
  -arson, arsonist, 21,24,111,146
  -car fire, 109
foul play, 59,119-120
gene(s), 67
Goleta, California, 34
Green Vega Rapists, 168
Guilty But Insane, 13
gun(s),
  -handgun, 68,104,141,153,169
  -pistol, 46,56,94,106,109,130,
    146,153
    -pistol whipped, 153
  -machine gun, 94,143
  -semi-automatic, 135,148
  -shotgun, 23,74,98,103,128
  -silencer, 94
  -rifle, 13,17,22,42,68,146,153
    -automatic rifle, 144
Highway Murders Map, FBI, 10-11
Highway Serial Killings Initiative,  10
History Channel, 50,122

Hitchhiker Vanishing, 28
homosexual(s), 7,31,41,80,89,176,178
        -gay(s), 36,39,79-81,83,117,157
        -lesbian(-ism), 72
hostage, hostage taking, 67-68
hunting humans, "*Hunting Humans,*"
        41,100,116,134
"*I kill because I can,*" 127
illegitimate, 30
        (see also out of wedlock),
impersonating a law enforcement
        officer, 28
        -fake police badges, 29
Innocent by Reason of Mental
        Defect or Insanity, 14
Investigation Discovery (ID) TV, 83,201
Jewell, 8
Joplin, Janis, 8
jurisdictional issue, 54
Kane, Lawrence (see Zodiac
        Killer suspects)
kidnap(-ped,-er), kidnapping, 13,20,30,
        32,34,37,41,46,52,54-56,65,73,76,
        78,87,89,92,89,101,103-104,113,
        125-126,128,130,138,147,150,
        152-153,155-157,168,174
"killing kit(s)," 21
"LA Murder Cop, The," 50
LaBarbera, Sal, 50
Lethal Injection (see executed)
London, Sandra, 68
long-haul (see trucker)
"lovers' lane(s)," 49,121
"*Lovers Lane Murders,*" 121
"Ma" Ferguson, 144
Mains, Kenneth, 50
Manslaughter, 104,108,117,126,128
        -Voluntary Manslaughter, 126,
        128
McCartney, Paul, 8
McVicker, David, 32-33
Mentally Disordered, 32
Miller, Benjamin Franklin, 57-58
molested (see sex crimes)
"*Most Dangerous Animal of
        All,*" 50
"Most Likely To Succeed," 41

Murder (see also Manslaughter),
        -Aggravated Murder, 128,166
        -Attempted Murder(s), 17,35,
          52,116,137-138,155
        -Murder for Hire, 142
        -Second Degree Murder, 42,
          123, 139,145,156
murderabilia, serial killer, 179,181-185
"murder mobile,"
        -William Bonin's, 32
        -William Howell's, 56-57
mutilation, 63,99
necrophilia, (see sex crime(s))
"Night Terrors," 137
"No Contest," 38,68,146
obsession with his mother, 81
"orders from God," 99
Passive Aggressive Disorder, 29
parentage, lying about, 160
pathological urges, 161
person of interest, 13,45,76,85,131
plea, pleading, plea agreement,
        plea bargain, plea deal, 26,31,
        36,38,46,57,64,66,70,72,80-81,
        85,101,108,113,123-124,128,137,
        147,156-157,162,165-166,174,182
poison (-ing), 29,48
        -carbon monoxide, 29
        -strychnine, 48
posed (body), 43,52-53,171,179
Pralle, Arlene, 72
presumed dead, 64
presumed murdered, 120
profile(s),
        -criminal,
18,41,59,61,80,110,168,173
        -DNA, 173
profiler, 41
prostitute(s), 7,16,20-21,27,29,35,37,43,
        51,53,57-58,61,63-66,69,73,80,89
        96,103,111,113,117,122-123,125,
        127,129,131-133,140-41,147,149,
        151,165-166,168-170,178,190
prostitution, 27,68,72,90-91,124,176
psychopath(s), -ic, 70,176-179
        (see also sociopath(s))
        -Borderline Personality

Disorder, 105
-Borderline Psychotic, 30
-Hysterical Neurotic, 74
-Classic Psychotic, 30
-Manic Depressive, 32
-Paranoid delusions, 42
-Paranoid Personality, 103
-Psychosis, 146
-Psychotic,
-Schizoid, 105
-Schizophrenia, 41,83,178
-Sophisticated Psychotic, 30
-Successful Psychopath, 70
Psychopathy, 171
Public Indecency, -exposed, flashing,
        (see Sex Crimes)
rage,
        -against bullies, 112
        -against individuals, 29,105
        -against society, 99,202
        -against women,  61,96,97
random killings,  7,13,17,24,35,41,44,49,
        55,62,89,106,121,133,137,153,
        178
Rather, Dan, 8
Reagan, Ronald,  7
rejection,  42,67,69,121
resentment,
        -toward mother, 160
Ressler, Robert (FBI profiler), 41-42,175
Richards, Keith, 88
"ride-alongs," 29
Rolling Stones, 88
Rule, Ann, 186
runaway,  25,31,39,52,67,69,113,148,165,
        178
Santa Barbara, California, 8-9,34,201
satanic cult, cultists, 43,107-108,121,190
        -"devil cult," 151
Sav-A-Lot Thrift Stores,
Schizophrenia, schizophrenic,
        (see Psychopathy)
Serial Killers Law and
        definition,
sex crime(s),
        -castration,
        -drugged and raped,

-foreign object,
-gang rape(d),
-genital mutilation,
-molestation, molested, child,
        34,59,72,78,113,148,164
        -165
-necrophilia, 38,68,146
-Public Indecency, flashing,
        exposing, 39,86,45
-sexually motivated,
-sodomized,
        -anal sex, 87
sexual abuse,
"signature" (killer's),
"Sixties Sweep" /"Baby Scoop" era,
skeletal remains,
sniper,
Sociopath,

(see also Psychopath)
spree(s) (shooting, killing, murder),
stalk(-ed), stalker, stalking,
standoff,
statistics, crime,
Substance Abuse Disorder,
suffocated, suffocation,
Sullivan, Ross (see Zodiac
        suspects)
suicide,
        -attempted/failed,
        -by hanging,
        -by injecting air,
        -by shooting, 18,41,112
        -by slashing, 15
        -"suicide by cop," 230
        -vehicular, 21
super computer (see code breaker)
"Sweetheart Murders," 50
terrorism, domestic, 24
torture, (-ed, torture-slayings), 16,30-31,
        39,47-48,55,63-64,66,68-0,77,93,
        97,101,137,145,148,175,177-178
        -burned, 39
        -castrated, 39
        -"map of torture," 39
        -speculum, 161
        -toolbox tools, 30

Touch DNA (see DNA)

transvestite, 91

"triad of behavior," 16  (see also
      Adopted Child Syndrome)

truck driver, trucker(s), 8,10,23,2,31-32,
      65,73,79,85,88,94,101,109,111,
      114,125,131,133,139-140,154,
      185-186
      -long-haul, 27,35,73,103-104,
          127-28,132,139,141,148-
          149

Trump, President Donald,  199

"unadoptable," (see adopt)

unremorseful, 96

"Unsolved Mysteries,"
62,86,106,110,120,138

Van Best Jr., Earl (see Zodiac Killer
      suspects)

"vanishing hitchhiker,"
      (see hitchhiking)

VICAP (Violent Crimes Apprehension
Program), 10
        -dash cam, 114
        -video surveillance, 110

*"wanted to kill someone just to*
      *see what it felt like,"*126

Walsh, Adam, 146

Walsh, John, 22

"woman hater," 168

Zodiac Killer suspects,
        -Edwards, Ed, 50
        -Kane, Lawrence, 50
        -Sullivan, Ross, 50
        -Van Best Jr., Earl, 50

# RESOURCES

## MISSING U.S. CRIME STATISTICS UNDER TRUMP

"Every year, the FBI releases a report that is considered the gold standard for tracking crime statistics in the United States: the *"Crime in the United States"* report, a collection of crime statistics gathered from over 18,000 law-enforcement agencies in cities around the country. But the first report released under President Trump's administration contains close to **70% fewer data tables** than the 2015 version did, a removal that could affect analysts' understanding of crime trends in the country. The removal comes after consecutive years in which violent crime rose nationally, and it limits access to high-quality crime data that could help inform solutions. Published under the auspices of the Uniform Crime Reporting Program, UCR's report contains national data on homicides, violent crimes, arrests, clearances and police employment collected since the 1960s. UCR's report has been a rich reference database for journalists and members of the general public who are interested in official crime statistics. Among the data missing from the 2016 report is information on arrests, the circumstances of homicides (such as the relationships between victims and perpetrators), *and the only national estimate of annual **gang** murders.* The fact that the FBI Office of Public Affairs determined which data tables to remove harkens back to patterns of suppression from the George W. Bush administration. Changes to the report typically go through a body called **the Advisory Policy Board (APB),** which is responsible for managing and reviewing operational issues for a number of FBI programs. **This time they did not.** At the beginning of his presidency, [Trump] established a Victims of Immigration Crime Engagement Office, to promote **awareness of crimes** *committed by immigrants* **who entered the country illegally...** Removal of the tables makes it more difficult to get information to support or refute one of the White House's most prominent causes."

--Source: excerpted from *"First FBI Crime Report Issued Under Trump Is Missing a Ton of Info,"* Clare Malone and Jeff Asher, FiveThirtyEight.com. 10-27-17.

## ABOUT THE AUTHOR

Lori Carangelo is no stranger to the criminal world. As an investigator, interviewer and biographer to killers, she compiled their stories, not solely to entertain, but also to ferret out clues to answer often asked questions such as *"why"* they did it, *"how"* a "normal" child grew to become a "monster," and *"where"* the bodies are hidden.

Retired from 25 years administrative positions in Santa Barbara and Palm Desert, California, Lori has authored over 600 published articles and more over 25 non-fiction adoption-themed and true crime books that give a voice to both the victims and their killers to help prevent creating and enabling more monsters.

More Books Lori Carangelo

SCHOOL SHOOTERS
*Why They Did It and America's War on Guns*

KILLERS ONLINE
*100 True Stories*

ADOPTED KILLERS
*430 Adoptees Who Killed – How and Why They Dd It*

KONDRO
*The "Uncle Joe" Killer*

BLOOD RELATIVES
*A True Story of Family Secrets and Murders*

JAMES MUNRO
*And the Freeway Killers*

EYEWITNESS
*The Case of the Carefully Crafted Central Coast Rapist*

RAGE!
*How An Adoption Ignited a Fire*

CHOSEN CHILDREN
*Children as Commodities in America's Failed
Foster Care, Adoption and Immigration Systems*

ADOPTION UNCENSORED
*4 Decades of Politics, People and Commentary*

THE 8 BALL CAFÉ
*Stories of Adoption, Addiction and Redemption*

ESPOSITO
*The First Mafioso*

THE ULTIMATE SEARCH BOOK
*Adoption, Genealogy and Other Search Secrets- U.S. and World Editions*

The ADOPTION and DONOR CONCEPTION FACTBOOK
*The Only Comprehensive Source of US & Global Data on the
Invisible Families of Foster Care, Adoption and Donor Conception*

www.ingramcontent.com/pod-product-compliance
Lightning Source LLC
Chambersburg PA
CBHW071529040426
42452CB00008B/947